THE MORASS

THE MORASS

United States Intervention in
Central America

Richard Alan White

1817

HARPER & ROW, PUBLISHERS, New York

Cambridge, Philadelphia, San Francisco, London
Mexico City, São Paulo, Sydney

FIRST EDITION

Designer: C. Linda Dingler

Library of Congress Cataloging in Publication Data

White, Richard Alan, 1944–
  The morass.

  Includes index.
    1. Central America—Relations—United States.
2. United States—Relations—Central America. 3. Central America—Politics and government—1979– . 4. Counterinsurgency—Central America. I. Title.
F1436.8.U6W47   1984   303.4'8273'0728   83-48942
ISBN 0-06-015312-1   84 85 86 87 88 10 9 8 7 6 5 4 3 2 1
ISBN 0-06-091145-X (pbk.)   84 85 86 87 88 10 9 8 7 6 5 4 3 2 1

To Sister Ita Ford

CONTENTS

Acknowledgments   xi

Introduction   1

1. *The Origins of Modern Day Counterinsurgency*   13
2. *Reform as Counterinsurgency*   16
   Land Reform   17
   Political Reform   20
   Self-Reform During Crisis   22
   Civic Action   34
   Propaganda   35
3. *The Role of the CIA 40*
   Extrajudicial Executions in El Salvador   43
   Disappearances   47
   Covert Operations   49
   The Nicaraguan Contras   52
4. *The Development of Counterinsurgency Military Strategy*   75
   Conventional Versus Unconventional Warfare   77
   Recent Changes in U.S. Warfare Doctrine   82
   U.S. Counterinsurgency Military Forces   85
   Insurgency According to the U.S. Army   88
5. *Guatemala*   95
   Massacres and Refugees   96
   Scorched Earth and Genocide   105
   Civil Defense Corps   107
   Strategic Hamlets   113
   The Fall of Ríos Montt   123

6. *El Salvador*   *131*
The Influence of U.S. Military Doctrine   137
Salvadoran Warfare Methods   147
The National Campaign Plan   159

7. *Honduras*   *180*
Taking Control   184
Fortress America   195
Polarization   206

8. *Costa Rica*   *212*
Brought into the Fold   214
In Over Its Head   220

9. *Reform Versus Repression*   *225*

10. *It Depends on the Way You Count*   *232*

11. *Rationalizing Washington's Policy*   *245*

Conclusion   *254*

Glossary of Acronyms and Terms   *269*

Notes 273

Index 301

A map of Central America faces page 1.

TABLES AND FIGURES

Phase III—Title Application and Grants   26

1983 Insurgent Structure of El Salvador   41

Extrajudicial Executions in El Salvador of Noncombatant
Civilians for Political Reasons   44

Extrajudicial Executions in El Salvador by Social Sector
(in Percent)   44

U.S. Economic and Military Aid to Central America,
1978–1980   183

1983 Foreign Economic Credits for Honduras   194

U.S. Security Aid Programs to Central America,
1950–1984   234–236

U.S. Economic Aid to Central America, 1980–1984   237

Total U.S. Security and Economic Aid to Central
America, 1980–1984   238

U.S. Security and Economic Aid to Central America   241

ACKNOWLEDGMENTS

In recognition of my appreciation to the people and institutions who gave moral, academic, technical, and financial support during the preparation of this book, special gratitude is owed to my colleague Jarco Almuli, who contributed greatly to the preliminary study; to Gloria Abella, Claudia Galindo, Christopher Olszyk, and Natalie White for research assistance; to Oxfam America, the Council on Hemispheric Affairs, the Commission on United States–Central American Relations, the Ford Foundation, and especially the Centro de Estudios Económicos y Sociales del Tercer Mundo for institutional and financial support; to the members of CEESTEM's Programa de Estudios Relaciones Mexico–Estados Unidos team—Sergio Aguayo, Adolfo Aguilar Zinser, and Cesareo Morales—for their valuable criticisms; to Terry Corcoran, Sue Ann Heimendinger, Leticia Inclán, and Georgina Romero for clerical assistance; to Nancy Meiselas for arranging publication; to Anthony and Rose DiRenzo for extensive technical assistance; to Mabel Treadwell for typing the manuscript; to Hugh Van Dusen and Janet Goldstein for coining the title and shepherding the book through the morass of the publishing process; and particularly to Henri J. M. Nouwen for his friendship and support. I would also like to take this opportunity to thank the many other people without whose courageous assistance this work could not have been completed, but who for obvious reasons cannot here be mentioned by name.

Regardless of these enormous contributions, the author accepts full responsibility for all translations and any conceptual or factual errors.

THE
MORASS

MEXICO

Belize

BELIZE

CARIBBEAN

Gulf of Honduras

Puerto Castilla

Puerto Lempira

1   2   3

GUATEMALA

HONDURAS

3

4

4

Guatemala City

Tegucigalpa

Puerto
Cabezas

San
Salvador

1

2

4

1

Acajutla

6

3

2

NICARAGUA

EL SALVADOR

5

2

Gulf of Fonseca

PACIFIC OCEAN

Corinto

Puerto Sandino

Managua

COSTA RICA

San José

GUATEMALA
1 Huehuetenango
2 El Quiché
3 Alta Verapaz
4 Chimaltenango

EL SALVADOR
1 Chalatenango
2 Cabañas
3 San Miguel
4 Morazán
5 Usulután
6 San Vicente

HONDURAS
1 San Pedro Sula
2 Choluteca
3 Gracias a Díos
4 Durzuna

NICARAGUA
1 Nueva Segovia
2 Matagalpa

PANAMA

Areas of contra invasions   Areas of Honduran incursions

INTRODUCTION

In keeping with his 1980 campaign promise to "project American power throughout the world," President Reagan intends that his foreign policy regain for the United States the dominant superpower status that it commanded during the 1950s and 1960s. What this means in concrete terms is that now, less than a decade after finally extricating its bogged down military machine from the morass of Southeast Asia, Washington is once again trying to stamp out revolution in the Third World.

This time, the official line goes, things are different. The insurgents can be beaten because Central America is not Vietnam: Latins simply are not made of the same stuff as the inscrutable Asians who proved to be such formidable foes. Moreover, not only is the battlefield in "our own backyard," the rebels cannot count on friendly neighbors—like North Vietnam and China—to constrain military strategy or offer them secure supply lines and fresh troops. While these are significant differences, as the Soviets are learning in Afghanistan, it does not take mysterious Asians with strategic borders on the other side of the world to stymie a counterinsurgency campaign.

Disregarding opinion polls, which consistently show public opposition to intervention in Central America, President Reagan has continued to escalate U.S. involvement in the region. At first he kept a regal distance from the entire business, leaving his subordinates to "draw the line against Communist expansion" in the hemisphere. By early 1983, however, the impressive military gains of the Salvadoran insurgents, combined with the continuing revelations of the CIA's "secret" and illegal war against Nicaragua, led to growing congressional opposition to his Central American policy and forced President Reagan to put his own personal prestige on the line. After several months of calling for enormous emergency increases in military aid, Reagan convened a rare joint session of Congress in April to dramatize that "the national security of all the Americas is at stake in Central America." An even harder hard line was soon adopted, and the nation was informed that the Soviet threat to U.S. vital security interests in Central America had become "of equal rank" to the Soviet threat in the Middle East.

Even though Congress seemed intimidated by the fear that it would be blamed in the 1984 elections for "losing" Central America, the Administration's alarmist message failed to rally the hoped-for public support. Subsequent polls continued to show overwhelming disapproval of the President's policy of pursuing a military solution to the problems engulfing the Isthmus. In great part, the popular rejection of the White House's approach is based on a gut reaction against the Vietnam adventure. Although most people recognize that Washington's militaristic policy is following the all-too-familiar course that led the nation into deeper and deeper involvement in Southeast Asia, only the well-informed realize that it is little more than an updated version of the counterinsurgency doctrine developed during the Vietnam war era. Even among those few who have made the connection, there exists widespread misunderstanding of the full scope of concepts that constitute "counterinsurgency."

It is not, as many people incorrectly believe, simply a military exercise to defeat guerrillas. Even the entire range of government repression—everything from My Lai–type massacres to the extrajudicial executions carried out by paramilitary death squads—makes up only part of a modern day counterinsurgency campaign. Along with repression, the other half of the equation is a series of seemingly progressive reforms. To understand the logic that governs counterinsurgency, the causes of insurgency require a brief exposition.

Central American societies are predominantly agricultural. Within this system, a relatively few wealthy families and transnational corporations own nearly all of the best land, upon which they produce the major exports of these nations: coffee, sugar, cotton, cocoa, and bananas. Traditionally, these elite minorities have guarded their positions by monopolizing politics and, when all else fails, by resorting to repressive actions of security forces to protect them from the efforts of their fellow citizens to better their lot in life. These peasants and other workers, who are most often employed under conditions that amount to virtual servitude, constitute a work force without which the agro-commercial economies simply could not function.

It would be far off the mark, however, to think that the tiny elite are sadistic tyrants who take pleasure in oppressing the impoverished majority. Acts of charity and generosity—albeit deeply engrained in paternalism—comprise a major aspect of their traditional relationship with the "popular classes."

But the realities of the world economy place severe restraints upon even voluntary concessions. Intense competition in the limited international markets for agricultural exports requires the elite to monopolize the most fertile land. Moreover, to produce their products at competitive prices, the oligarchy must pay the lowest possible wages to their laborers, who are denied land of their own from which they could earn a living. History also reveals another aspect of the oligarchs' tradition: When the people do threaten their privileged way of life, the oligarchs do not hesitate to unleash the dogs of war.

While the causes of insurgency lie in this unjust social system, the precipitant of the present social turmoil in the nations of Central America stems from the disaster that has befallen their economies. The effects of the current world economic crisis, which in the industrialized nations is felt as a severe recession, have wreaked far greater damage throughout the Third World. In Central America, plummeting export commodity prices, combined with high interest rates for foreign loans, and expensive imported oil, have plunged these countries into full-blown depression.

Given such circumstances, the appeal of socialism and liberation theology—which emphasizes physical as well as spiritual well-being—have become ever more attractive to the growing numbers of impoverished citizens. These are the major dynamics that during the past decade have formed the basis for the increasingly forceful attempts to bring about profound changes in the old and oppressive social order. The situation is complex, but in essence such is the hothouse of inherent social injustice in which insurgency flourishes.

This scenario also provides the rationale for employing land reforms or so-called democratic elections as counterinsurgency measures. Within the context of counterinsurgency, the purpose of such reforms is not merely to improve the well-being of the people but also to lessen the harshest of society's injustices, thereby attempting to undercut popular support for the insurgents. Reforms are designed to work in conjunction with a wider counterinsurgency campaign, which includes governmental repression.

Moreover, because of the crucial political component of all counterinsurgency campaigns, reforms play another important role. These apparently progressive measures lend domestic and international legitimacy to the local government and its patron. In the case of Central America, where the benefactor is the United States, the image of legitimacy is especially important. As the Vietnam experience made clear, the ability of a U.S. President to carry on a counterinsurgency war is greatly dependent upon public opinion, the attitude adopted by the media, and the support of the Congress.

While the amelioration of injustices in its client states is crucial for "winning the hearts and minds" of the local population, as well as for gaining support at home, U.S.–sponsored counterinsurgency reform programs find themselves plagued by an inherent contradiction: It is difficult, if not impossible, for entrenched Third World governments to enact self-reforms during periods of crisis because the very reforms themselves threaten the foundations of the old order. Consequently, Washington finds itself in the dilemma of simultaneously attempting not only to defeat the insurgents but also to force necessary reforms upon an intransigent local elite who are loathe to surrender their privileges. In many cases, enacting the reforms necessary to undermine the insurgents' appeal to the general population amounts to nothing less than the end of the oligarchy's way of life. Even so, as a top U.S. counterinsurgency expert in El Salvador emphasized: "Without political, social and economic reforms, there is no effective counterinsurgency campaign."

If reform can be depicted as the gloved left hand of counterinsurgency, then repression is its mailed right fist. Of course, the long and sordid history of covert activities constitutes an integral part of U.S. counterinsurgency doctrine. Reversing the post-Watergate trend of circumscribing the activities of the Central Intelligence Agency (CIA), the Reagan Administration has channeled enormous resources to restore the capabilities of its Operations Directorate, the CIA's clandestine-operations section. Reinstated with much of its former mandate, the CIA lost little time in picking up where it left off.

As yet, no hard evidence—such as the Pentagon Papers provided for the infamous Operation Phoenix in Vietnam—has been unveiled that would link CIA operations directly with death squads or the near-epidemic "disappearance" of people throughout Latin America. However, the CIA's "secret war" against Nicaragua's Sandinista government has been splashed across the front pages of the world's newspapers. Just as it organized, trained, armed, and financed the Meo tribesmen and Montagnards in Southeast Asia during its heyday in the 1960s, the CIA has now done the same with the Miskito Indians, former National Guardsmen of Anastasio Somoza's brutal dictatorship, and a number of other Nicaraguan counterrevolutionary groups.

These "contras" or "freedom fighters," as President Reagan has dubbed the counterrevolutionary groups, have launched a three-front war, making simultaneous invasions into Nicaragua from their havens in the U.S.-supported countries of Honduras and Costa Rica. (Since the Sandinistas constitute the government of Nicaragua and the CIA-sponsored contras are the rebels, in a technical sense the conflict does not fit within the counterinsurgency doctrine. More accurately, Washington's intervention falls under the generic label of counterrevolution. But because the growing regionalization caused by the Reagan Administration's policy forms such a tightly knit mesh of interrelations, it is impossible to understand any single piece of the puzzle without viewing the overall scenario.)

Not only has the Reagan Administration refurbished the CIA's clandestine and paramilitary capabilities, it has also rejuvenated the various "unconventional warfare" sections of the armed forces. Schooled in the conventional strategies of World War II and the Korean conflict, which relied upon massive fire power and increasingly sophisticated technology, the U.S. military high command traditionally has looked down upon their gung-ho comrades. In fact, these unconventional-warfare forces, whose counterinsurgency specialty employs small, highly trained commando units using little more than rudimentary equipment and primitive tactics, have been systematically discriminated against by the armed forces' hierarchy. Some officers have been forced to switch to more conventional aspects of their profession, others have left from disappointment or disgust, while most simply have been forced to retire from the service. Reflecting this reality, out of the three major branches of the military—the army's Special Forces (popularly known as the Green Berets); the navy's Sea, Air, and Land teams (more commonly referred to as the SEALs); and the air force's elite Air Commandos—only one counterinsurgency specialist has obtained flag rank. A Special Forces colonel, who described himself as a survivor whose career was resurrected when insurgency exploded in Central America, bitterly pointed out that there is only one general "in the counterinsurgency business" out of approximately three thousand top military officers in the U.S. armed forces.

Because of this shabby treatment, there still remains an ingrained resentment among the counterinsurgency elite against their more traditional military comrades. A high-ranking adviser at the U.S. Embassy in San Salvador graphically depicted their plight when he complained that "the SEALs sold half of their souls in order to stay alive, and so they still have their mission, but . . . they have to scrub ship bottoms. That is exactly what they have to do, but they survived." Ironically, the second in command of the United States Military Advisory Group, SEAL Commander Albert A. Schaufelberger III, managed to stay alive only long enough to win the questionable distinction in May 1983 of being the first U.S. adviser to be killed in El Salvador.

Such deep-seated animosities notwithstanding, with revolution boiling over in Central America, the fortunes of unconventional warfare soldiers are turning as they find their expertise in growing demand. In October 1982, for the first time in U.S. history, all of the military's special operations forces, from all three major branches of the armed forces, were brought under a unified command at the John F. Kennedy School of Special Warfare at Fort Bragg, North Carolina. Moreover, the Reagan Administration has revitalized other existing special warfare units, for instance, the Rapid Deployment Force, and created new unconventional warfare facilities such as the Regional Military Training Center in Puerto Castilla, as well as the modern air base in Durzuna, Honduras. It has even gone so far as to update its counterinsurgency curriculum by developing an official U.S. Army Special Forces five-phase explanation of insurgency which, of course, includes the theoretically appropriate counterinsurgency measures for defeating the rebels every step of the way.

One of the most significant dynamics of U.S. sponsored counterinsurgency in Central America is something of a mirror-image replay of the dispute over military strategy that dominated the war effort in Southeast Asia. On the one hand, during that period the Pentagon traditionalists, who virtually dictated military strategy after President Kennedy's assassination in 1963, steadfastly maintained that a well-trained conventional army was fully capable of combating insurgency using time proven battlefield methods—specifically, the concentration of fire power against the enemy through air superiority and large-scale operations, such as search-and-destroy sweeps and scorched earth missions.

On the other hand, the unconventional warfare soldiers argued that a comprehensive counterinsurgency strategy that incorporated both reform and repression had to be implemented to defeat the enemy. They contended moreover that only special warfare methods would be successful in overcoming a determined and popularly supported guerrilla army. In an even more radical departure from conventional military wisdom, the new breed of warriors insisted that the new tactics be based upon many of the insurgents' own methods: night fighting, small-unit saturation patrolling, and penetrating rebel territory in commando-style raids to harass and ambush the enemy. They also advocated more innovative measures, such as deliberately destroying "subversive" villages to create refugees of the former inhabitants—in order to disrupt the guerrillas' popular base of support as well as the forcible concentration of the local population into "strategic hamlets" to quarantine and better indoctrinate them against any contact with the rebels. Even though such a scheme, the Civil Operations and Rural Development Support program (CORDS), was developed, it was employed only on a sporadic and limited basis. The counterinsurgency campaign in Vietnam, therefore, never amounted to more than a poor cousin, eclipsed by the conventional warfare strategy imposed by the U.S. military brass.

Today in Central America the conflict over military strategy has taken an ironic twist. Now, the U.S. military officers who are calling the shots, having learned from bitter defeat in Vietnam, find it nearly impossible to persuade their Latin counterparts to abandon the time-honored conventional modes of warfare and adopt more effective counterinsurgency tactics. A top U.S. counterinsurgency expert in El Salvador summarized the situation in 1983 when he tried to explain why the Salvadoran armed forces were not effectively combating the guerrillas: "Part of it is institutional inertia. We've created an Army, um, or they have created an Army over the last fifty years, whose primary objective was to maintain internal control and to fight the Hondurans. . . . I have asked Salvadoran officers why, with all the years of counterinsurgency instruction that has been offered [at the U.S. Army's School of the Americas] in Panama and all the training teams that we have provided, how come you are so unprepared for this kind of struggle? And they said: 'We never believed that it could happen here.'"

While it is true that most of the Salvadoran officer corps stubbornly cling to the ideas of Douglas MacArthur and Dwight Eisenhower that they learned as cadets, such self-serving justifications only partly account for their remarkable incompetency. More important is that for the last half century this politically motivated and corrupt armed forces, which has distinguished itself by slaughtering peasants and keeping a dictator in power, have little stomach when the victims start shooting back. By fighting standards, the Salvadorans rank at the bottom of Central America's military institutions. With the exception of a few departmental commanders—the "war lords," as the U.S. advisers derogatorily call them because of their arbitrary and near-total control over the provinces they command—the conventional-minded Salvadoran officer corps has fought the war on a nine-to-five schedule, routinely taking weekends off to relax at the beach or at the hot spots of the capital city of San Salvador.

But it looks as if their laid-back war may be coming to an end. Faced with the ever more impressive insurgent victories and increasing pressure from Washington, they began in early 1983 to accept reality. In April, Minister of Defense José Guillermo García, an undistinguished army general who seldom left the safety and comfort of San Salvador, was dumped in favor of the notorious head of the National Guard, General Carlos Eugenio Vides Casanova, a pathological zealot, whose list of martial accomplishments include, according to authoritative sources, involvement in the rape-torture-murder of the four North American churchwomen in December 1980.

In spite of his "nun problem," Vides Casanova was selected to revamp the lethargic officer corps and gear up the army to fight a U.S.-designed counterinsurgency war. The gravity of the situation came through in no uncertain terms to the presidential interagency task force that assessed the Central American conflict for the National Security Council. In mid-1983, following a lengthy investigation, the task force found it necessary to recommend an increase of 40 to 65 percent in the projected 1984 military assistance allocations for El Salvador. To confront the immediate crisis, however, the Salvadoran armed forces in June launched their heralded "National Plan," a CORDS-type "full spectrum" counterinsurgency campaign that many experts boasted would finally do the trick. Official optimism and propaganda aside, the rebels remained unimpressed.

Not only had the insurgents already taken on and defeated the best troops that the Salvadoran Army could field—the elite U.S.-trained rapid reaction battalions—but by the end of the year their growing strength and devastatingly effective new tactics once again had won them the military and political initiative. Completely disrupting the new counterinsurgency campaign, the insurgents sent the government forces scurrying back to the safety of their barracks. The steady expansion of rebel control over ever larger areas of the country during the four years of war left little doubt that only a radical escalation in the forms of military assistance to the Salvadoran armed forces could possibly influence the outcome of the civil conflict.

Regardless of the jingoistic nationalism sparked by the U.S. invasion of Grenada, coming as it did on the heels of the massacre of several hundred U.S. Marines in Beirut only two days before, few in the Reagan Administration believe that the armed forces could pull off a repeat performance in Central America. The reasons lay in the fundamentally different nature of these movements for social change.

Rather than the result of a long and painful process of insurrectionary struggle that forges deep commitments among the population to defend their hard-won gains, the Granadan situation was an attempt by the leadership to impose revolution from the top downward. Prime Minister Maurice Bishop came to power through a 1979 palace coup that ousted the despotic Sir Eric Gairy. Although personally popular, Bishop never had as his power base an organized and armed population—which is perhaps the most important characteristic of an authentic revolution, as in the case of Nicaragua; instead, the government sought stability almost exclusively from the backing of the small Granadan Army.

When the socialist prime minister, in turn, found himself deposed on October 13, 1983, by a clique of ultra-left hard liners within the army led by General Hudson Austin, his supporters' only recourse lay in assembling a massive march to free their imprisoned leader. Austin reacted viciously, ordering his troops to open fire with machine guns on the protesting crowds, and later executing Bishop and several of his top aides and imposing an extremely harsh state of martial law. So, when U.S. forces invaded the tiny island on October 25, they found an almost ideal set of circumstances: a divided military junta attempting to consolidate power with little or no support among the small, unarmed general population. Given these conditions, most Granadans, including the vast majority of the army, assumed a most reasonable comportment. As the invading forces unleashed their powerful arsenal of airborne assault troops, rocket-firing helicopters, and supersonic fighter bombers, the people by and large just sat on the beach in their bathing suits watching the spectacular production—live and in deadly color—of *Apocalypse Now.*

Direct military intervention in Central America is quite a different story, one that does not include a quick and easy victory anywhere in the script. The Isthmus constitutes a sizable region composed of six countries with a population of 23 million inhabitants—not a minuscule island-nation of a mere 105,000 people. Its thousands of armed and experienced guerrillas represent only a tiny fraction of the resistance any invading force would have to face, for the insurgents' support structure and popular base, which have been painstakingly built up over the past decades, number in the millions. And Nicaragua, after almost five years of Sandinista leadership, which followed three years of brutal civil war, not only boasts the most powerful and experienced army in the region but has an armed and mobilized militia made up of virtually the entire adult population dedicated to defending its homeland.

Certainly all Central American revolutionaries recognize these facts, as do their counterparts in the Pentagon. And while this reality does militate against Washington embarking on a casual military adventure in the region, the Reagan Administration's saber-rattling and undisguised preparations to impose its will by means of military might—instead of abiding by international law—seem to point in the direction of further escalation. Clearly the predominant perception throughout the Isthmus is that U.S.-sponsored armies from "friendly" Central American nations, especially Honduras and Guatemala, will serve as the shock troops, likely supported by U.S. air power, to pave the way for U.S. ground forces. In any event, Washington's belligerent policies have all but convinced the revolutionaries that the inevitable problems that come with enacting meaningful social change in their countries will not be resolved peacefully through a political or negotiated settlement. From their point of view they must prepare for the worst—which is exactly what they are doing.

If the United States continues with its escalating, militaristic policy, regardless of the Reagan Administration's fantasies of building up its regional troupe of proxies to do the initial dirty work, it will undoubtedly find. itself drawn deeper and deeper into the Central American morass. Although the overworked cliché that "history repeats itself" is rarely more than a gratuitous means of trying to explain similar phenomena, it does offer a valuable insight into the uncanny parallels between U.S. intervention in Southeast Asia and U.S. intervention in Central America.

Today, just as then, Washington is rationalizing its intervention by casting the local conflicts in the East–West terms of global capitalist-communist confrontation, and expounding an updated version of the old domino theory: that to save the region from international Communism, the Nicaraguan revolution must be stopped in its historical tracks and the insurgencies in El Salvador and Guatemala must be crushed. Otherwise, the Reagan Administration insists, the other Central American nations will succumb, one after the other, until the United States finds itself fighting at the Panama Canal and the Mexican border. While such severe predictions amount to alarmist rhetoric by any objective standards, the United States' relentless pursuit of a military solution ends up, in fact, being a self-fulfilling prophecy because it creates the very conditions capable of setting off a regional conflagration. Considering the forces now set into motion, without a dramatic change in Washington's policy, just such a scenario is already more than a possibility; it is increasingly becoming a strong probability.

ONE

THE ORIGINS OF MODERN DAY COUNTERINSURGENCY

Though, historically, insurgent conflicts have been known under a variety of names (including "colonial wars," "brushfire wars," "internal wars," and "guerrilla wars"), John F. Kennedy was the first to employ the term "counterinsurgency."* Indeed, it is essential to recognize that President Kennedy's foreign policy was never really free of the obsessions of the Cold War that dominated international politics during the 1950s and early 1960s, and that the initial impulse behind the development of the U.S. counterinsurgency doctrine is traced to his Administration.

Kennedy's personal interest in counterinsurgency dates back to a time long before he reached the White House. As early as 1952, the year he was first elected to the U.S. Senate, he traveled to Vietnam to witness firsthand the dynamics of insurrection there, and the reasons that the French had failed to suppress it. During the following years, the future President continued studying the realities of revolution in underdeveloped countries. Moving beyond the understanding of most of his contemporaries, Kennedy came to believe that the causes of rebellion lay not simply in Communist agitation, but also in structural injustices of the status quo. As he understood it, these injustices became most pronounced and intolerable during a nation's period of transition from its traditional way of life to modernity, thereby touching off

* For this reason, the military headquarters of counterinsurgency, the John F. Kennedy School of Special Warfare at Fort Bragg, North Carolina, was named in his honor. Because of the U.S. public's negative association with the term "counterinsurgency," the current military nomenclature is "low intensity conflicts."

rebellion against the old regime. While Kennedy recognized that history was not static and that change must occur, he feared the instability caused by revolution because it was a process that the United States could not control. And worse yet, insurgency provided the Communists with the opportunity to exploit mass discontent by manipulating civil strife in order to seize control of the state. Kennedy advocated that, in theory, the role of U.S. foreign policy was to provide the assistance necessary to help these troubled countries through their transition period of establishing a modern society. In practice that meant developing and enforcing a doctrine of counterinsurgency to assure that those countries remained firmly within the Western sphere of influence.

As the 1950s came to a close, it was in this context that Kennedy interpreted the insurrections in South Vietnam, Laos, Algeria, Cuba, Colombia, and Venezuela. His preoccupation with Third World insurrection, and his analysis of the Communist role in it, remained consistent throughout these years. Senator Kennedy, in 1959, announced, "our nuclear retaliatory power is not enough. It cannot deter Communist aggression which is too limited to justify atomic war. It cannot protect uncommitted nations against Communist takeover using local or guerrilla forces. It cannot be used in so-called brush-fire wars. . . . In short, it cannot prevent the Communists from nibbling away at the fringe of the free world's territory or strength."[1]

Among his first actions as President, Kennedy implemented his demand, reiterated during the campaign, for a more "flexible response" to what he perceived as the Communist policy of sponsoring insurgency in order to destroy the capitalist world order. Two weeks before his inauguration, on January 6, 1961, the Soviets strongly reinforced this obsession. On that day, Chairman Nikita Khrushchev delivered his famous speech pledging Moscow's support for national wars of liberation in the underdeveloped world. Although Khrushchev's speech served as an important precipitant to the President's counterinsurgency program, the cause lies much deeper because Kennedy's adamant convictions went back at least a decade. With or without the Soviet leader's declarations, the new President undoubtedly would have gone ahead with the speedy development of his counterinsurgency doctrine.

Actually, Khrushchev's speech did not represent a major shift in Soviet policy. It was a defensive, and primarily rhetorical, response to the stinging criticism leveled against the Kremlin's foreign policy by the Chinese. During this initial period of the Sino–Soviet split, the Chinese charged that pro-Moscow Communist parties around the world had become complacent, excusing their failure to actively promote Third World revolution on the revisionist grounds that the "objective conditions" simply did not exist for successful insurrection.[2]

In any event, President Kennedy seized upon the incident to initiate his program. At the first meeting of his National Security Council, during which he read excerpts of Khrushchev's address, Kennedy directed the Department of Defense to begin investigating the means of "increasing counter-guerrilla resources."[3] This was only the initial step in rapidly developing his Administration's all-encompassing doctrine of counterinsurgency.

The humiliating Bay of Pigs fiasco, which occurred only a few months after Kennedy came to office, seems to have deepened the President's belief that an overriding Communist control of Third World revolutions existed. Immediately following the failed invasion of Cuba, on April 27, 1961, Kennedy declared that "we are opposed around the world by a monolithic and ruthless conspiracy that relies primarily on covert means for expanding its sphere of influence—on infiltration instead of invasion, on subversion instead of elections, on intimidation instead of free choice, on guerrillas by night instead of armies by day. It is a system which has conscripted vast human and material resources into the building of a tightly knit, highly efficient machine."[4]

It is this "Communist conspiracy theory," based on the East–West confrontation, that formed the ideological core of Kennedy's counterinsurgency doctrine. For the last two decades, it has remained the fundamental premise behind all subsequent U.S. initiatives opposing revolution throughout the world—as is so evident in Washington's intervention throughout Central America today. Before the current U.S. policy can be understood, however, it is necessary to examine the components of modern day U.S. counterinsurgency doctrine and practice.

================ TWO ================
REFORM AS COUNTERINSURGENCY

The subject of reforms is complex. Certainly reforms are not inherently negative or implicitly a means of forestalling social change. But when used within the context of a counterinsurgency campaign, their objective is not to improve the well-being of the people per se; rather, it is to make relatively superficial changes which would undermine popular support of the rebels. As Mao Tse-tung said, "the sea in which the guerrilla swims" will be dried up.

Of course not everyone involved in enacting reforms does so for such a Machiavellian reason. Indeed, those individuals who are implementing reforms in the Third World very often are idealists, unaware of, or even in disagreement with, the counterinsurgency intentions of high-level decision-makers. For example, José Viera, Michael Hammer, and Mark Pearlman, three dedicated land reform experts, were assassinated in 1981 in the coffee shop at the San Salvador Sheraton Hotel by "off duty" soldiers under the orders of rich Salvadoran oligarchs.

Because the spotty record of reform programs in quelling revolt in the Third World leaves their effectiveness an open question, this work focuses upon reforms as a counterinsurgency concept.* While the analysis draws upon concrete examples, it

*Bolivia after the 1952 revolution exemplifies the successful implementation of political and agrarian reforms, in contrast to the program in South Vietnam during the era of U.S. involvement, which clearly failed to accomplish its objectives.

does not pretend to reach absolute conclusions concerning the overall effect of reforms upon the process of social change.

LAND REFORM

The grossly inequitable distribution of land tenure is perhaps the most widespread and fundamental injustice throughout the Third World. Land reform, therefore, occupies top priority among the counterinsurgency reform programs. Furthermore, since the purpose of U.S.–promoted agrarian reform is to pacify discontent among the peasantry and landless agricultural workers, the objective of counterinsurgency involves more than simply expropriating and collectivizing the enormous estates of the oligarchy. From a counterinsurgency perspective, the distribution of land to individual families is of far greater importance.

For the peasant, nothing is so highly valued as land and its ownership. This was made clear by Thomas O. Enders, then Assistant Secretary of State for Inter-American Affairs, in a 1982 speech before the Council of the Americas.* On that occasion, he unequivocally stated the counterinsurgency function of land reform when he said that "for the United States it is vital to carry the agrarian reform through [in El Salvador]. Peasants who have become landowners will be a strong bulwark against the guerrillas."[1] Granting peasants their own piece of land has an immediate, enduring, and conservative influence. The new landowners feel that they must protect their newly acquired possession of land, which by extension means preserving the existing social order. Their false sense of security, and insecurity, is exploited by the government through campaigns against the "communist subversives" who threaten the new status of the "peasant capitalist."

The basic objection leveled against counterinsurgency agrarian reform schemes is that they do little to improve the well-being of the people in the long run. Peasants who receive a small plot of land on which they can cultivate their own food most often find

---

*As part of a larger personnel shake-up that reflected the harder line being adopted toward Central America by President Reagan, on May 27, 1983, the administration announced that Enders was being replaced by Langehorne A. Motley, then United States Ambassador to Brazil.

themselves better off than when they were landless migrant workers or peons on the big agro-business estates. But when these large, relatively efficient production units are broken up into individually held family-size land holdings, their crops cannot compete in the international marketplace. Even when the former workers are allowed to run the estates as collectives, lack of managerial skills and credit to purchase seed, fertilizers, and machinery dooms their efforts. Even when the peasants attempt to eke out a living on individual parcels of land, they face many of the same obstacles because they become marginal to the economy, reduced to subsistence farming. A solution to this dilemma is true collectivization, with adequate technical and financial support from the government that would allow them to become profitable enterprises. But the purpose of counterinsurgency-inspired agrarian reform is the pacification, not the prosperity, of the people.

Both the importance of U.S–sponsored agrarian reform and its counterinsurgency orientation are uniquely illustrated in the career of Professor Roy L. Prosterman, a liberal land reform expert from the University of Washington who has worked on such programs in at least eighteen countries around the world.[2]

During the early 1970s, Professor Prosterman directed a frantic eleventh-hour effort to avoid defeat in South Vietnam by conducting a massive land reform program that gave titles to almost one million landless peasants. Although, in Prosterman's opinion, the program was implemented with insufficient resources and far too late in the course of the war to be a decisive factor, he claims that as a result the Viet Cong recruitment fell from 7,000 to 1,000 soldiers per month. While these statistics are open to question, the effectiveness of this type of agrarian reform is reflected by the post-war policy of the Democratic Republic of Vietnam. To this day it has postponed the collectivization of these small land holdings.

More recently, Prosterman served as the architect of the U.S. promoted and financed land reform in El Salvador. Following the 1979 coup, the Carter Administration became convinced that if revolution was to be avoided in El Salvador—a country that has a higher population density than India—it was necessary to force a profound restructuring of the land tenure system. To accomplish this, it utilized the American Institute for Free Labor Development (AIFLD), which is the overseas affiliate of the powerful AFL-CIO trade union organization, to provide "technical assistance" in the formulation and implementation of the U.S.-backed government's new agrarian reform program. Further, it supplied millions of dollars in funding for the program through the Agency for International Development (AID), a dependency of the Department of State.[3]

Under the guidance of Prosterman and the AIFLD team, the Salvadoran junta decreed, in March 1980, the Basic Law of Agrarian Reform, which established a three-phase program. In the first phase, all latifundia over 500 hectares were expropriated. The second phase, which was never implemented, called for the expropriation of estates ranging from 100 to 500 hectares. The third part of the reform—and, according to Prosterman, most important in terms of counterinsurgency goals—was the "land-to-the-tiller" program. In theory, this granted the immediate transfer of ownership from the landlords to the peasants who worked land they previously were only renting.

Although impeded by bureaucratic delays, violent repression by the oligarchy-supported death squads and security forces that carried out frequent murders and evictions, and the failure to grant final titles to the peasants in the critical land-to-the-tiller phase, according to Prosterman the agrarian reform was a resounding counterinsurgency success. He bragged, "The far left had brought a hundred thousand into the streets of San Salvador in January 1980; it could muster fewer than two thousand on May Day. Three unsuccessful 'general strikes' in the summer were followed by a similarly unsuccessful 'final offensive' in January 1981. As Alan Riding noted in the *New York Times* on February 8, 1981, the far left had 'apparently miscalculated the impact on the peasants of land reforms decreed by the junta in March.' There was no popular uprising."[4]

Certainly Prosterman gives too much credit to himself and the effects of his agrarian reform when he neglects other factors essential for understanding the phenomenon that he describes. In particular, during 1980 the diverse sectors of the Salvadoran insurgent movement often issued contradictory messages to their supporters. For example, following the massacre at Archbishop Oscar Romero's funeral in March, it became apparent to the armed insurgents that they could not protect their followers during mass protests against the government. This necessitated a shift away from mass action—such as general strikes and demonstrations—to more clandestine forms of resistance. Although most of the opposition leaders adopted the new strategy, a few organizations continued to call for mass demonstrations and strikes. Similarly, in January 1981, two of the five guerrilla groups optimistically, and unrealistically, called their initial offensive a "final offensive." Yet, regardless of Prosterman's glaringly self-serving omissions, few observers of the Salvadoran revolutionary process doubt that his land reform program provided the government with a powerful counterinsurgency weapon.

POLITICAL REFORM

Just as with other aspects of reform, in the context of counterinsurgency political reform is not meant simply to provide the citizenry of "authoritarian regimes" with a better way of life through democracy. More accurately, political reform is an attempt to bestow national and international legitimacy upon the state. Opening up the political process is meant to convince the people that they have increasingly greater control over their lives by sharing in the decisions of government. Therefore, the dangers, hardships, and sacrifices of armed insurrection are not only unnecessary, they are also counterproductive.

The U.S. record of forcing political reforms as counterinsurgency measures is typified in its dealings with the regime of Ngo Dinh Diem in South Vietnam (1954–1963). As insurgency and U.S. intervention in South Vietnam grew in the early 1960s, Diem faced increasing pressure from his Washington allies to enact a widespread reform program. These measures included reforms of the military and the land ownership system. At the top of the list, however, were political and administrative changes in Diem's corrupt dictatorship. But Diem would not, or could not, carry out the reforms deemed vital by U.S. counterinsurgency doctrine. Consequently, by the summer of 1963, U.S. policymakers seriously began considering overthrowing him.

Henry Cabot Lodge, the new U.S. Ambassador in Saigon, cabled then Secretary of State Dean Rusk: "Believe that chances of Diem's meeting our demands are virtually nil. . . . Therefore, propose we go straight to Generals with our demands, without informing Diem."[5] Four days later, on August 29, the Ambassador was even more explicit in another cable to the Department of State. After flatly stating, "We are launched on a course from which there is no respectable turning back: the overthrow of the Diem government," he explained that "there is no possibility, in my view, that the war can be won under a Diem administration. . . . The chance of bringing off a Generals' coup depends on them to some extent; but it depends at least as much on us."[6]

But President Kennedy was not yet ready to dump the Vietnamese dictator. On September 17, the White House's National Security Council cabled the Ambassador: "Highest level meeting today has approved broad outline of an action proposals program designed to obtain from GVN [Government of Vietnam], if possible, reforms and changes in personnel necessary to maintain support of Vietnamese and U.S. opinion in war against Viet Cong." The reforms that it specified bear an uncanny similarity to those implemented under the prodding of the United States in Central America. For example, it recommended "Cabinet changes to inject new untainted blood, remove targets of popular discontent," and elections to choose a constitutional assembly, which the regime could then get to endorse its policies, since "an assembly resolution would be most useful for external image purposes." Washington then went on to caution that "specific 'reforms' are apt to have little impact without dramatic, symbolic move which convinces Vietnamese that reforms are real." In order to conceal the degree of U.S. intervention in the internal politics of South Vietnam, the White House, in the understated tone of diplomatic language, informed Lodge that it "would not expect to make public our specific requests of Diem."[7]

But in the following weeks, diplomacy played only an insignificant role in Vietnamese history. President Kennedy, frustrated by the obdurate Diem, stepped up pressure by selectively suspending U.S. assistance. On October 5, he explained to Ambassador

Lodge that these measures did not represent a change in policy, but rather were meant to demonstrate to the Vietnamese regime "our displeasure at its political policies and activities and to create significant uncertainty in that government and in key Vietnamese groups as to the future intentions of the United States."[8]

Lodge was also engaged in distinctly undiplomatic actions during these weeks. Because of the rapidly deteriorating situation, he continued plotting the coup with the generals. On the same day that he received Kennedy's message, Lodge secretly met to discuss the coup plans with General Duong Van Minh and immediately notified Washington that "Gen. Minh ... states he does need American assurances that the USG [United States Government] will not attempt to thwart this plan."[9] The following day, October 6, the White House cabled its virtual approval for the coup to oust Diem: "While we do not wish to stimulate coup, we also do not wish to leave impression the U.S. would thwart a change of government or deny economic and military assistance to a new regime if it appeared capable of increasing effectiveness of military effort, ensuring popular support to win war and improving working relations with U.S."[10] Less than a month later, on November 1, 1963, a group of South Vietnamese Army officers led by General Minh toppled the government and assassinated President Diem.

While such detailed documentation is not available to illustrate the downfall of General Carlos Humberto Romero's regime in El Salvador on October 15, 1979, or the coup in Guatemala of August 8, 1983, that ousted General Efraín Ríos Montt from power, the parallels with the fall of Diem seem evident. These regimes were under strong pressure from Washington to carry out programs of self-reform during crisis. In the absence of a positive response, both dictatorships subsequently found themselves overthrown by their own army officers who immediately received the support of the United States.

SELF-REFORM DURING CRISIS

Without doubt the most severe impediment to implementing a successful counterinsurgency reform program is the resistance of the local elite. This inherent contradiction and limitation upon the reform aspect of the counterinsurgency doctrine was recognized from the beginning of the Kennedy Administration. In November 1961, John Kenneth Galbraith—the Harvard economist, confidant to John F. Kennedy, and U.S. ambassador to India—was asked by the President to visit Saigon to evaluate the situation in South Vietnam. Among other things, Galbraith reported that "Diem will not reform either administratively or politically in any effective way. That is because he cannot. It is politically naïve to expect it. He senses that he cannot let power go because he will be thrown out." [11]

This same problem was vividly analyzed in a more methodical fashion by U. Alexis Johnson, then the Under Secretary of State for Political Affairs and a key figure among the Kennedy counterinsurgency strategists. In a major contribution to the developing counterinsurgency doctrine, Johnson pointed out that it is not always possible to implement the required reforms: "To bring about some degree of social, economic and political justice or at the very least ameliorate the worst causes of discontent and redress the most flagrant inequities, will invariably require positive action by the local government. In some cases only radical reforms will obtain the necessary results. Yet the measures we advocate may strike at the very foundations of those aspects of a country's social structure and domestic economy on which rests the basis of a government's control." [12]

In other words, powerful sectors of the local elite often simply refuse to give up their privileges by accepting the reforms deemed necessary by the United States. This is precisely what occurred in El Salvador and Guatemala during the height of President Carter's attempt to impose minimal human rights standards on those nations receiving military aid. Part of the reasoning behind his Administration's human rights policy was the belief that arbitrary violations of fundamental human rights by local dictatorships prove counterproductive in the long run, ultimately creating larger and more determined opposition movements that can form a popular base for armed insurrection. So deeply ingrained in these regimes was the belief that massive repression of all opposition was essential for them to remain in power that, in 1977, rather than submit to the Carter Administration's demands to restrain the indiscriminate slaughter of "subversives," both the Guatemalan and Salvadoran dictatorships elected to reject U.S. military aid. Instead, they sought out other sources to fill their military requirements. As a U.S. counterinsurgency expert in the region explained, it was "the Taiwanese and the Israelis who filled the vacuum during that period."[13]

In a similar vein, the Salvadoran elite still thumb their noses at the human rights standards imposed by the U.S. Congress for the continuation of military aid, resumed after the U.S.–backed coup in 1979. These oligarchs, often from the safety of their plush Miami Beach condominiums, continue to finance the murderous activities of the death squads, and the armed forces still routinely carry out massacres of civilians suspected of sympathizing with the rebels.

Because of these extrajudicial executions by the death squads and mass murders by the military, by late 1983 President Reagan faced a pressing problem. From 1981 to 1983, the Administration duly submitted the required reports every six months to Congress certifying that the human rights situation in El Salvador was improving. While only the myopic and cynical believed this, by the autumn of 1983, human rights violations had so dramatically increased that even the enormous weight of the presidency could no longer cover up another false certification. Fortunately for Reagan, the two-year period of the original law had run out, and Congress had to pass an identical bill to extend the same restrictions; unfortunately for the cause of human rights, the President must sign such legislation before it can become law. The Administration solved its dilemma through words and actions: It mounted a verbal campaign criticizing the death squads—and on November 30, 1983, the President vetoed the new bill that would have extended the certification requirements, and thereby allowed military assistance to continue without troublesome congressional oversight of the crimes committed by Washington's ally.

Another obvious example of the intransigent Salvadoran elite's refusal to surrender its privileges is the virtual repeal of the U.S.–sponsored land reform program. Ironically, the instrument by which agrarian reform has been decimated was created by the U.S.–forced elections in March of 1982, which resulted in an ultra-rightist coalition, led by the terrorist Roberto d'Aubuisson, gaining control of the Constituent Assembly.

As president of the Assembly, d'Aubuisson led the attack against land reform. On April 26, 1982, he pushed through a decree that nullified Phase II (the expropriation of the prosperous middle-size estates of from 100 to 500 hectares) by requiring a constitutional amendment for any further land expropriations.[14] Translated into practical terms, this means that as long as the Constituent Assembly is controlled by the extreme rightists, Phase II will not be carried out.

Phase I, the expropriation of latifundia over 500 hectares, has also been sabotaged. Although 326 such estates have been turned into cooperatives, their failure to prosper is due to a severe lack of credit and technical assistance. Under the provisional government of President Alvaro Magaña, the Ministry of Agriculture was placed under the direction of a member of the Nationalist Republican Alliance (ARENA), d'Aubuisson's rightist party.[15] The cooperatives, according to Roy Prosterman, have been forced to accept new "managers," who have made access to credit contingent upon support of the right wing. Even so, half of all the cooperatives do not receive credit for seeds, fertilizers, and equipment, making planting and cultivating new crops impossible. Moreover, since the rightist electoral victory, technical assistance and other services have ceased to be provided by the government.[16]

Phase III, the critical land-to-the-tiller program, was "temporarily suspended" by two laws passed by the Assembly. These decrees permit the landlords to continue renting, instead of transferring the ownership of the land to the peasants who work it, the land that produces cotton, sugar cane, or grain, or on which cattle are raised. That is, virtually all of the land originally intended for expropriation under this program.[17]

The disastrous effects on the land-to-the-tiller program caused by the extreme right-wing electoral victory, the subsequent increase in evictions, and the Assembly's legislation can be seen in Table 1, which details the number of applications and legal titles granted under Phase III.

TABLE 1. PHASE III—TITLE APPLICATION AND GRANTS[18]

	Applications Taken	Provisional Titles Distributed	Final Titles Distributed
March 1, 1981, to November 31, 1981	30,873 (3,430)	16,144 (1,794)	0
December 1, 1981, to March 28, 1982	4,573 (1,143)	11,071 (2,768)	0
March 29, 1982, to May 28, 1982	1,305 (653)	3,000 (1,500)	0
May 29, 1982, to June 28, 1982	105 (105)	1,225 (1,225)	103 (103)

Note: Parentheses show rates per month.

While the ultimate fate of the U.S.–sponsored agrarian reform is still to be decided, as a counterinsurgency measure it has been seriously compromised by the subversion of the Salvadoran oligarchs and their ultra-right-wing accomplices. Yet regardless of the outcome, this fiasco serves as a vivid illustration of the contradictions of reform as a counterinsurgency strategy.

The complexities of El Salvador's ability to carry out self-reform during crisis extend beyond the agrarian reform program into the political arena. The U.S. Congress placed conditions on President Reagan's military assistance to El Salvador that required him to certify to Congress every six months that the government of El Salvador "is making a significant and concerted effort to comply with internationally recognized human rights"; as well as that it "is making continued progress in implementing essential economic and political reforms, including the land reform program."[19] Confronted with the ludicrous task of attempting to explain away the extreme-right's violent efforts to sabotage the land reform program and continued violations of human rights, the Reagan Administration has drawn a wide range of criticism, from Congress to the press, from civil and human rights organizations to the Catholic Church.

Consequently, as previously explained, in November 1983, the President vetoed the renewal of this law. Since Congress is sensitive to public pressure, however, while the law was in effect it did influence the Reagan Administration's domestic and Central

American policies. For example, in light of widespread and growing opposition, it does not seem entirely coincidental that shortly before the U.S. congressional elections in November 1982, the Administration stepped up pressure to undermine the Salvadoran ultra-right while supporting rightist elements. It should be noted that since the March 1982 elections in El Salvador, Washington has redefined these political labels. For example, the "moderates" are no longer former President José Napoleón Duarte and the Christian Democratic party; this label was given to the rightist faction led by General José Guillermo García, the former Minister of Defense.* Disregarding the Reagan Administration's semantics, the political faction headed by García during this period will be referred to as "rightist," and the d'Aubuisson coalition called "ultra-rightist," its true political orientation.

Barely a week before the elections, the Reagan Administration kicked off its publicity campaign. On October 26, it announced that Under Secretary of Defense Fred C. Iklé had been sent to El Salvador to threaten that the United States would end military assistance if the human rights situation did not improve.[20] The following day, the State Department made an empty gesture: In response to the FMLN–FDR† offer of unconditional peace negotiations, it announced that "the U.S. favors reconciliation in El Salvador."[21] Two days later, Deane R. Hinton, then U.S. ambassador to El Salvador, had exhausted his patience after 17 months of "quiet diplomacy."‡ The Ambassador was outraged by the kidnapping of FDR and labor leaders in early October and by the failure, several weeks previously, of the Salvadoran courts to issue an indictment against a politically well-connected

*On April 18, 1983, García was finally forced to resign his post. His fall from power came about not because of his political stance, but rather his ineffectual leadership of the armed forces.

†Frente Farabundo Martí de Liberación Nacional–Frente Democrático Revolucionario (Farabundo Martí Liberation Front–Revolutionary Democratic Front). The FMLN is composed of the five guerrilla groups in El Salvador; the FDR is the political arm of the opposition and is made up of Salvadoran political dissidents groups.

‡As part of the larger personnel shake-up that reflected the harder line being adopted toward Central America by President Reagan, in late May 1983 the Administration announced that Hinton would be replaced by Thomas R. Pickering, the former Ambassador to Nigeria.

military officer for the January 1981 assassinations of two U.S. agrarian reform workers.

During a speech to the U.S.–Salvadoran Chamber of Commerce, Hinton threatened to cut off U.S. military aid unless human rights abuses stopped and the judicial system was reformed. The Ambassador raged that in the three years of civil war as many as 30,000 Salvadorans have "been murdered—not killed in battle, murdered."[22] In a direct attack against the collaboration of the courts with the death squads, he declared, "Neither internal confidence nor external support can long survive here in the absence of an effective system of criminal justice . . . The 'Mafia' must be stopped. Your survival depends on it. The gorillas of this Mafia, every bit as much as the guerrillas in Morazán and Chalatenango, are destroying El Salvador."[23]

Adding credibility to the suspicion that these actions by the Reagan Administration were at least in part influenced by the U.S. congressional elections is the fact that on November 9, one week after the elections, the White House ordered Ambassador Hinton to stop publicly criticizing the Salvadoran regime.[24] Furthermore, two days later a presidential spokesman announced that the Ambassador's declarations were "not intended to represent any change in either the substance or style" of the Reagan Administration's policy toward El Salvador.[25]

It would be incorrect, however, to conclude that the Reagan Administration was engaged exclusively in U.S. domestic campaign manipulation. Taking a page from President Kennedy's counterinsurgency handbook on dealings in Vietnam, the Reagan Administration used the ploy of threatening to cut off U.S. aid in an attempt to force the recalcitrant Salvadoran elite to institute minimal reforms, at least in appearance, in order to placate the U.S. Congress. Specifically, this means that land reform must be "rehabilitated," the judicial system must provide the impression of adhering to the rule of law (especially through the indictment of the murderers of U.S. citizens), and that the death squads and security forces diminish the number of their extrajudicial executions.

To accomplish these goals, the principal obstacle to reforms—the extreme-right coalition led by d'Aubuisson—must be restrained from continuing its fanatical program against all types of social reform. Already there were indications that U.S. pressure was producing results. In late October 1982, the Ministry of Defense announced that eight of the kidnapped opposition leaders were in the custody of the armed forces, and that they would be put on trial as "terrorists" for collaborating with the insurgents.[26] As ridiculous as this may appear, within the Salvadoran context it does represent an "improvement," both of the human rights situation and the functioning of the Salvadoran courts. Normally these people simply would have disappeared, or their bodies would have been found along the roadside or city dump after they had been executed.

Another apparent concession to U.S. pressure came on November 15, when a criminal court judge announced that five National Guard soldiers would be put on trial for the torture-murder of four U.S. churchwomen in December 1980. Even though there exists strong evidence that the National Guardsmen were acting on orders, no superior officer has been charged with the killings.[27] In fact, it appears likely that no one ever will be convicted of the crimes. After a series of delays, on March 11, 1983, a court of appeals ruled that there still was insufficient evidence to try the National Guardsmen.[28] Regardless of the fact that U.S. military aid is in part contingent upon bringing to trial the assassins of the churchwomen and other U.S. citizens murdered by the Salvadoran armed forces, the risks to the Salvadoran regime of trying the assassins may even be higher. As is characteristic of dictatorships that employ gross violations of human rights as state policy in order to stay in power, punishing the guilty would raise vital questions in the minds of the hired murderers, who would become far less trustworthy in carrying out their grisly orders.

Perhaps, because of U.S. public outrage, enough pressure will be generated so that these particular assassins will be brought to justice. But there is little chance that any of their colleagues will find themselves on the dock for committing Salvadoran government–sponsored atrocities.

A precedent has been set by the Argentine dictatorship. In an act of "national reconciliation" in 1982, Argentina declared amnesty for political crimes committed during the "dirty war" following the 1976 military coup. Since the top insurgent leaders were excluded from the amnesty provisions, the major beneficiaries were those members of the Argentine armed forces who tortured and killed on behalf of the government and are responsible for the "disappearance" of more than 20,000 "subversives," all of whom were officially declared dead in early 1983.* If the military prevails in El Salvador, a similar scenario can be expected to take place there.

Of greater importance in operational terms for U.S. counterinsurgency policy in El Salvador was the partial victory of General García, then Minister of Defense, over his principal rival for power, Roberto d'Aubuisson, president of the Constituent Assembly. The conflict between García and d'Aubuisson dates back to April 21, 1982, when the General imposed the pliable Alvaro Magaña as provisional president, a position that d'Aubuisson felt should be his. Subsequently, according to former President Duarte, at least three attempts were made—in July, September, and October—to overthrow the Minister of Defense. Duarte explained: "D'Aubuisson sees García as his problem and wants to get rid of him. The army, at this moment, is behind reforms. But a new command can change many things." [29]

During the October attempt to oust García, d'Aubuisson conducted a campaign to foment a coup against the Minister of Defense through public declarations and by means of private conversations with powerful military officers. The situation became so tense that the General felt forced to launch a direct counteroffensive to defend himself. Relying upon the support of a loyal cavalry regiment—the largest mobile armed military unit in the country—which he keeps deployed close to San Salvador as a "guarantee against a coup," in early November 1982 García spent several days in emergency consultations with President Magaña and his most important regional military commanders. Playing its cutting-off-military-aid card, the U.S. Embassy

---

*Since the December 1983 inauguration of the democratically elected president of Argentina, Raul Alfonsin, judicial prosecution has been initiated of many of the police and military officials responsible for these crimes.

openly supported the General by threatening that the removal of García would mean the end of all North American military assistance to El Salvador.[30]

Supported by President Magaña, the U.S. Embassy, and elements within the armed forces, on November 8 García carried out a purge of high-level officers in the army. Heading the list of at least six ultra-rightist colonels who were "rotated" out of positions of power was Nicolas Carranza, the chief of Salvadoran military intelligence, and perhaps the closest confidant of d'Aubuisson in the armed forces. Among other colonels who did not pass the U.S. Embassy's and García's loyalty test and found themselves purged were the regional commanders of Sonsonate, El Paraíso, and Santa Ana.[31] Even though García was forced to resign five months later, this episode dealt a severe blow to d'Aubuisson's power and prestige. The Reagan Administration was given some badly needed ammunition to defend itself against congressional pressure to enact reforms, so that it could continue its fundamentally military approach to counterinsurgency in El Salvador.

Yet the resistance of the national elite to external pressures should not be underestimated. A case in point was President Magaña's futile attempt in late 1982 to inflict another political set-back on the ultra-right. On December 17, Magaña called for the resignation of all cabinet members, secretaries, and subsecretaries of his administration in what he euphemistically labeled a "routine change" of personnel.[32] The real reason behind this attempt at high-level governmental house cleaning, just as during the military purge the previous month, was to attack the power of d'Aubuisson and his allies. The Kennedy Administration, during its attempt to revamp the cabinet of Vietnamese President Diem, characterized its similar effort as an attempt "to inject new blood, [and] remove the targets of popular discontent." One high-ranking Salvadoran official bluntly put it: "Magaña wants to form a Cabinet that is dedicated to implementing reforms."[33]

D'Aubuisson reacted furiously, forbidding his ARENA party functionaries to submit their resignations. He claimed, with justification, that the move amounted to an attempt at a "silent coup d'etat."[34] When asked to resign his own position as president of the Constituent Assembly, he angrily replied, "I will leave my post when I feel like it and not when a group of intriguers and liars decide to sell the idea to the United States public."[35]

Finally, all members of the cabinet submitted their resignations, and during late December rumors abounded that when Magaña announced the composition of the new cabinet on December 31, ARENA would be crippled as a political force.[36] But as the year passed, suspicion grew that something was amiss. When on January 3 the president made the announcement, it turned out that ARENA had lost only the Ministry of Public Health. Of greater significance, it had retained its two most important cabinet positions: the Ministry of Foreign Commerce and the Ministry of Agriculture, which are central to the implementation of the U.S.–sponsored reforms.[37]

The next act in the continuing drama of Salvadoran self-reform under crisis came in early January 1983 with the revolt of Lieutenant Colonel Sigfrido Ochoa Pérez. The ultra-rightist officer is considered one of the most powerful of the "warlords," and, along with Colonel Jaime Ernesto Flores Lima, has proven himself the most effective counterinsurgency tactician. Widely commended by U.S. officials for his successful "pacification" of the province of Cabañas, when Ochoa took command in mid-1981 he began the campaign by systematically "eliminating suspected subversives" from the area. Evidently frustrated by the Minister of Defense's attempts to adhere to the Reagan Administration's demand on human rights and land reform, the rebellious Colonel saw these concessions as hampering the war effort and destroying the traditional social structure.[38] Consequently, Ochoa, who is an intimate of Roberto d'Aubuisson and a number of powerful military officers (his 1964 graduating class included d'Aubuisson and the commanders of the three U.S.–trained "rapid reaction" battalions), felt strong enough to publicly challenge the authority of Defense Minister García.

On January 7, he declared himself and the 1,200 troops under his command "in rebellion." After closing off all official access to Cabañas to the rest of the armed forces, he demanded García's resignation, denouncing the General as "corrupt, arbitrary, and capricious."[39] At first, Ochoa's position seemed to gain strength, counting in the support of other major units of the armed forces. In fact, the situation became so tense that the General decided to retreat to the safety of his personally loyal garrison of Santa Clara, where he was joined by President Magaña. According to a highly placed member of the U.S. Embassy in San Salvador, who asked to remain anonymous, the president and the minister of defense received a visit there from U.S. Ambassador Hinton. This same source explained that after the conference, Hinton personally made the rounds of the principal Salvadoran military headquarters and "explained the facts of life to their commanders": U.S. assistance would be suspended if Ochoa and his cohorts were not brought under control.[40] It is a reasonable assumption that the Ambassador's threats influenced the Salvadoran armed forces, and the ultra-right ended up getting its wings clipped once again. General García remained in his post as Minister of Defense, while Colonel Ochoa was sent out of the country after being awarded a one-year grant to attend the prestigious Inter-American Defense College in Washington, D.C.[41]

Through a series of purges and political maneuvers in 1980, García already had driven the liberal members of the officer corps into insignificant posts or out of the country. Now, with Ochoa in Washington and the threat of the armed forces falling into the hands of the ultra-right finally eliminated, the time was approaching to dump the militarily inept General García, whose uninspired leadership had led many of his fellow officers and U.S. advisers to fear a guerrilla victory.

On April 18, 1983, Minister of Defense García, abandoned by his former U.S. backers, was forced to resign. He was immediately replaced by General Carlos Eugenio Vides Casanova, who until then occupied the position of head of the feared National Guard.[42] The role of the National Guard within the Salvadoran armed forces is to "maintain internal order." Historically, it has been so zealous in this task that even many army officers openly express their revulsion at the atrocities its troops regularly carry out against any type of real or imagined opposition. With such an impressive record already to his credit, U.S. officials held high hopes that Vides Casanova was the man to shake up the officer corps and transform the conventionally minded Salvadoran armed forces into an efficient counterinsurgency fighting force.

CIVIC ACTION

Another element of the counterinsurgency doctrine that should be mentioned under the overall rubric of reform is military civic action programs. This effort, fundamentally one of public relations, is designed to present the face of the "good army" in the overall pacification campaign. Not even pretending to institute any type of structural social change, civic action concentrates upon small-scale projects conducted by the military, such as road and bridge construction, digging wells, improving water supplies and other public health facilities, building and staffing free health and dental clinics, and other similar civilian-oriented projects. But just as with other types of reforms within the counterinsurgency context, these seemingly innocuous activities disguise an ulterior motive: improving the military's image and undermining the insurgents' popular base of support by "winning the hearts and minds" of the people.

The first civic action programs, begun by the Kennedy Administration in 1961 and 1962, were implemented in Colombia, Ecuador, Guatemala, Haiti, Turkey, Iran, and a number of African nations.[43] Even though this multimillion-dollar initiative (in 1962, for example, 1.5 million dollars were allocated to Ecuador alone)[44] grew to encompass dozens of Third World countries, it produced disappointing results. In large part, civic action programs fail, handicapped by the fundamental role these military establishments play within their respective countries. Throughout the Third World, and especially in Latin America, the function of the armed forces traditionally has been less that of a guarantor of national security against foreign threat, and more of an internal police force; basically they are designed to repress dissident groups in order to maintain the status quo.

In partial recognition of this reality, the U.S. Congress in 1975 established the Inter-American Foundation to fund small-scale civilian projects, without the involvement of the military. Even so, military civic action programs have continued to be used, although on a much reduced scale. During the Carter Administration, for example, the Military Advisory Group operating out of the U.S. Embassy in San Salvador provided the Salvadoran armed forces with limited quantities of medicines and food stuff. These goods, rather than being distributed to the population at large, found their way instead to "loyal" peasants in order to further assure their continued allegiance to the government.

If civic action by itself has produced only marginal results as a counterinsurgency tool, when employed immediately after massive military operations that have prostrated the local population, its record appears somewhat different. The Vietnam experience bears out this observation. There, the most successful civic action programs were incorporated into the CORDS campaigns after their initiation in 1967, whereas their precursors, such as President Diem's Catholic rural workers and the Political Action and Census Grievance teams that operated from 1964 to 1965, proved almost totally useless as pacification attempts.[45] Similarly, while in the early 1960s civic action efforts in Guatemala met with indifference, during 1983 in those areas that suffered the greatest and most frequent massacres by the Guatemalan armed forces, there could be seen not only the traditional civic action projects at work but even officers giving soccer instruction in schoolyards full of students, and military bands entertaining hundreds of young people by bleating out off-tune North American rock music.

The dynamics behind this deceptive success story will be discussed later. It is enough to say, here, that the U.S. counterinsurgency strategy in El Salvador, beginning for the first time on a "full spectrum" scale with the launching in June 1983 of Operation Well-Being employs a CORDS–type campaign that includes a large civic action component.

PROPAGANDA

Because of the strong political constraints imposed upon U.S.-sponsored counterinsurgency operations, it is imperative to confer international legitimacy upon client governments, while at the same time discrediting the insurgent forces. This is necessary to gain the support of, or at least to neutralize the criticism from, the international community as well as the U.S. public, news media, and Congress.

During the early years of the Cold War, much of the responsibility for disseminating U.S. propaganda fell upon the United States Information Service (USIS)—a dependency of the White House that operates out of U.S. embassies abroad, known within the United States as the United States Information Agency (USIA). The original purpose of USIS was to direct programs in foreign countries that would cast the United States in the best possible light. This was done through its "cultural centers," exchange programs, lecture series, and the dissemination of U.S. government propaganda. Within the context of the developing counterinsurgency doctrine, the USIS's duties expanded to include developing similar propaganda to improve the image of client governments among their own citizens and the international community.

Visitors to the USIS office at the U.S. Embassy in San Salvador are treated to endless horror stories depicting guerrilla atrocities and are offered packages of unconvincing photographs of alleged arms caches infiltrated from Nicaragua. The presentation continues with tales extolling courageous soldiers and skillful pilots, and the growing effectiveness of the U.S.-trained "Rapid Reaction Battalions." The good listener, moreover, is rewarded with exciting accounts of how the U.S. Military Group "put out of business" a renegade Salvadoran armed forces "night and fog" unit, and angry complaints bemoaning what a better job could be done if only the military advisers were not so hamstrung by the lack of leverage they are able to exercise upon their Salvadoran counterparts because of their ridiculously small numbers and the limited aid programs that prohibit them from training police and security forces. If the briefing seems to be going well, USIS officials might even confide that "perhaps the time has come to reinstate the Office of Public Safety"—a program run during the 1960s and early 1970s under the auspices of the Agency for International Development, that in 1975 was curtailed by Congress when an investigation revealed that its curriculum included training foreign police and security forces in torture techniques.

But not all of the responsibility of counterinsurgency propaganda falls upon U.S. shoulders. In Guatemala, for example, the dictatorship of General Efraín Ríos Montt designed a highly effective program of selling itself and its exceptionally vicious counterinsurgency policies. The core of this operation was a slick booklet, in English, that the Minister of Public Relations proudly handed out to the stream of visitors from around the world who were required to pass through his office for the mandatory press accreditation and military safe conduct passes required to travel outside of the capital. The January 1983 publication, entitled *This Government Has the Commitment to Change,* began with the official theme of the "born-again" General's regime: "I do not steal, I do not lie, I do not abuse." It details a questionable list of government accomplishments, reproducing in full the army's new code of conduct, which instructs its members on how to improve relations with the people by such means as paying for food obtained from the villagers and yielding the right of way to civilian vehicles.

Even the most severe critic can acknowledge the apparent sincerity that permeates this propaganda, as exemplified in its denunciation of the previous dictatorships: "For years dishonest authorities have taken for themselves money, goods and services that do not belong to them. For years the norm has been that Government and authorities distorted the truth, lied and did not fulfill their promises. For years the authorities have believed that their positions gave them rights over the rest of the citizens and that they were not responsible to the law. This is stealing, lying and abusing. This must not continue." But these are lofty words for a government which in its first four months alone systematically massacred thousands of civilians and made refugees out of hundreds of thousands more.[46]

As Washington learned during the Vietnam era, reforms in themselves can often serve as the best propaganda material. To lend legitimacy to the Vietnamese military dictatorship, the United States forced the 1966 constituent assembly elections and the following year's presidential charade, which was handily won

by generals Nguyen Van Thieu and Nguyen Cao Ky. In a similar
ploy, in order to counter charges that the U.S.-supported junta
in El Salvador was in reality nothing more than a thinly dis-
guised dictatorship, the Reagan administration sponsored elections there in March 1982 to choose a Constituent Assembly.
Regardless of the unexpected victory of the extreme right over
the more acceptable Christian Democrats, the initial impression
as of overwhelming popular participation in the electoral process. Loudly and persistently proclaimed by the United States as
a rejection by the people of El Salvador of the insurgent's armed
struggle, the elections have proved one of Washington's most
successful propaganda efforts. Upon closer examination,
however, evidence was uncovered that showed the elections
were seriously flawed by inflated numbers of votes and manipulative procedures.[47]

With presidential elections scheduled for March 1984, Washington is repeating its Vietnamese electoral propaganda program.
In Vietnam the opposition was officially prohibited from participating in the elections. In El Salvador they are excluded de facto
because right-wing death squads and government repression
make it impossible for them to organize and run an effective
campaign. Consequently, in El Salvador, just as in Vietnam,
U.S.-sponsored elections have far more to do with propaganda
than democracy. They are irrelevant as a means of settling political conflicts because the fundamental issue of power remains
untouched.

Propaganda is too important a counterinsurgency tool to be
dealt with only abroad. Given the widespread opposition to U.S.
counterinsurgency wars, the Department of State and even the
President himself find it necessary to throw their weight behind
the effort. In an embarrassingly inept attempt to discredit the
Salvadoran insurgents as Communist dupes, the State Department, in February 1981, released its White Paper on "Communist Intervention in El Salvador." This hastily contrived "proof"
of the Moscow–Havana–Managua conduit of material support
and operational control of the Salvadoran revolution was also
meant to justify increased U.S. intervention in the region. Its
miserable failure to accomplish either objective is reflected in the

fact that its credibility was not accepted internationally; even within the United States such important newspapers as the *Wall Street Journal* and the Washington *Post* rejected its authenticity.

Another typical operation was the State Department's media attack against Nicaragua in March 1982. Using U-2 spy plane aerial photographs, like those employed by the Kennedy Administration to convince the world of the installation of Soviet missiles in Cuba during 1962, the Reagan Administration attempted to demonstrate that Nicaragua was a military threat to Central American stability by becoming a "regional superpower." Yet, because of the inconclusive nature of the evidence and the general attitude of distrust caused by previous unsubstantiated claims, this unsuccessful propaganda exercise met with undisguised skepticism.

Subsequent State Department efforts, such as a second White Paper in May 1983, proved equally disappointing. In fact, by the spring of 1983 when Salvadoran guerrilla victories and revelations of illegal CIA covert operations against Nicaragua threatened the entire U.S. policy toward Central America, the State Department had so badly discredited itself that the President personally had to enter the fray. In a frantic attempt to rally support, Reagan, for the first time, found it necessary to place his and the presidency's prestige on the line and play an active role. Yet, regardless of his frequent and well-staged speeches and actions—for instance, the April appointment of Richard Stone as special envoy to Central America, the lip service paid to Latin peace initiatives (such as those put forward by the Contadora Group), and the creation in July of the bipartisan Kissinger commission—the President has failed to form a national consensus supporting his Administration's policies. On the contrary, public opinion polls continue to show overwhelming opposition, the media has become more critical, and Congress remains divided along partisan lines. Internationally, the Administration's situation is just as dismal. Washington has become increasingly isolated; virtually no friend or ally supports Reagan's militaristic policy toward Central America.

THREE

THE ROLE OF THE CIA

Reforms in themselves, it should be emphasized, never were considered an adequate method of defeating insurgency. U.S. counterinsurgency doctrine designed reforms to function hand in glove with repression. While inducements to "win the hearts and minds" of the population are offered through reform, repressive measures are meant to intimidate, or terrorize, the people into submission. Through this carrot-and-stick strategy, modern day counterinsurgency doctrine attempts to eliminate the insurgents' popular support, while at the same time physically destroying the insurgents themselves.

The primary counterinsurgency role of the CIA, as with other U.S. intelligence organizations, is to gather information concerning the insurgents' organization and mount paramilitary operations to disrupt enemy operations.

Perhaps the most notorious CIA counterinsurgency operation in Vietnam was the Phoenix program. To understand the rationale behind Operation Phoenix, the basics must be known about the structure of an insurgency organization. In Vietnam, as in the accompanying diagram (Figure 1) of the Salvadoran insurgent structure, for every rebel actually carrying a weapon and fighting, there were eight to ten people organized into a support system, technically known as the insurgents' "infrastructure." This administrative apparatus, or infrastructure, provides intelligence and medical care, coordinates supply and communication lines, manufactures rudimentary weapons, staffs "safe houses," and even invests surplus insurgent funds in legitimate businesses. The rebel militiamen are people who go about their normal lives but whose functions sometimes overlap with the

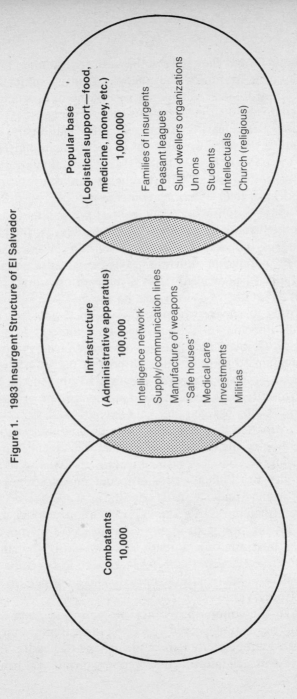

Figure 1. 1983 Insurgent Structure of El Salvador

Combatants
10,000

Infrastructure
(Administrative apparatus)
100,000

Intelligence network
Supply/communication lines
Manufacture of weapons
"Safe houses"
Medical care
Investments
Militias

Popular base
(Logistical support—food,
medicine, money, etc.)
1,000,000

Families of insurgents
Peasant leagues
Slum dwellers organizations
Un ons
Students
Intellectuals
Church (religious)

combatants in that they have some military training and can be called upon to reinforce the guerrillas during major military actions. They are also considered part of the infrastructure.

The complete insurgent organization rests upon its popular base, which has at least the same geometric relationship of about ten to one as the infrastructure has to the combatants. The function of the popular base is to provide logistical support for the insurgents in the form of food, medicine, and other supplies. To a small degree, their activities coincide with the purpose of the infrastructure, insomuch as members of the popular base often provide intelligence and money when possible. At the center of the insurgents' popular support lie the families of the insurgents. The rebels' popular base, while heavily weighted among the organized poor (the so-called mass organizations), comprises people from all sectors of society (see Figure 1).

According to congressional testimony of the former head of Operation Phoenix in Vietnam and later director of the CIA, William E. Colby, "The Phoenix program includes an intelligence program to identify the members of the VCI [Viet Cong Infrastructure], an operational program to apprehend them, a legal program to restrain them, and a detention program to confine them." Colby bragged that between 1968 and 1971, while he and approximately five hundred other U.S. advisers supervised the execution of the program by Vietnamese officials, a total of 26,369 South Vietnamese noncombatant civilians were assassinated under the Phoenix program, and an additional 36,369 were imprisoned under terrible conditions.[1]

The way that the CIA's Phoenix operation worked was that once an intelligence agent identified a suspected member of the Viet Cong infrastructure, a death squad would be dispatched to "neutralize" the victim. If the suspects were less fortunate, they were arrested, tortured, interrogated, and confined in 3-foot-square "tiger cages."

Although the counterinsurgency program had been targeted specifically against high-level Viet Cong infrastructure members, there existed a major problem in identifying this cadre. Proof of membership in a clandestine insurgent organization is nearly impossible to obtain, certainly in the judicial sense. Consequently, less rigorous standards, which amounted to little more than suspicion, were applied to target the "subversives." Such imprecise procedures left ample opportunity for denouncing personal enemies and settling vendettas. As in Central America today, many innocent people found themselves condemned by government death squads.

Most of those "neutralized" were peasants who only paid taxes to the Viet Cong or who joined the insurgents' mass organizations. Worse still, in order to fill the monthly quota, Vietnamese officials killed peasants at random and then labeled them as Viet Cong, or they listed as Viet Cong the people killed or captured in routine military sweeps. In fact, as one observer noted, "it has not been unknown for province or police chiefs to seek each month to exceed their quotas in order to demonstrate their competence."[2]

Although firm documentary evidence linking the CIA to death squads and disappearances in Central America today is not available, this counterinsurgency component is based upon the same rationale that guided the infamous Phoenix program. In reality, it matters little if the CIA is once again employing its social scientists and computers to compile lists of "subversives" in these "dirty wars." The concept of attacking the insurgents' infrastructure by killing suspects on the flimsiest of suspicions was first conceived and implemented by the CIA in Southeast Asia, and was taught as part of counterinsurgency doctrine in U.S. training facilities to the same people who today run the death squads throughout Central America.

EXTRAJUDICIAL EXECUTIONS IN EL SALVADOR

As demonstrated in Tables 2 and 3, which show extrajudicial executions of noncombatant civilians in El Salvador, documented by the legal aid office of the Salvadoran Catholic Church (Socorro Jurídico), the insurgent infrastructure and popular base have become a prime target of repression since the beginning of the civil war in 1979. As shown in Table 3 it is clear that the

TABLE 2. EXTRAJUDICIAL EXECUTIONS IN EL SALVADOR OF NONCOMBATANT CIVILIANS FOR POLITICAL REASONS

Year	Jan.	Feb.	Mar.	Apr.	May	Jun.	Jul.	Aug.	Sep.	Oct.	Nov.	Dec.	Total
1979	15	18	38	58	160	141	53	45	52	159	10	281	1,030
1980	268	236	487	481	1,197	763	682	546	830	764	779	991	8,024
1981	2,644	903	1,922	2,311	536	744	587	582	472	438	819	1,395	13,353
1982	466	532	526	805	375	355	198	701	474	617	631	296	5,976
1983	378	657	471	455	485	377							2,823

Sources: For the years 1979–1981, "Boletin Internacional del Socorro Juridico del Arzobispado de San Salvador," El Salvador, No. 40, May 15, 1982, pp. 3–6. For 1982–1983, "Boletin Internacional del Socorro Juridico Cristiano Arzobispo Oscar Romero, de El Salvador," No. 2, second fortnight of September 1982; and "Boletin," No. 3, first fortnight of October of 1982 (The "Boletin" changed names on June 1, 1982); *Situacion de los Derechos Humanos en El Salvador: period Jan.–Dec. 1982,* published on Jan. 15, 1983, by "Socorro Juridico Cristiano, Arzobispo Oscar Arnulfo Romero de El Salvador"; and "Boletin," No. 21, first fortnight of July 1983.

TABLE 3. EXTRAJUDICIAL EXECUTIONS IN EL SALVADOR BY SOCIAL SECTOR (IN PERCENT)

Year	Peasants	Workers	Students	Teachers	Professionals	Religious
1979	58.0	20.1	14.6	5.1	1.7	.5
1980	74.6	8.0	14.3	2.0	.8	.2
1981	88.4	5.4	4.9	.9	.3	.1
Jan.–Sep. 1982*	63.8	6.3	3.8	.5	.5	–
Average	75.9	10.6	10.0	2.3	.9	.2

The percentages for 1982 are calculated on an annual basis; that is, 75 percent of the January to September statistics.

Sources: The sources are the same as for the above table. Percentages have been calculated after subtracting the number of victims whose professions could not be determined or who fall into marginal categories such as merchants, journalists, etc. For 1979, they amount to 387 people, or 37.6 percent of the total; for 1980, they amount to 2,835, or 35.3 percent of the total; for 1981 they amount to 6,434, or 48.2 percent of the total; and for the first nine months of 1982 they amount to 3,191 or 72 percent of the total.

massive and systematic violation of human rights there, as with
the Phoenix operation in Vietnam, is almost totally directed at
the working classes (86.5 percent of the victims) and particularly
at the rural population, which makes up 75 percent of the dead.
Likewise, the steady growth of the rebel forces provides undeni-
able evidence of the ineffectiveness of this barbaric counterinsurgency tactic.

These statistics represent minimal figures, only tabulating
murders that can be documented. The reality of the situation is
far worse. In the countryside, where military commanders govern with an iron fist, many cases go unreported because the local
residents fear reprisals. Other victims are buried, quickly and
quietly, before human rights workers can arrive at the scene,
because of the fear that permeates the nation and the health
hazard presented by decomposing human bodies. It is generally
agreed that the actual number of dead is considerably higher
than shown in these tables. For example, U.S. Ambassador
Deane Hinton conservatively estimated by October 1982, that
"as many as 30,000 Salvadorans have been murdered—not
killed in battle, murdered."[3] Rather than the figure of 31,206
victims registered in Table 2 from October 1979 to June 1983,
however, a more accurate number would be closer to 40,000
murders by extrajudicial executions; and with the stepped-up
killings by death squads and army massacres during the last half
of the year, the total continues its grim climb.

Even with these limitations, the statistics clearly reveal other
counterinsurgency patterns. Following the 1979 coup that overthrew the old regime of President Carlos Humberto Romero, the
murders increased. Beginning that December, the month that the
Social Democrat civilian members of the new junta all announced their intention to resign in protest over the military's
failure to check the appearance of right-wing death squads, the
numbers of civilians killed jumped from dozens to hundreds
each month. Ever since, the death squads have been an institutional part of the Salvadoran way of life—and death.

It is no secret that these bands of killers are "off duty" soldiers
and police (often financed by rich Salvadorans who have chosen
the safety of voluntary exile in the United States) who operate in

close collaboration with the government and armed forces. While the rest of the country remains at home behind locked doors because of fear or military curfew, these men select their victims on the slightest hint of suspicion and "go on night patrol," as one young red-eyed Salvadoran army lieutenant, who had recently returned to El Salvador after graduating from West Point, euphemistically referred to their grisly nocturnal missions.[4] During the initial period of frenzied death squad activity, the government actually tried advertising. In a doublespeak campaign—which was understood by everyone, since at that time there were virtually no political prisoners in El Salvador—throughout the summer of 1980, the following message appeared daily on television, radio, and in the nation's major newspapers:

Salvadorans, Denounce Violence. This is the opportunity for us to defend our sacred right to live in peace. In the name of the Fatherland, denounce all suspicious or abnormal situations that could lead to violence. Your information should be given to the armed forces at the telephone number 26-8484. You do not have to identify yourself, just denounce.

Pressure from world opinion subsequently forced the government to stop publicly advertising for victims and to hold a token number of prisoners as evidence of the "improving human rights situation."

The slaughter of hundreds of civilians each month continues. The statistics also record months in which the number of victims reaches into the thousands. For example, the 1,197 victims registered in May 1980 reflects in large part the massacre by the army at the Río Sumpúl. The extraordinary number of murders in December 1980 and January 1981 (991 and 2,644, respectively) corresponds to the increased repression associated with the insurgent offensive of the latter month. The figures for March and April 1981 (1,922 and 2,311, respectively) reflect the various massacres by the army during its first major offensive after receiving massive U.S. military assistance, among which was the widely publicized massacre at the Río Lempa. The high December 1981 figure of 1,395 is also in great part the result of another army offensive that took place at this time in the province of Morazán and includes the Mozote massacre.

In terms of counterinsurgency warfare tactics, murders by death squads and massacres by the armed forces serve different functions. Even though in both cases they involve noncombatant civilians, death squad killings are aimed at destroying the insurgents' infrastructure, while massacres by the armed forces are direct attacks against their popular base in an attempt to terrorize the people into retracting their support. While this distinction carries military and legal significance, for the families of the victims it matters little. There is a popular saying in El Salvador that when a person is killed by the military or a paramilitary death squad, the younger members of the family first go to the funeral; their next stop is the guerrillas.

DISAPPEARANCES

A related counterinsurgency tactic widely employed throughout Latin America is the "disappearance" of suspected subversives. This brutal practice was originally developed by the Germans during World War II, and during the late 1960s adopted in the Americas by the moral heirs of the Nazis. The descriptive name given by Adolf Hitler in 1941 to this program was *Nacht und Nebel,* because its purpose was to make people suspected of "endangering the security of Germany" vanish into the "night and fog" of the unknown.

Field Marshal Wilhelm Keitel, who at his Nuremberg trial claimed that these disappearances were "the worst of all" the war crimes that he committed, nevertheless clarified the Führer's initial orders with several decrees of his own. Expostulating on the methods of sowing terror among the population, Keitel instructed: "Efficient intimidation can only be achieved either by capital punishment or by measures by which the relatives of the criminal and the population do not know his fate."[5] Several months later the Field Marshal explained in another directive that such disappearances would have the desired deterrent effect upon resistance to the Third Reich because: "(a) the prisoners will vanish without leaving a trace, (b) no information may be given as to their whereabouts or their fate."[6] In order to inflict the maximum anguish, the prohibition on revealing information, as documented in captured S.S. files, was especially applied to keeping secret the burial place of the victims.[7] (For his crimes Field Marshal Keitel was executed by hanging at the Nuremberg prison on October 16, 1946.[8])

This crime against humanity, which so shocked the world only several decades ago, is perpetuated as an everyday occurrence by many of the United States' best friends throughout Latin America. Typical of this counterinsurgency tactic was the kidnapping and disappearance in San Salvador of fifteen opposition political and labor leaders during October 1982 by squads of armed men dressed in civilian clothes. Five of the victims were among the few Democratic Revolutionary Front (FDR) officials that had remained in the country. The Washington Office on Latin America led an international campaign that forced the Salvadoran security forces to admit their responsibility for the disappearances and, furthermore, that they held eight of the kidnap victims in their custody.[9] The fate of the other seven people remains unknown, but in keeping with the pattern of such incidents, it is almost certain they were executed. This crime is reminiscent of the kidnapping by the Salvadoran security forces of twenty FDR high-ranking members in November 1980. On that occasion, the building in which these legal opposition leaders were meeting was surrounded by uniformed National Guard soldiers and armed men dressed in civilian clothing. The day after the twenty were abducted, the mutilated bodies of the six most important leaders were found discarded along the roadside, while the others have simply disappeared.[10]

These cases represent only a few of the incidents that have forced the moderate opposition into a firm coalition with the more radical guerrillas, and in large part accounts for their refusal to participate in any type of public activity. With adequate justification, they claim that to do so would be tantamount to suicide.

Indeed, the epidemic proportions that political disappearances have reached has prompted the families of those who have disappeared to join together in the Latin American Federation of Family Associations of the Detained-Disappeared (FEDEFAM). Along with El Salvador, among the most gross violators during the past years are other close friends of the Reagan Administration, especially Guatemala, Argentina, and Chile. In preparation for its third Latin American Congress, which was held in Lima, Peru, during November 1982, FEDEFAM announced that at least 90,000 people have been kidnapped, and subsequently have disappeared, because of political motivations. The ambitious purpose of this congress was to pressure the United Nations to take action to force the governments responsible for these crimes to release information concerning the whereabouts of those missing relatives. Furthermore, they hope to halt this type of state terrorism by the violator regimes through direct pressure on them, and indirectly on the United States to adhere to its own human rights standards and end Washington's uncritical support of these governments.[11]

COVERT OPERATIONS

The clandestine activities of the CIA in Central America today bear a striking resemblance to its role in Southeast Asia two decades ago. One of the best documented types of covert operation of that era consisted of recruiting, financing, and providing logistical support for dissident religious and ethnic minorities to fight the insurgents. Among the earliest of these operations in Vietnam occurred well before the United States made its major military commitment in the early 1960s. Immediately after the French defeat and the 1954 partition, Catholic priests led whole communities from North Vietnam to settle in the South. In co-operation with the Diem regime, the CIA began the first of its "secret wars" in the region by arming and training hamlet militia in the Catholic refugee villages.[12]

But not until 1960 did the U.S. Army and the CIA become involved on a large scale when they organized the Meo tribesmen of Laos into a mercenary paramilitary guerrilla force to counter the Pathet Lao (the Lao Communist National Liberation Front) and the North Vietnamese. Just as the Miskito Indians of Nicaragua and Honduras, these people cared little for political ideology of any kind. Impoverished natives living outside of the national economy, they resisted the imposition of any type of outside authority, be it the Lao government or the Communist

insurgents. The fiercely independent Meo proved to be prime
material for the CIA to forge into anti-Communist mercenaries.
The CIA was so generous in providing them with all the weaponry of war, even with transport and communications facilities
through the subsidiary Air America airline, that the Meo tribesmen actually became a force unto themselves. Even though they
were dependent upon CIA support, they freed themselves from
any interference by the Lao government. To many of their leaders, it seemed that the Meo finally had found a way of maintaining their independence. But during the course of the 12-year "secret war," this illusion shattered. The Meo met with disaster.
More than 20,000 lost their lives and approximately another
125,000 people were forced to flee from their homes and become
refugees.[13]

A similar example of CIA covert paramilitary operations can
be seen in the organizing of the Montagnard tribesmen of the
Vietnamese highlands. In November 1961, the CIA began arming these people; within thirteen months, 38,000 tribesmen were
under arms and over 200 villages with a population of about
300,000 were incorporated into the scheme. In this operation the
U.S. Agency for International Development collaborated with
the CIA by funding complementary civic action programs. Initially organized into hamlet militias called Citizens Irregular Defense Groups, the Montagnards were later unsuccessfully utilized
by the CIA as regular soldiers in the fight against the Viet Cong
insurgents and North Vietnamese regular army units.[14]

As one consequence of the Southeast Asian debacle, the CIA
got its wings clipped for a while. Following the revelations of the
Pentagon Papers and the senatorial subcommittee headed by
Frank Church that investigated the CIA's sordid operations
throughout the world, during the post-Watergate reform period
the CIA found its finances and activities sharply curtailed. According to the Reagan Administration's director of the CIA, William J. Casey, during this period the budget for U.S. intelligence
agencies as a whole was cut by 40 percent and the number of
their employees reduced by half.[15] Moreover, in 1978, President
Carter placed strict limitations on the Agency's covert operations.

Covert operations are not simple espionage exercises like stealing secret documents from other governments. They are interventions meant to bring about changes in the affairs of other nations. Often referred to as the "black side" of intelligence or the "third option," clandestine activities are designed to function in the area between doing nothing at all and engaging in outright warfare. Known examples of clandestine intervention range from placing provocateurs in dissident groups, blackmailing, fomenting labor strife, assisting "friendly" organizations in order to "destabilize" governments, conducting "disinformation" campaigns by planting false media stories, and, sometimes, even coordinating political assassinations.

What President Carter's limitations meant for CIA clandestine activities can be seen in the fact that, compared to the yearly average of approximately 300 covert operations during the 1950s and 1960s, during the late 1970s the United States conducted an average of from twenty to thirty per year.[16]

But since 1981, the CIA's fortunes have changed. Much of its budget and mandate have been restored by the Reagan Administration. While the exact amount of its financing is hidden in the budget of the Defense Department, what information that is available clearly reveals the generosity of the current Administration. For fiscal year 1982, the CIA's budget grew to about 1.5 billion dollars, and according to congressional sources, the sum for FY 1983 was even greater. Furthermore, the Agency is scheduled to be granted substantial yearly increases throughout the 1980s. Already, according to White House budget officials, the CIA is the fastest growing arm of the government. Its fiscal year 1983 budget increase of 25 percent dwarfs even the 18 percent growth for the Department of Defense. Reflecting this largess and lack of restraints, recently the CIA has hired an additional 1,500 officers, bringing the total number of its employees to more than 16,000 members.[17]

Upon assuming the office of director of the CIA, Casey announced that among his objectives was improvement of intelligence analysis and strengthening of counterintelligence capabilities. Highest on the Director's list of priorities, however, has been the revitalization of the Operations Directorate, that section of the CIA responsible for covert operations. As the *New York Times Magazine* explained: "From the start he took personal command of the clandestine services, adding staff members and resources, and has worked to rebuild the covert operations staff, euphemistically known within the CIA as the international-affairs division." [18]

In fact, the fascination with covert activities is not just an obsession of CIA Director Casey. Unlike the Carter Administration, the Reagan Administration views clandestine operations as a routine instrument of foreign policy. The Director justified this concept in the following manner: "To be, or to be perceived as, unable or unwilling to act in support of friendly governments facing destabilization or insurgency from aggressor nations, or to prevent groups acting or standing for American interests or values from being snuffed out, would be damaging to our security and leadership." [19] By employing this imperial logic in the formulation of U.S. policy toward Central America, the CIA has been unleashed to mount its biggest covert action since the days it ran amuck in Southeast Asia.

THE NICARAGUAN CONTRAS

In the past, in large part due to a generalized if misguided sense of patriotism and the self-censorship of the mass media, precise information proved extremely difficult to obtain concerning undercover operations. But the Vietnam war and the Watergate scandal changed the nation's uncritical assumptions about its intelligence agency's actions along with government activities in general. In this climate of skepticism, it has now become questionable whether any large-scale covert operation could be carried out in secrecy.

Certainly the most dramatic case in point is the Reagan Administration's "secret war" against the Sandinista government of Nicaragua, which undoubtedly has become the worst-kept secret operation in CIA history. Although the story came out in dribs and drabs, by mid-1983 the U.S. press had fully documented the major steps in the organizing, training, financing, and continuing support of Nicaraguan counterrevolutionaries, called the contras, into a powerful guerrilla army determined to overthrow the Managua regime. Alan Riding, the senior Latin American correspondent for the *New York Times,* wrote that "diverse Nicaraguan exile groups now concede that the Reagan Administration, working through the Central Intelligence Agency, forged them into a single force, the Nicaraguan Democratic force." [20] Actually, the situation is more complicated, involving yet a second contra army: the Democratic Revolutionary Alliance.

The saga begins only six weeks after Reagan's inauguration, when the President dispatched a "finding" to the congressional Intelligence Oversight committees, contending that U.S. national security called for clandestine operations in Central America. The "9 March 1981 Presidential Finding on Central America" emphasized that these activities would consist primarily of clandestine political and propaganda campaigns, as well as efforts to improve intelligence-gathering capabilities on the flow of arms to the Salvadoran insurgents and a paramilitary operation to interdict this traffic.[21] By mid-November the National Security Council (NSC) had worked out the details of a ten-point covert plan that Reagan approved and signed on December 1, 1981.[22]

According to NSC documents, the objective of the secret program was to "build popular support in Central America and Nicaragua for an opposition front that would be nationalistic, anti-Cuban and anti-Somoza." [23] Even though the former dictator of Nicaragua, General Anastasio Somoza, was assassinated in 1980, the CIA recognized that his followers, especially the hated National Guard, are still so universally despised that to associate them with a popular movement amounted to a contradiction in terms.

Moreover, the plan called for initial funding of 19 million dollars to create a 500-man force to conduct paramilitary operations.[24] These Honduras-based commandos, NSC records go on to explain, were to be deployed against the "Cuban–Sandinista support infrastructure in Nicaragua and elsewhere in Central America." As CIA Director Casey presented the operation to the congressional oversight committees at the time, the contras would be carefully limited in their numbers and in the scope of their activities; no mercenaries were to be involved and their primary function was to stop the arms flow from Managua to the rebels in El Salvador and Guatemala.[25]

Several months later, in February 1982, during a follow-up briefing before Congress, the CIA's Latin American director, Dewey Clarridge, stuck his foot in his mouth when he announced that the number of counterrevolutionary commandos stood at 1,000 troops. When pressed to explain the increase, CIA officials insisted that there was none, that they had not lied to the committee in previous testimony, that all along they had informed them that the 500-man task force would be augmented by another 1,000 dissident Miskito Indians. At this point serious doubts about the honesty of the CIA briefings began to form in the minds of many committee members. Indeed, if it is true that this was the first that the Congress had heard about the Miskito contras, NSC documents reveal that as early as its November 1981 meeting the Administration knew that in Honduras "the Argentines are already training over 1,000 men."[26] Eventually, because of the United States' support of England in the Malvinas/Falkland Islands War, the Argentines temporarily pulled out their military advisers in protest, and the support of the Indian commandos passed over to the larger CIA paramilitary operation.

The next step in Congress's growing suspicion that the Administration had a "hidden agenda," regardless of the fact that the law required it to report the full plans of covert operations, came in the summer of 1982. In further CIA briefings, Congress learned that U.S.-supported contras had blown up two major bridges inside Nicaragua in March, and that the "carefully limited" commando forces had grown to 1,500 soldiers who were preparing to move some of their camps out of Honduras and into northern Nicaragua. Concerned about the legality of these activities and the danger of war between Honduras and Nicaragua that the CIA and their contras could touch off, in August 1982, both oversight committees amended the secret intelligence bill to set clear limits on U.S. covert operations in Central America.[27]

These congressional restrictions were passed into law in December 1982 as the Boland Amendment, which specifically forbids the U.S. government to provide "military equipment, military training or advice, or other support for military activities, for the purpose of overthrowing the Government of Nicaragua or provoking a military exchange between Nicaragua and Honduras."[28]

By this time Congress had received a double jolt. The first came in November, when a series of spectacular press reports blew the cover off the undercover operation; the other arrived during the December CIA briefing, when it announced that the number of U.S.-supported irregular forces had in the preceding four months swelled to approximately 4,000 contras.[29]

In early November 1982, *Newsweek* published a special report entitled "America's Secret War—Target: Nicaragua," in which it charged that the true objective of the CIA–backed contras was, in fact, nothing less than the overthrow of the Sandinista government.[30] For the preceding nine months, when reports of clandestine Central American operations first broke in the press, Administration officials steadfastly declined to comment. But the devastating *Newsweek* cover story put them on the defensive, forcing them to admit the truth of the original allegations. The Administration attempted to contain the damage by claiming that the CIA plan was limited only to harassing Nicaragua by providing financial support for moderate political and business institutions and leaders in Nicaragua, helping to train anti-Sandinista forces in Honduras, using these contras "to interdict Cuban supply lines to guerrillas in neighboring El Salvador," and to conduct hit and run raids into Nicaraguan territory. But in no way, Reagan officials insisted, was there any idea of overthrowing the Sandinista government.[31] In retrospect, it is obvious that the Administration admitted only what it could not creditably deny and simply lied about the rest.

Even at that time, drawing upon information obtained from numerous U.S. and Honduras government and military officials, *Newsweek* convincingly presented a far more insidious scenario. According to its report, CIA clandestine operations in Nicaragua actually began in 1978, when President Carter, in an attempt to prevent the Sandinistas from coming to power, authorized the secret support of anti-Somoza—but non-Sandinista—elements, such as the press, the private business sector, and labor unions. This covert support of the so-called moderate elements was not only continued by the Reagan Administration, it also radically broadened the scope of U.S. undercover intervention.

Obsessed with the idea of the Nicaraguans sending arms to the Salvadoran insurgents, then Assistant Secretary of State for Inter-American Affairs, Thomas O. Enders, insisted that it was necessary to "get rid of the Sandinistas."[32] But organizing the diverse contras, who were plagued by bitter factional strife, proved easier said than done.

In April 1982, the CIA first attempted to recruit Edén Pastora—the legendary former Sandinista Commandante Zero—to unite and lead the various contra groups. But Pastora, although he had become a virulent anti-Sandinista, dedicated to bringing down the Managua regime, refused to have anything to do with the CIA at this time.[33] Because of CIA backing of the Nicaraguan Democratic Force (FDN), the Honduras-based contras, composed mostly of former Somoza National Guardsmen, almost another year would pass before Pastora formed his Democratic Revolutionary Alliance (ARDE) and began hostilities against the Sandinistas from Costa Rica along Nicaragua's southern border.[34]

The CIA encountered further disappointment in recruiting counterrevolutionaries among the Indians who live along the Caribbean coast of northern Nicaragua and southern Honduras. These natives, commonly referred to as the Miskito Indians, actually include the Rama and Suma Indians as well. All three tribes, historically, have opposed whatever central government happened to be ruling from Managua, forming a loose coalition called the Misurasata to better protect themselves. While the vast majority of the natives remain neutral, with many actually supporting the Managua government, two dissident factions actively opposed the Sandinistas.

The CIA's problem was that these two groups not only hate the Sandinistas, they despise each other just as much. The leader of the smaller faction, Brooklyn Rivera, denounces his rival, Steadman Fagoth, as a sell-out for accepting U.S. support and joining up with Honduras-based FDN.[35] Consequently, Rivera has refused to have anything to do with the northern contras, and has teamed up with Pastora's ARDE commandos in the south along the Costa Rican border.[36] Meanwhile, Fagoth's group, accepting CIA support and entering into a loose alliance with the FDN in the north, had grown by early 1983 to an unofficial estimate of between 2,000 to 3,000 members.[37] To top this off, Pastora not only considers as enemies the FDN Somocista National Guard that he fought against, he denounces equally Fagoth's anti-Sandinista Indians as "worse than the Sandinistas."[38]

In any event, the disaffected Indians, unlike the Meo tribesmen of Laos or the Vietnamese highland Montagnards, have proved to be disappointingly poor soldiers. As Fagoth casually remarked, we "fight one day and plant seeds the next."[39] Certainly their participation is far from proportionate to their numbers. In December 1982, about 600 Indians joined in the first major contra raids into Nicaragua, and the following month a frogman team sabotaged port installations at Puerto Cabezas near the Honduran border.[40] As the year progressed, they attended more to their crops than to fighting. Although some Indians fought in the February–April offensive, since then there has been no significant Indian participation.

Without doubt the CIA has channeled the lion's share of its succulence to the former Somoza National Guardsmen. After their defeat by the Sandinistas in July 1979, many of the Guardsmen found themselves scattered around Central America, with a high concentration along the Honduran side of the border with Nicaragua. Typical of their activities during the following two years is the history of the 15th of September Legion, whose more than 300 Honduras-based members distinguished themselves by robbery, murder, and indolence. In August 1981, they gained some measure of legitimacy when the CIA recruited the entire 15th of September Legion, along with other Somocista gangs, to form the FDN.[41] In fact, the FDN officer corps, led by Colonel Enrique Bermudez, who served as Somoza's military attaché in Washington until the Sandinista victory, is completely made up of ex-National Guardsmen. This presents both advantages and disadvantages for the counterrevolutionary crusade.

The principal advantage of utilizing the ex-National Guardsmen as the primary strike force lies in the fact that they are highly motivated and experienced combat troops. In any case (as the CIA informed Congress in December 1982 when pressed to explain why) in contrast to their initial plan, the CIA was employing these Somocistas because "they were the only ones who wanted to fight." [42]

The initial *Newsweek* report sketched U.S. involvement with the FDN. In addition to the doubled size of its CIA station in Honduras, the official staff is supplemented by an undetermined number of retired U.S. military and intelligence officers, as well as teams of Green Beret Special Forces advisers and other technicians, who have supervised the establishment of training camps located along both sides of the border. The function of these U.S. personnel is not only to train the counterrevolutionaries and supply them with ordnance, but also to provide the Somocistas with logistical support for their incursions into Nicaragua; they even repair their U.S.–provided electronic equipment and helicopters when they break down.

An article by Raymond Bonner of the *New York Times*—which was based on information given by a Honduran who was directly involved in planning the CIA covert operation and which was confirmed by two members of the Senate Intelligence Committee as well as a top Reagan Administration official—fills in some other gaps in the story.[43] According to these sources the United States has provided the contras with nearly all of their weapons and equipment. Following the joint United States–Honduran military exercises in August 1982, a number of huge U.S. C-130 cargo planes arrived to deliver enormous quantities of ordnance to the anti-Sandinista forces. As the Honduran source explained: "Because of the exercise, they figured that the planes would not attract notice." Moreover, rather than taking their equipment with them after the maneuvers had ended as is normal practice, the U.S. forces left most of it behind to be distributed to the contras. Other arms reached the FDN directly from the Honduran armed forces, who "just opened the doors" of their warehouses. The United States, in turn, simply resupplied the Hondurans. Once the contras began moving some camps into Nicaraguan territory that November, the pattern changed accordingly. After being delivered by air to Honduras, the Honduran army transported the weapons and equipment by truck to the border and the contras carried them into Nicaragua.

In mid-1983, facing increasing congressional resistance to further funding for its "secret war," the Reagan Administration developed an innovative way of getting arms to its counterrevolutionaries. At that time, Washington persuaded Israel to supplement U.S. military aid by sending weapons captured by them in Lebanon to the Honduran government, for transshipment to the Nicaraguan contras.[44]

Even the details of the secret operation's command structure have become a matter of public record. The November 1982 *Newsweek* article first outlined the general scheme of things. Not surprisingly, the U.S. Ambassador to Honduras, John D. Negroponte, is at the top of the heap. Handpicked by Alexander Haig, then the Secretary of State, Negroponte, a counterinsurgency expert who proved his ruthlessness in Vietnam and Cambodia, heads the covert operations. Establishing himself as a virtual U.S. proconsul, shortly after his appointment, he brought both the Honduran president and the commander in chief of the armed forces under his personal control. At the January 1982 inauguration of Roberto Suazo Córdova, the Ambassador presented the new Honduran president with a written list of eleven specific policies that he demanded be adopted by the new government. These included fiscal reforms such as lowering taxes on mining companies, and austerity measures such as the elimination of government price controls. Reflecting the Ambassador's power, the Honduran government has already complied with many of these demands.

But of greater importance, Negroponte has also established dominance over General Gustavo Adolfo Alvarez, the head of the armed forces. Regardless of the election of Suazo Córdova as president—the first civilian head of state in nine years—there is no question that General Alvarez is the most powerful person in the nation. A member of the Honduran army high command explained their relationship: "They discuss what should be done, and then Alvarez does what Negroponte tells him to." Serving as the Ambassador's intermediary with the Somocistas, the General provides a buffer so that Negroponte can deny any direct involvement. The reason that Suazo Córdova and Alvarez accept such indignities is pitifully obvious. For fiscal years 1981 and 1982, direct U.S. assistance amounted to 187 million dollars to that nearly bankrupt country and for fiscal year 1983 alone, the Reagan Administration funneled a whopping 114 million dollars into Honduras.[45]

Later investigation filled out the picture. According to FDN sources, a three-tier chain of command is in operation. At the summit sits Ambassador Negroponte who, together with a team of CIA and U.S. military experts, develops the day-to-day strategy. This command board then passes its general orders down for tactical refinement to the second-level command center. This international junta is led by General Alvarez and the Honduran high command, but also includes the CIA station chief in Tegucigalpa, Colonel Bermudez, and a military representative from Argentina. (Since the end of the Malvinas/Falkland Islands War, the Argentines have swallowed much of their resentment toward the United States and have resumed their participation in training and advising the contras.) In turn, the orders flow down to the third level, an operational general staff, comprised of FDN officers who actually command the military operations, virtually all of whom are former National Guardsmen.[46]

All this looks fine on paper, if the Reagan Administration's original purposes for launching the clandestine operation can be believed. But in reality, a Somocista army has been created in the process, and this army has presented serious problems for the U.S. functionaries. While the ex-National Guard soldiers may have been "the only ones who wanted to fight," it quickly became apparent that what they wanted to fight for was not simply the interdiction of the purported arms traffic from Nicaragua but the defeat of the Managua government. Receiving independent financing from rich Somocistas living in Miami,* these counter-revolutionaries are so fanatically committed to regaining their former positions of power by overthrowing the Sandinistas that

---

* Financing of the former National Guard contras by wealthy Miami-based Somocistas has long been an open secret.

the CIA, even if it so desired, could not maintain tight control over their activities.[47]

Once on the offensive after three years of humiliating exile, the Somocistas developed an ambitious plan that they intended to carry out, with or without approval of the United States. As reported in the first big *Newsweek* story, their so-called plan "number one" was to establish more camps on the Nicaraguan side of the border, then rapidly move farther down toward Managua and on to the south. Finally, they would draw in their loose circle of camps around the capital to drive out the Sandinistas. "And then? Come the counterrevolution, there will be a massacre in Nicaragua, promises one contra officer. 'We have a lot of scores to settle. There will be bodies from the border to Managua.'" As one U.S. diplomat later bemoaned: "These guys are like the Cuban exiles. In the end nobody can control them. They have their own agenda."[48]

As long predicted by Managua, beginning in early December 1982 large numbers of contras, led by former officers of Somoza's National Guard, began daily commando raids into the northern border provinces of Nicaragua. On December 17, eleven days after the raids began,[49] the first large-scale incursion penetrated Nicaraguan territory with a force of approximately 1,000 counterrevolutionaries.[50] In the following days the contra forces, estimated to number between 1,500 and 2,000 troops,[51] stepped up their attacks from their Honduran bases in what one high-ranking Sandinista official prophetically labeled "a silent and growing, although undeclared war."[52]

The immediate objective of the contra military operations was to quickly secure a portion of one of the northern Nicaraguan provinces, which they then would declare a "liberated territory" under their control. They hoped this would be accepted by the United States and its Central American client states as the basis for the recognition of an anti-Sandinista provisional government, or at the very least a state of belligerency.

But by mid-January the offensive had clearly failed, even in the most promising northern province of Nueva Segovia. Here the contras hoped to spark popular support because traditionally a high proportion of the National Guard came from the area, which is one of the nation's poorest provinces. The population in Nueva Segovia is noted for its pioneer life-style and conservatism, which has expressed itself in an historical resentment toward any authority. Even these favorable conditions and the fact that the Sandinistas did not deploy their seasoned veterans, but rather sent poorly trained militia units to combat the contras, proved to be inadequate for the counterrevolutionary commandos to gain a foothold in Nicaragua. But the biggest test was yet to come.

Even as CIA officials reported to Congress in February 1983 that the contra forces had leaped to 5,500 combatants, the Somocistas began their most determined offensive.[53] Beginning in late February, the incursions intensified step by step until, by late March, they amounted to what only can be accurately described as a full-scale invasion. Depending on whose figures are accepted, somewhere between 2,000 and 4,500 contras invaded wide stretches along the northern frontier. The Sandinistas gave the lower figure, claiming that the FDN exaggerated the number of invaders to create the appearance that the nation had finally erupted into civil war. Regardless of the exact numbers, the invasion shook the Sandinistas, especially since at least several hundred contras penetrated as far as Matagalpa province, which lies nearly 100 miles from the border and only 70 miles from Managua. This time the Sandinistas called out crack units from the regular army, some of whom had already fought and defeated the National Guard during the three-year war against Somoza. Unlike the local militias, these veteran Sandinista troops once again proved more than a match for the National Guardsmen. By early April, the heavy fighting was over, with the contras taking a terrible beating; those that were not killed or captured were forced to beat a hasty retreat back to their havens along both sides of the Honduras–Nicaragua border.[54]

The repercussions of the invasion by the CIA's "secret army" reverberated across the continent. In the light of the deluge of press reports[55] and the undisguisable fact that the invasion was aimed at toppling the Sandinista government, it became impossible to credibly maintain the fiction, although both the Honduran and United States governments tried. For the past twenty months, in the faces of persistent Sandinista charges and press reports, Washington and Tegucigalpa adamantly denied the existence of the contra training camps in Honduras. Indeed, Honduras continued denying them even after Bill McLaughlin stood in the center of one during the *CBS Nightly News* and announced: "The Honduran government claims they do not exist. The U.S. government refuses to confirm or deny its support for them. This is one of them: a guerrilla training camp in Honduras less than ten miles from the Nicaraguan border."[56]

May 1983 opened with a series of ominous events. First Edén Pastora's ARDE opened its long-awaited "second front" in southern Nicaragua along the Costa Rican border in coordination with a renewed month-long FDN offensive in the north.[57] At this time the contras, whose numbers by now had reached 7,000, were still planning on a short war.[58] Projecting their own enthusiasm, they based their hopes on the false assumption that their commando raids would provide the catalyst to touch off a popular uprising—much like the delusion held by the 1961 Cuban Bay of Pigs invaders—which would result quickly in bringing the revolutionary government to its knees.[59] Evidently, many in Washington shared in this fantasy, for CIA Director Casey and other senior Administration officials predicted in congressional testimony that the contras stood a good chance of defeating the Sandinistas by the end of the year.[60]

In the aftermath of Reagan's dramatic April 27 speech to the joint session of Congress—which, as then NSC head William Clark emphasized, placed the importance of Central America on a par with the Middle East[61]—the President could not help being disappointed in the continued opposition to his policies among the public, media, and Congress. Perhaps he was also caught up the counterrevolutionary optimism when on May 4 he, for the first time, acknowledged that the United States was in fact giving direct assistance and "providing subsistence" to the anti-Sandinista "freedom fighters."[62] Marking a major shift in the publicly stated purposes of the CIA's contras, subsequent Administration statements deemphasized their role of harassing the Sandinistas and interdicting arms traffic—which reliable sources claim had diminished to a trickle by this time.[63] In any event, this rationale was already wearing thin since the contras had failed to capture even a single arms shipment.

The coming months produced further complications for the now absurdly public secret war. The expectations of a quick victory faded when in June, just a week after the northern contras launched another short-lived offensive, Edén Pastora and his southern-based ARDE commandos went on strike.[64] Apparently disheartened by the failure of large-scale defections from the Sandinista army that he had counted upon, Pastora announced that he was suspending hostilities because the United States was preventing money and arms from reaching his rebels.[65] Initially the CIA supplied ARDE with about 500 weapons and a few hundred thousand dollars to get them started, with the understanding that the independent-minded Pastora would cooperate with the Somocista FDN. In late May the CIA's stance toughened to stipulating that further aid depended on Pastora's agreement to restrict his armed activities to the south and formally placing him way down the list to fourth in command of the contra forces.[66] Pastora balked, the CIA blocked, and Pastora buckled.

In mid-July, ARDE announced its intention to work more closely with the northern contras. Their supplies resumed and its troops returned to the fray.[67] By this point, however, even though the contra armies reportedly had mushroomed to an estimated 10,000 combatants, it had become painfully obvious that the contras were not about to spark a popular revolt.[68] In fact, while they may be tolerated by the people living in some areas of Nicaragua, unlike the guerrillas in El Salvador and Guatemala, they enjoy no significant popular support. Rather than the classic insurgent organizational structure where each combatant is backed up by an infrastructure that in turn rests upon a popular base, these so-called "freedom fighters" simply do not constitute such an indigenous force. The contras are, more accurately, externally organized, financed, and supported commando armies that function under an almost conventional military structure.

Given this reality, which became increasingly evident, the best that could be hoped for was that the contras might defeat the Managua government through a long, if limited, war of attrition. But to accomplish this they would need the help of other more forceful means to squeeze the Sandinistas. This was not long in coming. On July 18, 1983, the same day that the Administration revealed plans for two sets of coordinated military maneuvers in the region, President Reagan announced that "more Cuban and Soviet supplies have arrived in Nicaragua" and that "this cannot be allowed to continue."[69]

The joint United States–Honduran "Big Pine II" military exercises, although presented as routine, were scheduled to last into 1984. Rather than the normal two or three week duration as in the past, these unprecedented eight-month "maneuvers" in reality amounted to nothing less than a temporary stationing of U.S. armed forces in the Isthmus. To call routine the simultaneous deployment of two naval battle groups, one on either side of Nicaragua, is ludicrous. It is classic gunboat diplomacy.[70] The destructive force represented by the guns and planes carried on these two armadas is phenomenal: It should be noted that at no time did the United States deploy as much naval-based fire power in Southeast Asia throughout the entire course of the Vietnam war.

Unable to admit openly that their objectives were the same as those of the contras—the overthrow of the Managua government—the White House adopted a new line. President Reagan explained that by supporting the CIA–sponsored counterrevolutionary war, the United States hoped "that we can persuade the Nicaraguan, the Sandinista government, to return to the principles of the revolution and which they in writing guaranteed to the Organization of American States [OAS]."[71]

What the President was referring to was the promise to the OAS the Sandinistas made shortly after coming to power in 1979, i.e., to maintain a pluralistic society and, especially, to hold elections within a reasonable length of time. The Sandinistas argue that most of these promises have been kept: that two thirds of the economy still remains in private hands; that only following the first contra sabotage raids in March 1982 were they forced to declare a state of emergency and impose partial press censorship; and that although elections are scheduled for 1985, because of the state of war created by the U.S.–sponsored contra armies, it is now impossible to move up the date. Besides all this, they point out further that, in good part because of the 80,000 "contras" that fled to hostile neighboring Canada, it was thirteen years before the United States held the first election after its own revolution, during which time George Washington shot his way into power.

Of course the rhetorical battle between Managua and Washington paled beside the force of arms. Presenting a major address on July 19, 1983—the fourth anniversary of the Sandinista victory over General Somoza and his National Guard—the Coordinator of the Nicaraguan governmental junta, Daniel Ortega, delivered a grave message to the nation. After announcing that the fighting had already taken the lives of more than 600 of their fellow citizens and inflicted upward of 70 million dollars in damages since the beginning of the year, the Sandinista leader prophetically warned that in the near future the contra attacks would be claiming an even greater toll.[72] Due to the stepped-up contra commando raids beginning in the fall, according to the Sandinista armed forces, by the end of 1983 the nation's material losses had topped the one billion dollar mark.[73]

Perhaps encouraged by the closer cooperation among the different contra factions, in early August Reagan Administration officials openly began talking about eventually fielding 20,000 guerrillas.[74] Overcoming more of their ideological differences, in mid-August the three contra armies—the FDN, the Misurasata, and the ARDE—issued a joint communiqué stating their common objective of installing a "democratic government" in Nicaragua. At this same time, while the ARDE stepped up its activities from their southern base in Costa Rica, the Honduras-based contras launched a major offensive, sending several thousand troops into the northern Nicaraguan border provinces. This time the FDN held high hopes of finally securing a "liberated area" inside Nicaragua from which they would claim the establishment of a provisional government that would be recognized by the United States and its friends.[75]

Several new factors also boosted expectations. Along with their customary strategy of attacking Nicaraguan border stations, small towns, and outlying military posts with the special demolition teams whose mission was to demolish bridges and other strategic targets, the invaders introduced what in the coming months would develop into a focused attempt to destroy the nation's economic infrastructure.[76] Moreover, another cause for optimism lay in the fact that previous offensives had suffered from the lack of adequate logistical support for their soldiers fighting inside Nicaragua. As the FDN leader, Adolfo Calero Portocarrero emphasized: "We did not have the capacity to supply our people. Now we are better prepared logistically."[77] Not just another of the interminable contra propaganda declarations, the approximately forty violations of Nicaraguan airspace that August to support and resupply the rebel ground forces provide ample testimony to the accuracy of Calero's boast.[78]

Only in October did the full facts come to light concerning these resupply missions, which the Sandinistas had assumed originated exclusively in Honduras; and the reality of the situation carried even more volatile implications for the regionalization of the Isthmus conflicts. According to U.S. officials in Central America, the CIA had been employing Salvadoran pilots, using Salvadoran air force planes bought with U.S. aid money, to fly as many as a dozen sorties a week from El Salvador deep into Nicaragua to resupply the contras with medicines, ammunition, and communications equipment.[79]

Despite these advantages, the August offensive never really got any further than the preceding efforts of the contras to set up shop in the Sandinista heartland.[80] By the end of the month, they had been driven back to their Honduran sanctuaries, where they sat licking their wounds and suffering the lowest ebb of their war; for the fundamental problem remained the same—unable to break the barrier of mustering even minimal support among the people for their cause, the contras proved incapable of making the critical transition from an invading commando army to an indigenous insurgent force that could establish and maintain control over any appreciable area. In fact, during the long months of fighting, although they did sow terror by killing and kidnapping civilians, the contras had not even managed to hold a single town for more than a few hours.

No longer able to mask reality, the CIA, in its secret report to the House and Senate Intelligence subcommittees in September

1983, finally admitted that by themselves the contras stood no chance of inflicting either a military or political defeat on the Sandinistas. In order to keep up the pressure on Managua, however, the CIA insisted on continued funding for its charges.[81] But now the "freedom fighters" found themselves in a double bind. The contras faced yet another, potentially more serious, problem as the U.S. Congress began to gear up for its perennial budget debate that would determine their official financial fate.

Some liberal congressional members, feeling that the contras were not really fighting for "freedom" but rather doing the Reagan Administration's dirty work in order to ultimately benefit themselves, wanted to cut off all CIA succulence because of its illegality and immorality. At the other end of the spectrum, a growing group of conservative legislators, assessing their inability to produce a serious challenge to the Sandinistas, began wavering, because continued support for these "losers" could quickly end up as a political albatross around their own necks. Ruling out (for obvious reasons) any further attempts at legal or moral legitimization, under CIA tutelage the contras decided that the pragmatic route of a highly visible economic-sabotage campaign against the Nicaraguan infrastructure offered the best chance of retaining the backing of the congressional right wing.

The implementation of the new strategy began with a bang: On September 8, 1983, two ARDE aircraft flying out of their Costa Rican bases attacked Managua. Sandinista ground fire blasted the first out of the air only after its bombs had inflicted heavy damages and casualties at Augusto Cesar Sandino International Airport; the other escaped unscathed when its strafing run missed the Santa María telecommunications center located in a nearby suburb.[82] The Sandinistas charged that the CIA provided the contras with the planes and bombs. Of course, ARDE denied the allegations, claiming that they purchased the aircraft with the $600,000 that the former Nicaraguan Ambassador to Washington, Francisco Fiallos Navarro, stole from the embassy when he defected in 1982.[83]

A penetrating article in the *New York Times* a month later, however, substantiated CIA involvement by tracing the downed plane to the shadowy Investair Leasing Corporation of McLean, Virginia. Although incorporated in 1982 in Delaware, in violation of Virginia law, the company had failed to register with that state's authorities. Furthermore, the background of Investair's general manager, Edgar L. Mitchel, a former vice-president of the now dissolved Intermountain Aviation Company (which a 1976 Senate investigation disclosed as one of the CIA's largest assets), lent further credence to the idea of the Agency's involvement; as did the previous employment of Investair's marketing manager, Mark J. Peterson, who had served as the secretary and treasurer of the world's biggest airline before its forced demise—the totally CIA–owned property, Air America.[84] Confronted with these revelations, Washington officials finally acknowledged that the CIA had in fact supplied ARDE with the aircraft, although they pleaded ignorance as to its intended use.[85]

The next day, ARDE planes shelled oil and chemical storage facilities in the Nicaraguan Pacific port of Corinto, while yet another of its aircraft attacked Sandinista soldiers near the Costa Rican border.[86] During the same week, from the north, the FDN complemented the southern contras' brazen actions by hitting the oil pipeline terminal at Puerto Sandino, on the Pacific coast just thirty miles from Managua and by sending in hundreds of commandos[87] to sabotage bridges and an electrical generating plant in the northern part of the nation.[88]

The other part of the revised strategy called for squeezing the Sandinistas through ever more frequent incursions, particularly along the northern agricultural zones, to disrupt the coffee harvest, Nicaragua's major foreign exchange earner.[89] In an even more ambitious effort, during early September the FDN contras began a push into the northeastern provinces in a frantic attempt to fight their way down the Atlantic coast and hook up with the Costa Rica–based ARDE rebels driving up from the south.[90] Following their defeat by the Sandinistas, the U.S.-backed commandos followed up with even more determined attacks. Under covering fire from the Honduran armed forces, several thousand FDN troops crossed into four northeastern provinces in what developed into one of their most ambitious offensives.[91] Meanwhile, on September 28 from their southern Costa Rican bases, ARDE troops devastated the Nicaraguan Peñas Blancas customs station.[92]

Reacting to the intensifying incursions from the Honduras- and Costa Rica–based rebels, on October 1 tensions heightened further when the Nicaraguan Minister of Defense, Humberto Ortega, declared that, in the future, Sandinista forces would counterattack the contra camps in these countries, because their concentrated presence along the borders had in effect created a "no-man's-land" where the concept of national territorial sovereignty lost its meaning.[93] Although the Sandinistas did not follow up on their threat, extremely heavy fighting continued throughout the month;[94] and on October 4 the Nicaraguans, for the first time using their heat-seeking surface-to-air missiles, shot down a U.S.–registered DC-3 attempting to resupply FDN ground troops ninety miles from Managua.[95]

During this same month several other ominous events punctuated the course of the escalating conflict. Beginning in early October—while two Senate-sponsored resolutions permitted the temporary flow of assistance to the rebels until the "contra question" could be resolved by the full Congress—the counterrevolutionaries, embracing the wisdom of their U.S. mentors, pushed the hostilities to a new phase. In light of the ineptitude of the contras since the beginning of the year, the Agency now took direct control over the planning and operational aspects of the economic-sabotage campaign meant to show concrete results in "destabilizing" the Sandinista government. Providing their protégés with specialized training and equipment to carry out the commando raids, the CIA's charges set out, as the FDN saw fit to put it, "to paralyze the war apparatus of the leftist regime."[96]

Within three weeks, the devastatingly efficient CIA–planned and directed campaign decimated all four major Nicaraguan ports. On October 2, specially outfitted FDN speedboats blew up two fuel storage tanks in the Caribbean port of Benjamin Zeledón;[97] ten days later, the contras employed virtually the same tactic—except that their aircraft complemented their boats—in an attack against Corinto, destroying five storage tanks containing millions of gallons of fuel and forcing the evacuation of the city's 25,000 inhabitants;[98] and three days later, on October 14, the FDN raided the country's other Pacific port of Puerto Sandino,[99] rendering the oil pipeline terminal unserviceable.[100]

The massive damage to three of the nation's four principal ports prompted Defense Minister Ortega to formally request from foreign governments the "military means to defend our coasts and our airspace,"[101] which generally was taken to mean the acquisition of fighter planes and more antiaircraft batteries. Rounding out the picture, one week later the U.S.–backed FDN launched their fourth raid since the beginning of the year against the other Caribbean port of Puerto Cabezas, firing machine guns and rockets that killed and wounded numerous sailors and longshoremen.[102]

Declaring Nicaragua's economy in a "war situation," the Sandinista government took severe steps to husband the precious remaining fuel supplies—all of which are imported—by imposing stricter rationing of gasoline and diesel fuel, reducing and staggering work hours, and eliminating street lighting and the Sunday newspaper.[103] While it certainly would not be overstating the case to say that Nicaragua's problems had reached crisis proportions at this time, it is equally accurate to recognize that events following the October 25 U.S. invasion of Grenada geometrically intensified the nation's concern; especially now that everyone recognized that the contras alone posed no serious threat to the government's stability.

The groundwork had already been laid by the deployment of U.S. naval battle groups off both of Nicaragua's coasts, the presence of thousands of U.S. troops on "routine maneuvers" in Honduras, the revival of the reactionary Council of Central American Defense (CONDECA), and the increasingly bellicose declarations of high Reagan Administration functionaries. The Grenada invasion seemed to confirm Nicaragua's worst fears, providing a tangible basis for and adding immediacy to the nation's alarm that Washington harbored similar plans to overthrow their government. Now, air, sea, and land incursions by the contras—such as those of October 28 against the Momotombo geothermal plant, the small Pacific port of Potosí, and in the Cerro Cumbo region[104]—took on the dimension of prelimi-

nary "softening up" operations. Moreover, Managua saw the
ever more frequent border fighting, especially in the north when
the Honduran armed forces shelled the Sandinista observation
post of Chinandega and on the same day attacked two Nicaraguan coast guard patrol boats in the Gulf of Fonseca, as provoca-
tions to create "a pretext to launch open warfare against Nicaragua."[105]

The events of following weeks provided further cause for concern—especially in the statements of Secretary of Defense Caspar W. Weinberger that "I am not discarding the possibility" of
an invasion, and by the chairman of the Senate Foreign Relations Committee, Howard Baker, that "this is a decision that the
President will make"—particularly because they coincided with
renewed FDN economic-sabotage raids in another attempt to
ruin the coffee harvest.[106] Likewise, the provocative November 7
violation of Nicaragua's airspace by fifteen aircraft from Honduras and the sinking on the same day of an unarmed Nicaraguan
fishing boat in its own territorial waters by the Honduran coast
guard,[107] coupled with the deadly joint FDN–Honduran army
mortar bombardments four days later of the Murupuchi and
Cifuentes border stations,[108] lent yet more credence to the belief
that Washington actively sought to goad Managua into some sort
of rash retaliatory action that would provide the excuse to
unleash its belligerent plans.

On November 17, the Democratic-controlled House of Representatives surprised even the most optimistic. After twice voting
against further funding for the illegal support of the contras,[109]
the House, in a complex parliamentary maneuver engineered by
the minority conservative factions, ended up reversing itself and
joining the Republican-dominated Senate to appropriate an extremely generous 24 million dollars for the CIA's charges so that
they could continue operations until at least June of 1984.[110]
Perhaps the more liberal House members made some sort of a
trade-off with the Senate conservatives to hold back funds for
the production of the Reagan Administration–sponsored chemical warfare weapons, or maybe they got caught up in the flag-
waving generated by the President's Grenadan conquest. In any
event, their about-face sent a sobering message to Managua.

Furthermore, reinforcing what everyone had reluctantly come to believe, the following day the Washington-based Council on Hemispheric Affairs revealed the plans of "Operation Pegasus," the Pentagon's code name for one of the plans to invade Nicaragua. Citing the same high Reagan Administration source that leaked the details of the Granadan invasion six days before it occurred, the COHA press release asserted that because of negative public opinion, most likely U.S. ground troops would not spearhead the operation. Instead, the plan called for massive air and naval bombardments from the U.S. forces already stationed in the area to pave the way for invading contra and CONDECA armed forces from Honduras, Guatemala, and perhaps even El Salvador.[111]

As 1983 came to an end, the Reagan Administration, shifting its focus to the rapidly deteriorating military situation in El Salvador, began lowering the level of rhetoric. But its actions, and those of its allies, continued to sharpen the Sandinista perception that Nicaragua still faced a mortal threat. On November 18—the first day of the simulated five days' amphibious assaults in Honduras as part of the Big Pine II military exercises involving thousands of U.S. soldiers, ships, and aircraft of all types—the nation's real ruler, General Gustavo Alvarez, proclaimed that the maneuvers were meant "to send a message demonstrating [military] force to the Managua regime."[112] On the same day, from their southern sanctuaries in Costa Rica, the ARDE contras launched operation "Blazing Tooth," their most ambitious offensive to date.[113] Within days approximately 1,000 commandos, according to ARDE spokespersons, had driven forty miles into Nicaraguan territory, simultaneously attacking a dozen towns that lay in their ninety-mile-wide path.[114] And in late December, several thousand FDN soldiers once again invaded Nicaragua from their Honduran bases in the north in yet another futile, and bloody, attempt to establish a provisional government.[115]

By this time, not only the Nicaraguan economy but the entire society had been set on wartime footing. In August, when the Big Pine II joint Honduran–United States "routine military maneuvers" commenced, the government announced plans to institute national conscription;[116] in November when Congress appropriated the millions of dollars for the CIA-sponsored contras, the Sandinistas mobilized the entire nation. Beginning on November 17, Civil Defense units in Managua started constructing air-raid shelters,[117] and in a couple of days, 20,000 citizens were already at work digging trenches and foxholes throughout the capital and around the airport, as well as at other strategic sites throughout the country.[118]

When and if the invasion comes—be it whatever combination of contra, CONDECA, and U.S. forces—the ensuing struggle will be neither a totally conventional war nor a military piece of cake like the Grenadan invasion. The war will be fought guerrilla style, with the Sandinistas also employing their formidable conventional warfare capability, in which, as foreign minister Father Miguel D'Escoto warned, every "Nicaraguan, including my 84-year-old mother, will fight."[119]

FOUR

THE DEVELOPMENT OF COUNTERINSURGENCY MILITARY STRATEGY

The military strategies and tactics being taught at the various U.S. counterinsurgency schools and military missions abroad are currently being employed in Central America. And they reflect the long-standing dispute within the U.S. armed forces that dates back to the Kennedy Administration. The intramural conflict centers on the beliefs of the military traditionalists, who contend that well-trained regular soldiers can accomplish any military task, and the new breed of counterinsurgency specialists, who advocate radically new methods of combatting insurgency. This fundamental difference in warfare philosophy was best described by Roger Hilsman, a West Point graduate with extensive experience during World War II in Burma where he conducted guerrilla operations under the direction of the Office of Strategic Services (the OSS), the precursor to the CIA. Not only are Hilsman's credentials impressive, so were the positions he held: One of Kennedy's top counterinsurgency strategists, he headed the State Department's Bureau of Intelligence and Research, and was a key member of that Administration's elite Special Group (Counterinsurgency) as well.

In his widely circulated speech, delivered in August 1961, entitled "Internal War: The New Communist Doctrine," (subsequently published in book form, with an introduction by President Kennedy), Hilsman explained the limitations of the traditionalists' concept of warfare. "Regular forces are essential for regular tasks,"[1] he says, and continues:

But guerrilla warfare is something special. Conventional forces with heavy equipment in field formation tend to cluster together, centralizing their power in terrain that allows rapid movement. They rely on roads, consider strong points and cities as vital targets to defend, and so, when they do disperse, it is only to get tied down in static operations. In combat, rigid adherence to the principle of concentration keeps units at unwieldy battalion or even regimental levels, usually with erroneous stress on holding land rather than destroying enemy forces."[2]

On the other hand, Hilsman argued that for "effective counterguerrilla operations, we need radical changes in organization, combat doctrine and equipment. Our key units might be decentralized groups of 50 men, self-reliant and able to operate autonomously, fanned out into the countryside."[3] Further, he advocated that these special troops, supported by constant helicopter-delivered supplies and reinforcements, be deployed in the classic quadrillage technique first developed by the French. This strategy entails sending special counterinsurgency soldiers into clearly delineated quadrangles of enemy-held territory to eliminate them one sector at a time, until an entire region is secured by government forces.

Indeed, during the Kennedy Administration, counterinsurgency warfare even became fashionable in certain sectors of the armed forces. For the first time, these strategies and tactics were incorporated into U.S. military training programs and taught not only to U.S. military personnel but also to large numbers of foreigners, especially Latin American officers. But with President Kennedy's assassination in 1963, the military high command retreated to the comfort of tradition. Subordinating not only the reform aspect of the Kennedy counterinsurgency doctrine, these officers, schooled on the battlefields of World War II and Korea, imposed their conventional warfare methods during the course of the Southeast Asian war. As vividly recorded by history, the deployment of more than half a million U.S. soldiers to defend strategic points and cities, battalion-size search-and-destroy sweeps, massive artillery barrages, precision A-37B aircraft bombing, and even high altitude B-52 saturation bombing, all ultimately proved ineffectual against the elusive and determined guerrillas.

CONVENTIONAL VERSUS UNCONVENTIONAL WARFARE

The perennial debate between those who adhere to conventional warfare methods to fight insurgent forces and those who argue for the use of unconventional military strategies has been revived in El Salvador, but with an ironic twist. As noted above, in the early 1960s during the Southeast Asian war the debate took place between the dominant military traditionalists within the Pentagon and the largely civilian counterinsurgency theoreticians and pacification experts in the Kennedy Administration. In El Salvador, it is the U.S. military establishment that insists upon employing unconventional warfare methods to wage the counterinsurgency campaign, while the Salvadoran high command resists their recommendations, stubbornly sticking to the more familiar traditional warfare strategies.

In military practice, the principles of conventional warfare are the deployment of regular forces in large units, in set-piece combat. Roads must be relied on for the transportation of troops, supplies, and artillery, and there is a heavy dependence upon air and artillery tactical support to "soften up" targets prior to attack. The principal mode of this main-force combat in counterinsurgency wars is the aggressive search-and-destroy tactic, which consists of attempting to seek out and eliminate large insurgent units through the concentration of troops who invariably have the advantage of superior fire power. Reflecting the traditional U.S. Army concept of employing its overwhelming superiority in technical capability, fire power, and mobility, this tactic was used in South Vietnam in a futile attempt to inflict massive casualties on the Viet Cong and the North Vietnamese forces. The idea was that, unable to sustain such heavy losses, the insurgents would be forced to abandon their strongest positions and retreat to the safety of more remote areas. Then, by cutting their main supply channels, the theory contended, victory over the isolated guerrillas finally would be achieved through a war of attrition. Following this logic, during the last five months of

1966, the U.S. Military Assistance Command, for example, committed 95 percent of all combat battalions to search and destroy operations.[4]

While these quick-striking operations extensively employed helicopters to move troops rapidly into and out of combat zones, they also relied heavily upon the preliminary employment of B-52 bombers, chemical defoliants, and napalm. One tragic result was that immense areas were subjected to saturation bombing and destroyed by chemicals and fire.[5] An even more severe consequence of these indiscriminate attacks was the large numbers of civilians who lost their lives. But worst of all from the military's point of view, the large insurgent units never were destroyed, and the losses in manpower, installations, and supplies never were great enough that they could not be absorbed by the guerrillas. In large part this was because the tactical softening up bombardment forewarned the rebels of the impending arrival of enemy troops, thereby giving them the option of either dispersing or engaging the South Vietnamese and U.S. forces. In this way, the insurgents controlled the pace and scope of combat and limited their losses by evading battle when it was to their disadvantage.

The most serious strategic flaw in the search-and-destroy tactic as employed in Vietnam lay in the Pentagon's underestimation of the insurgents' ability to respond to the massive force deployed against them. As the allies built up their war machine, so did the insurgents. Consequently, the U.S. and South Vietnamese armies found it necessary to constantly increase their technological and manpower force levels. Furthermore, the larger and more complicated their military apparatus grew, the more necessary it was to deploy it in a conventional manner. This put them at a disadvantage in relation to the insurgents, whose growth, because they began with a guerrilla army, resulted in a type of strength and flexibility that permitted them to interchangeably employ guerrilla-style and mobile warfare methods.[6]

Another conventional tactic widely used in Vietnam was the sweeping operation. Conducted in areas where strong Viet Cong presence was suspected among the civilian population, this method concentrated on sealing off an area with troops, searching all structures, and screening the entire population to comb out weapons, supplies, insurgent infrastructure, and troops. The purported goals were to sweep the territory and, just as important, to occupy the area with soldiers to prevent the return of the insurgents. In general, sweeping operations failed because the occupying South Vietnamese troops were unable to stay long enough in the "cleaned" areas to establish lasting government control. A 1964 U.S. military pamphlet recognized that, from the political and the military points of view, clear-and-hold operations were far more effective than sweeping operations, which allowed the insurgents to return, since allied troops left an area shortly after passing through it. But the realities of the Southeast Asian war required that South Vietnamese troops assigned to such operations be sent to other battle zones, resulting in the futile cleaning of the same areas over and over again.[7] Not surprisingly, this same dynamic has been a major problem in El Salvador's counterinsurgency war.

Unconventional warfare methods, however, call for the use of small units, light weapons, and precise, measured fire power eschewing almost entirely artillery and combat air support. The principal mode of operation is guerrilla-style warfare, especially the setting up of ambushes, nighttime patrolling, and surprise commando attacks carried out deep inside enemy territory to destroy equipment and supply dumps. Given the Pentagon's open resistance to these warfare methods in the 1960s, counterinsurgency specialists of that period did not even bother to recommend the complete reorientation of the regular U.S. and South Vietnamese armies from conventional to unconventional warfare methods. Instead, they proposed the creation of special units whose principal responsibility was to fight in the unconventional, guerrilla-style combat mode.

The first attempt at sustained guerrilla-style methods employed by U.S. forces in Vietnam was that of the Combined Action Platoons (CAPs).[8] Initiated in 1965, this experiment involved highly trained squads of U.S. Marines consisting of 14 men led by a sergeant, who lived and worked closely with South Vietnamese paramilitary platoons of 34 men. Operating at the hamlet level, the CAPs (of which a total of 114 were eventually formed) operated in the Viet Cong–controlled northernmost provinces of South Vietnam. Usually deployed in groups of six to eight men, their principal duties were nighttime patrolling and setting up ambushes. Although the CAPs initially suffered heavy casualties, they did succeed in forcing the Viet Cong to abandon the hamlets that they patrolled.

However, despite the interest which this experiment aroused in a number of high-ranking U.S. Army officers, the Commander of U.S. Military Assistance Command Vietnam (COMUS-MACV), General William Westmoreland, refused to adopt the CAP concept on any sizable scale.[9] In his view, this program represented a static and defensive employment of forces, unlike the traditional infantry approach best exemplified in Vietnam by the search-and-destroy tactic, which he considered to follow the principles of aggressive pursuit and destruction of insurgent forces.[10] As it turned out, the CAP program was never fully put to the test because the 1967 buildup in the DMZ (Demilitarized Zone: the border between North and South Vietnam) shifted the marines' attention back to the main-force war.

While at this time the more successful counterinsurgency CORDS program was initiated, focusing on the strictly military aspects of the war reveals that there was more involved in the CAP episode than simple stubborn refusal on the part of General Westmoreland to employ unconventional guerrilla-style tactics against the Vietnamese guerrillas. When General Creighton Abrams took over as COMUSMACV in June 1968, he attempted to switch the U.S. Army's mode of operation from large-scale search-and-destroy campaigns to saturation patrolling tactics. Much like its CAP predecessor, this tactic consisted of small-unit patrolling operations in densely populated areas, where they cooperated closely with South Vietnamese paramilitary units.[11] The reasons for its failure provide insights into the resistance encountered within the Salvadoran armed forces to adopt irregular warfare methods.

Besides going against the deeply ingrained traditional warfare doctrine, a counterinsurgency warfare mode also posed subjective problems to U.S. officers in the field. Compared to the main-force war, the guerrilla-style methods seemed demeaning, relying as they do on small-unit operations, most frequently conducted during the night in which an elusive enemy could inflict heavy casualties. This type of fighting denied them the opportunity to engage in dramatic battles during which U.S. officers could employ the full arsenal at their command. In fact, viewed from the traditional military standpoint, unconventional counterinsurgency warfare is irrational, since it means reverting to a more elemental form of combat; reducing the force levels of the combat units to the weapons they can carry and abandoning the principle of the concentration of force in favor of deploying numerous platoons on constant patrol. In the military mind, which is hardly famous for its creative flexibility, it defies common sense to reduce a sophisticated and immensely powerful war machine to rudimentary commando teams. The Pentagon traditionalists' frustration with such changes was dramatically illustrated a decade ago by Brian Jenkins, the expert who subsequently has developed the current Special Forces' counterinsurgency strategy. At that time, he quoted a U.S. Army general, who, when asked about the possibility of the army's conversion to unconventional warfare methods in Vietnam, said: "I'll be damned if I permit the U.S. Army, its institutions, its doctrine, and its traditions to be destroyed just to win this lousy war."[12]

As the officers knew, their performance was being judged according to World War II criteria, which put a premium upon maneuvering the enemy into major battles that, because of massive materiel superiority, the U.S. forces would win. The dominant battle mode in that war was the bulldozer concept of military confrontation that won the U.S. Civil War for the North. Consequently, the competition for promotion among U.S. officers in Vietnam encouraged the widespread pursuit of large-scale search-and-destroy operations. South Vietnamese officers and troops, consistent with their training and the prevailing U.S. military doctrine on which they modeled their own institutions, almost exclusively aped their North American patrons.

Finally, the seeming inertia of the Pentagon during the 1960s, even in the face of the increasingly successful Vietnamese insurgency, stemmed from the nature of the military bureaucratic apparatus itself. As a renowned civilian counterinsurgency expert perceptively pointed out, the U.S. military establishment "knew how to mobilize resources, provide logistic support, deploy assets, and manage large efforts. So they employed all these skills to develop irresistible momentum toward fighting their own kind of war."[13]

RECENT CHANGES IN U.S. WARFARE DOCTRINE

In the wake of the Vietnam debacle, the traditional U.S. Army doctrine has been undergoing some fundamental revisions.[14] Ever since the U.S. Civil War (1861–1865), through World War I (1917–1918), and World War II (1941–1945), and then in Korea (1950–1952), and Southeast Asia (1965–1975), the Golden Rule of the armed forces was the Doctrine of Attrition. According to this military doctrine, any enemy can be defeated by a head-on confrontation with its main combat forces—preferably along a well-defined front—and simply wearing the enemy down through superior fire power and sheer technological weight. The new army approach, based on the AirLand Battle Doctrine, shifts the emphasis from the old bulldozer approach to maneuverability, mobility, surprise tactics, and quick counterattack behind enemy lines. Instead of waging drawn-out attrition offensives in which superiority in fire power levels decide the final outcome, under the new doctrine most army units would be expected to complete their battle missions within 72 hours. For defensive combat operations, the AirLand Battle Doctrine calls for a counteroffensive that includes deploying strike forces as far as 150 miles behind the line of enemy advance (the functional range of radar because of the earth's curvature). This was a significant departure from traditional military doctrine, which dogmatically stuck to maintaining its primary defense along the front line.

A number of related developments during the last decade prompted these radical changes in fundamental conventional warfare concepts. Perhaps most important, Washington faced what it perceived as clear Warsaw Pact superiority in the total number of battle-ready divisions, war materiel, and overall capability to wage a prolonged war. Moreover, suffering the effects of economic recession that gradually eroded the U.S. industrial base, which had produced ever more elaborate warfare technology, Pentagon and North Atlantic Treaty Organization (NATO) military strategists came to doubt that the imbalance of power could be checked with increasingly sophisticated tactical nuclear weapons systems. Following what they saw as a series of Soviet strategic nuclear weapons buildups since the 1960s, many Western defense analysts claimed that the nuclear umbrella that protected Western Europe had become obsolete; they argued for an urgent reexamination of the NATO forces to wage and win a conventional war against the Warsaw Pact.

The generational change within the U.S. military establishment was another important factor influencing the reorientation that is taking place in U.S. military doctrine. The Pentagon's highest-ranking officers, those who shape present military policy, have been tempered by the Southeast Asian war experience, where many served as field commanders. Through their ineffectual campaigns against the Vietnamese insurgents' high maneuverability, high flexibility, and surprise tactics, officers such as General John Wickham (U.S. Army Chief of Staff) and General Don A. Starry (who was the U.S. Army head of training and doctrine) are among the chief advocates of the new doctrine, and have come to realize the necessity of fundamental changes.*

Both the Rapid Deployment Force (RDF) and the *Defense Guidance* paper reflect the shift in the Pentagon's overall military conceptualization and are the natural products of this new generation of top-level U.S. military officers. Although the European and Persian Gulf war theaters apparently inspired the formulation of the new military doctrine—in most of the scenarios made public so far, the deployment of the RDF and the application of the AirLand Battle Doctrine were hypothetically placed there—it is not inconceivable that they will first be utilized in the Caribbean Basin, given that the Reagan Administration now considers Central America of equal strategic importance to U.S. vital security interests.

*General Starry is now head of Readiness Command, a joint command in charge of moving U.S. forces to meet contingencies anywhere in the world.

Indeed, a wide spectrum of opinion predicts that it will not be possible to avoid indefinitely a direct U.S. military commitment to Central America. On the far right, Dr. Edgar Chammorro Coronel, a director of the contra FDN flatly stated: "Eventually the United States will have to get involved in the fighting because sooner or later the United States will have to intervene directly."[15] In his farewell address, Colonel John D. Waghelstein, the commander of the Military Advisory Group in El Salvador, warned that should the Nicaraguans invade (which he doubted) or in the event that Congress cuts off aid (which he was concerned about) that it would be necessary for the United States to "use our military option."[16] At the other end of the spectrum, former Vice-President Walter Mondale issued the dire prediction that "under present policies it is inevitable that American troops will be sent to Central America, because the policy is failing."[17]

But important domestic considerations continue to restrain the Reagan Administration from committing U.S. forces to the region. Surprisingly, after Congress, the Department of Defense has expressed the most reluctance to follow this course. The U.S. military's qualms are not based upon any moral principles, but upon practical considerations rooted in the Vietnam experience, and they date back to its refusal to draw up the military "contingency plans" that Secretary of State Alexander Haig pressed for during 1981 and 1982. What the Pentagon fears is that the unprecedented five-year 1.7 billion dollar buildup of the armed forces intended to reestablish uncontested United States military might around the world could be placed in jeopardy, since such unpopular action would alienate the public, media, and Congress, especially in view of the Administration's sharp budget cuts for domestic social programs. Consequently, before sticking themselves out on a limb again, the generals demand that clear political and military objectives first be established, that they will not be hamstrung in the use of force in meeting these goals, and, most important of all, that they count with solid congressional and public support to fulfill these goals. As the retiring Army Chief of Staff, General Edward C. Meyer, reflected in June 1983: "We didn't do that in Vietnam. We inched our way in. Then all of a sudden we were there."[18]

As detailed in the introduction, the October 1983 invasion of Grenada met all these criteria—while direct military intervention in Central America is a different story altogether. Even so, Honduras is already being prepared to serve as the forward base in the event that the United States decides to invade Central America with its own forces. For the time being, however, U.S. strategists still believe that the only viable policy is to attempt to defeat the insurgents in El Salvador and Guatemala through the massive application of and strict adherence to U.S. counterinsurgency doctrine.

U.S. COUNTERINSURGENCY MILITARY FORCES

Certainly the counterinsurgency advocates within the armed forces still encounter entrenched opposition to their kind of warfare. But under the patronage of President Kennedy, and the requirements of his counterinsurgency doctrine, all four branches of the military—the Army, Marine Corps, Navy and Air Force—established elite special operations units. While each of the services emphasizes its own specialties, some skills must be mastered by all of these counterinsurgency fighters. First are those necessary to effectively organize counterrevolutionary groups in the Third World: languages, communications, paramedical aid, leadership qualities, and, most important, extreme proficiency in guerrilla fighting tactics such as night operations, hand-to-hand combat, sabotage, and terrorism.

Using an analysis strikingly similar to that employed by the Kennedy Administration, in March 1982 Secretary of Defense Caspar W. Weinberger approved a five-year military program to rebuild the armed forces' unconventional warfare potential. The rationale underlying this classified plan, entitled *Defense Guidance,* is cast in the same East–West Cold War terms of twenty years ago: "The United States must be able to defeat low-level aggression, both to prevent the step-by-step expansion of Soviet or surrogate influence and to prevent escalation to higher levels of conflict. The United States must be able to achieve these objectives when to its advantage without direct confrontation." Moreover, the *Defense Guidance* is specific about the method of carrying out this plan. It goes on to explain that "we must revitalize and enhance special operations forces to project United States power where the use of conventional forces would be premature, inappropriate or unfeasible."[19]

The most important operational aspect of the *Defense Guidance* is the creation of the Special Operations Command (SOC), under the command of the U.S. Army at Fort Bragg, North Carolina. The Special Operations Command, which was formally established on October 1, 1982, is led by the veteran Special Forces Brigadier General Joseph C. Lutz, the only counterinsurgency officer to achieve flag rank. Making more U.S. military history, SOC marks the first time that counterinsurgency forces from the different branches of the armed forces have been unified under a single command.[20]

During the Kennedy Administration, the air force created its Special Operations Wing. This counterinsurgency unit, known as the Air Commandos, is based at Elgin Air Force Base, Florida. Trained and equipped to handle a variety of unconventional aircraft, the Special Operations Wing commando "flies black, unmarked airplanes that carry cargo to special ground forces or their allies, drop secret agents and saboteurs by parachute, or extract Americans or allies from behind enemy lines."[21] The Air Commandos, just as their navy and army counterparts, make up the key units in the ongoing series of joint United States–Honduran military maneuvers.[22] Their participation in the clandestine war against Nicaragua, while not documented, is precisely the type of military operation that they were created to fulfill.

Also during the Kennedy Administration, the navy established its elite Sea, Air, Land teams, the SEALs. Their specialty is to "swim into a harbor to plant explosives to sink ships, to sabotage harbor operations, and to move inland to destroy enemy facilities. The SEALs are also trained as parachutists so that they can be dropped inland for a mission and then escape by sea."[23]

The marine corps, which is officially under the command of the Department of the Navy, never has fielded a full-fledged counterinsurgency force on the scale of the other three services. This is largely explained by the dominant role of the U.S. Army in this area. Even so, the marines did run the Combined Action Platoons in Vietnam and do boast elite airborne commando units specially trained in counterinsurgency warfare to operate within enemy-held territory.

The army's Special Forces, popularly known as the Green Berets, are of course the most well-known and active of the U.S. counterinsurgency forces. The Green Berets were a special favorite of President Kennedy's, and he added to their mystique by dramatically increasing their size and scope, upgrading the Special Forces headquarters at Fort Bragg, North Carolina, to a Special Warfare Center, and restoring to them the prestige of wearing the green beret. (The Army High Command, as part of an overall policy, had forbidden the Special Forces from using the green beret because it was such a highly visible insignia.)

Originally, the Special Forces grew out of the World War II guerrilla units that operated behind enemy lines under the direction of the OSS. But as reorganized under Kennedy's counterinsurgency doctrine in 1961, the Special Forces, rather than being a guerrilla force, became a counterguerrilla force. Although they are highly proficient combat soldiers, their primary responsibility is to instruct armies friendly to the United States in counterinsurgency techniques. Employing the political–military tactics of guerrilla warfare, they advise, train, and lead the armed forces of foreign countries in campaigns to eliminate insurgent forces. The Special Forces conducted the intensive four-month training course for the Ramón Belloso battalion of El Salvador in the United States during early 1982 and are in charge of the continued instruction of Central American troops at the new Regional Military Training Center in Puerto Castilla, Honduras, and elsewhere throughout Central America. During the post-Vietnam period the Green Berets, along with the other special operations forces, fell into disrepute and were relegated to minor importance within the U.S. military establishment. But, just as with the CIA covert Operations Directorate, the Reagan Administration has reversed this trend, reviving the counterinsurgency units of the various branches of the armed forces.

In early 1983 the Green Berets were still limited to a maximum strength of 8,600 troops. But according to Reagan Administration officials, the Special Forces were to be expanded considerably in the immediate future. This growth will mean not only an increase of Special Forces personnel, but also more rigorous training, sophisticated miniature communications equipment, and special aircraft to transport infiltration teams into combat areas around the world.

INSURGENCY ACCORDING TO THE U.S. ARMY

Already the Special Warfare Center at Fort Bragg is working to develop a more effective theory of counterinsurgency at its research center, the Institute for Military Assistance. About a dozen Green Beret specialists study the classic works of such revolutionaries as Ho Chi Minh, Ché Guevara, and Carlos Marighella. They also rely upon the constant flow of intelligence reports and special analytical studies prepared by civilian experts who work at private think tanks under U.S. government contract. Among the institutions that are currently working on counterinsurgency is the Hudson Institute of New York and the Rand Corporation of Santa Monica, California. From the latter has come a detailed counterinsurgency strategy, which in 1982 was adopted as a working model by the Special Forces.

This official conceptualization, developed by the civilian expert Brian Jenkins, divides insurgency into five progressive, interlocking and overlapping phases; and, accordingly, each of these stages requires progressively more difficult counterinsurgency methods to defeat the rebels.[24] While not all insurgencies must pass through all of the five steps, the sooner counterinsurgency measures are employed against the rebels, the easier it is for the government forces to crush the dissidents.

According to Jenkins's conceptualization, to draw public attention to their organization and cause, the rebels begin with spectacular actions, such as blowing up power stations or assassinating politicians. Jenkins's bias is reflected in his imprecise analysis sequence, for he fails to mention that many, less sinister actions often characterize this embryonic stage of insurrection. These include the protest occupation of official buildings, as occurred at the Spanish Embassy in San Salvador in 1979 and the 1982 occupation of the Organization of American States office in Guatemala City. An even more daring tactic is the capture of entire groups of prominent establishment figures, which the insurgents then attempt to exchange for the release of their own political prisoners. The two most dramatic examples of this tactic were the Sandinista commando raid in 1977, carried out by former Sandinista hero Edén Pastora, that took prisoner virtually the entire diplomatic corps in Managua; and the September 1982 capture, by the Cinchoneros guerrillas, of many of the most important business and governmental leaders in Honduras, which took place in San Pedro Sula.

Countermeasures for this stage of "terrorism" are not considered by Jenkins to be a military matter, but rather a function of the police. At the same time, the government is counseled to conduct a propaganda campaign designed to politically discredit the rebels as mere terrorist fanatics determined to disrupt society for their own extremist goals.

Many authentic popular insurgencies have employed such tactics. Even so, Jenkins seems to have indiscriminately merged together all forms of armed protest against an established state in the general category of insurgency. His first stage correctly corresponds to the actions of the many student and middle-class ultra-left organizations that out of frustrated miscalculation have deluded themselves into thinking that they represent a revolutionary vanguard. The terrorist activities described in the Jenkins analysis are characterized by the actions of such fringe groups as the Weathermen of the U.S. and the Bader Meinhof of West Germany during the late 1960s and early 1970s.

The second phase of this model of insurgency is the recruitment of cadres, tightening and expanding of the organizational apparatus, and increasing propaganda activities against the state. To finance their growing operations, the rebels begin assaulting banks and conducting kidnappings, as well as raiding military arsenals for weapons and ammunition. At this stage, the Special Forces counterinsurgency strategy calls for tight governmental control over the movements of the population through curfews and frequent identification checks. Even though they are not mentioned, other more repressive measures are customarily taken by security forces and paramilitary death squads that include raids on possible hideouts, mass arrests of suspected subversives, torture, summary executions, and "disappearances." The repression, Jenkins advises, should be explained to the public as the necessary consequence of combatting the insurgents' activities. Historically, true insurgencies crushed in this stage have been extremely vicious affairs claiming unfathomable numbers of noncombatant civilian victims, as exemplified by the Argentine military dictatorship's "dirty war" against the Montoneros and the People's Revolutionary Army urban guerrillas during the 1970s.

A guerrilla war, to be successful, must have the active support of a considerable portion of the population. Therefore, from the counterinsurgency point of view, it is critical to stop the rebels by the third stage. At this point, the insurgents are actively challenging the authority of the government through military actions. While some of the armed confrontations are carried out in the cities, to a far greater degree they are concentrated in the countryside. There the rebels gain legitimacy—and begin establishing themselves as an alternative authority—by ambushing military patrols, temporarily capturing small towns, executing the agents of government repression and criminal elements, and, when feasible, collecting modest taxes from the people to help the war effort.

Once the guerrillas are strong enough to secure zones of control, they gain further popular support by establishing self-defense militias, local revolutionary governments, education facilities, and medical clinics. To be effective, these strategic objectives must build an infrastructure through the active involvement of mass organizations—which are an essential link with the overall population—such as peasant leagues, unions of rural workers, and increasingly, the Christian Base Communities, which function upon the humanitarian concepts of liberation theology. In the cities, the guerrillas' popular base rests upon the countryside's urban counterparts—labor unions, organizations of slum dwellers, and students and intellectuals.

U.S. Army Special Forces Major Thomas J. Kruster, Jr., a member of the Green Beret research unit at Fort Bragg, emphasized that "this is the point where the Government has to respond, not react." [25] In concrete terms, this means the aggressive application of the dual counterinsurgency doctrine of reform and repression. Reforms, in an attempt to lessen the injustices, must be rapidly implemented to undermine the insurgents' appeal. Repression must be increased to destroy the guerrilla infrastructure and terrorize the population. Again Jenkins's strategy glosses over the harsh reality, neglecting to mention that this means even more indiscriminate killing by paramilitary death squads and security forces, and greater use of torture, arrests, and disappearances. Militarily, it is essential that the government forces maintain firm control of the cities, while stepping up their attacks against the insurgent organization in the countryside.

According to the Jenkins scheme of insurrection, this is when the Special Forces play their crucial role. With U.S. weaponry and money, the Green Beret teams arrive to advise and train the local armed forces in counterinsurgency doctrine: military strategy, interrogation techniques, the establishment of strategic hamlets, and civic action programs. The current revolution in Guatemala provides an example of an insurgency in this third stage.

The Green Berets' insurgency doctrine claims that the fourth phase consists of mass mobilization, particularly in the form of general strikes. The intended effect of this tactic is to paralyze the economy, thereby placing growing numbers of protesting unemployed workers in the streets. The appropriate counterinsurgency response, according to Jenkins, is for the government to declare martial law, in an attempt to contain the situation through increased repression.

The FMLN–FDR strategy of calling for a boycott of the March 1982 elections and a general strike in El Salvador would seem to correspond to this phase of Jenkins's scheme. The strategy failed because it was overly ambitious for the guerrillas' resources at that time: They were unable to penetrate the government's military defense of the cities in sufficient strength to physically provide protection for their unarmed supporters, so their call for a general insurrection was doomed.

The fifth and ultimate phase in all successful insurgencies is the shift by the rebels from the exclusive use of guerrilla warfare strategies to the incorporation of those of conventional warfare as well. That is, rather than simply employing the hit-and-run tactics of the guerrilla, the insurgent armies must possess sufficient strength to restructure themselves and engage in direct head-on battles with conventional armies. Of course, once the insurgents have reached this level of military strength, the distinction between unconventional and conventional war becomes blurred, with the government increasingly relying upon its regular armed forces in order to stay in power. At least in some areas, the Salvadoran guerrillas had reached this most advanced stage of insurgency by October 1982; by fall of 1983, insurgent conventional forces operated in all three theaters of the war.

This qualitative reorganization from purely guerrilla to conventional warfare is the essential final phase of all revolutions. Yet the timing in committing the insurgents' conventional forces to major battles is perhaps the most critical factor, as history has amply demonstrated. Among these factors, the most important are the will of the government and the military ability of its armed forces to resist the final offensive. Even such a master revolutionary warfare strategist as General Vo Nguyen Giap once miscalculated the complex political–military conditions that are of vital determination.

In 1951, while still fighting against the French colonial regime in Vietnam, Giap erroneously felt the time was right to shift to conventional warfare against the enemy. Because of this mistake in judgment, the revolutionary forces were badly defeated at Da Nang, and ultimate victory was set back by months, if not years. Not until 1954 did the Viet Minh finally win their decisive victory at Dien Bien Phu. Evidently, learning from these experiences, Giap correctly timed the January 1968 General Uprising and General Offensive (better known in the West as the "Tet offensive"), which consisted of coordinated assaults against forty-three cities in South Vietnam. Although the insurgents did not even attempt to hold these citadels permanently, the General Uprising and General Offensive so disrupted the enemy militarily and politically, that it marked the turning point of the revolution. The political ramifications of counterinsurgency were emphatically demonstrated in the United States, where congressional, media, and public opinion turned so adamantly against the war that it was impossible for President Johnson to run for a second term. After this setback, neither the Nixon nor Ford administrations could pursue an aggressive war policy. Instead, they were forced to steadily withdraw U.S. troops and support from South Vietnam, which directly led to the victory of the insurgent forces in April 1975.

The way the South Vietnamese regime fell demonstrates another important dynamic of insurrection. Rarely is there a prolonged final assault on the enemy's last stronghold, such as the Nazis holding out in Berlin to the bitter end as the Soviets pulverized the city. Although the insurgents certainly won a military victory in Vietnam, the rapidity of the final offensive and the fall of the government surprised the world. The panic of a Vietnamese divisional commander in the Central Highlands touched off a headlong retreat to the coast. Breaking the will of the South Vietnamese forces quickly led to the collapse of the entire state apparatus, catching even the insurgents by surprise. Rather than the two years that they planned for the final offensive, it was all over in fifty-five days. There was no real siege of Saigon, just such a rapid sweeping through by the insurgent forces that the last of the U.S. personnel managed to escape literally at the last moment only by helicopter airlift off the embassy rooftop.

Similarly, the Cuban and Nicaraguan revolutions did not end with the siege of Havana and Managua. Once the insurgents had proved their military strength by slugging it out in head-on battles with government troops, the will of these dictatorial regimes to resist simply collapsed. As the rebels marched into the capitals, Batista and Somoza flew off to their Florida homes with their top henchmen. In early 1983, U.S. military experts in El Salvador were already privately talking about the possible collapse of the government; by the end of the year they were publicly airing their concerns.

A disquieting signal for their Washington backers was the fact that the Salvadoran Minister of Defense, most of the high command, and provincial commanders had long since sent their families, and bank accounts, out of the country, mostly to the Miami area where their wealthy compatriots had already established a luxurious exile community. Despite the guerrillas' devastating economic sabotage campaign, there is no danger that the Salvadoran economy will crumble, since it receives massive U.S. support. Neither is it likely that the end will be marked by the siege of San Salvador. The insurgent victory, when and if it occurs, probably will come when the will of the regime cracks.

FIVE
GUATEMALA

President Efraín Ríos Montt came to power in March 1982 through a military coup; in August 1983 he left the same way. While General Ríos Montt did not start Guatemala's counterinsurgency activities—they began decades ago, have continued through successive regimes, and certainly did not end with his departure—this born-again Christian fanatic did oversee a radical reorganization of their strategy. Most characterizations of this campaign to eliminate subversion in God's name draw parallels with tactics developed in Vietnam, such as the scorched earth and strategic hamlets programs. But in reality such parallels are only partly accurate and do not truly describe the practices perpetrated under the General's counterinsurgency campaign.

Denouncing the preceding regimes as abusive, corrupt, and sinful, initially Ríos Montt held as his top priority the bringing of some measure of legitimacy to the government, for the domestic and international image of Guatemala had already earned the reputation not only of being the hemisphere's worst human rights violator but of being a world-class pariah. At first it appeared that Ríos Montt meant business. He did clean up the urban death squads directly controlled from the U.S.–built telecommunications annex of the National Palace by his predecessor, President Romeo Lucas García.[1] He repeatedly issued the most sincere-sounding promises to improve the human rights situation and turn the reins of power over to a democratically elected government at the soonest possible date. Moreover, Ríos Montt vowed that his self-professed reformist regime would apply "enlightened" counterinsurgency measures that placed as much emphasis on civic action (reform) as on military action (repression).

In May 1982, declaring that "a strictly military solution only creates more enemies," he announced his "rifles and beans" policy.[2] Several days later, he surprised almost everyone when he declared that Guatemala did not need additional helicopters, weapons, or any other type of military help to defeat the insurgents, stressing that "the only solution to civil strife is love." Offering further details of this innovative counterinsurgency program, the fundamentalist General added that it would be carried out in "model villages" under the sociopolitical and economic system that he called "communitarianism"; that is, "the human relation that does not come from communism nor democracy, but of the family; it is sharing everything, it is working for the community."[3]

Under this paternalistic plan, the peasants would be given a house and a piece of land to work, while the government would provide a school, as well as civic and health centers for the community. According to the evangelical head of state, all this was not even going to cost the government anything, since it would be financed and staffed by his U.S. coreligionists who had offered "more than a billion dollars" for the endeavor.[4]

All this sounded too good to be true; events shortly proved the skeptics right. Not only did the money not come through, the new dictator's "counterinsurgency love campaign" turned out to be the most brutal in that nation's long and bloody history of repression. Hidden from the public scrutiny was the National Plan for Security and Development, a secret political–military scheme that the army had already drawn up and Ríos Montt approved on April 1, 1982, only a week after the coup. The counterinsurgency scheme called for a drastic escalation of rural repression, where 80 percent of Guatemala's people live, and the creation of a corporatist civilian–military structure to further control the countryside.

MASSACRES AND REFUGEES

The major difference between Ríos Montt's strategy and a classic counterinsurgency campaign lay in the fact that it shunned attempts to confront the guerrillas directly, and to a large extent did not even try to destroy their infrastructure in any systematic fashion. Instead, it focused upon eliminating the insurgents' popular base by massacring whole communities of suspected sympathizers, forcing those who did manage to escape the slaughter to become refugees. With some significant differences, the tactic of attempting to eliminate the rebels' popular base does have antecedents in Southeast Asia.

Throughout the war in Vietnam, especially during the 1966–1970 period, U.S. and South Vietnamese forces engaged in the extensive relocation of the civilian population in order to create free-fire zones (FFZs); that is, areas in which anyone and everyone is considered a legitimate target. In 1967, for example, operations Cedar Falls and Hickory forcibly relocated 6,000 and 13,000 people, respectively, the rationale being that this action would deny the Viet Cong recruits, food, and revenue, and would score a political victory by making the people "vote with their feet."[5]

Counterinsurgency proponents of these tactics proved ingenious in the "legal" and "moral" justifications they devised for their widespread implementation. Following the recommendations of the International Committee of the Red Cross,[6] and anticipating those of the United Nations, they developed the so-called Rules of Engagement.[7] These included legal guidelines for the deployment of U.S. military forces, establishing the duty to remove civilians from a combat zone, or to give at least 72-hours advance notice that any civilians still remaining in an FFZ must abandon it.[8] As happened in Guatemala, the inevitable outcome of these massive population movements was the generation of internal refugees. During the Cedar Falls military operation alone, while 6,000 people were relocated, more than 100,000 more simply fled their homes and became refugees.

To impart some idea of the magnitude of these operations, it should be mentioned that between 1964 and 1969 as many as 3.5 million South Vietnamese internal refugees—over 20 percent of the population—ended up as virtual prisoners in concentration camps. This figure does not include those unfortunates only temporarily displaced by acts of war, such as the almost one million persons whose houses were destroyed during the 1968 Tet and post-Tet offensives, or the even larger number of homeless people who simply blended in with the general population and received no government assistance whatsoever.[9]

One immediate cause for the growing numbers of Vietnamese internal refugees was the indiscriminate usc of heavy artillery and aircraft bombardment that accompanied the large-scale sweeps by military ground forces in heavily populated areas. As one particularly candid "pacification" officer explained, "search and destroy operations produced tactical conditions in which the civil population could not live—and sometimes in which they could not be permitted to live. Hence the refugees."[10]

More than enough evidence exists to conclude that the generation of internal refugees through the systematic relocation of noncombatant civilians became an intentional and generally accepted policy. Gunter Lewy, one of that era's top counterinsurgency analysts, noted that "in view of the great difficulties experienced in bringing security to the people it was considered easier to bring people to security. . . ."[11] In fact, the special assistant to the U.S. Joint Chiefs of Staff for Counterinsurgency and Special Activities (SACSA) coldly recommended, in 1967, that Viet Cong activities could be seriously hampered in the densely populated Mekong Delta if two million refugees were created in the following year.[12]

While the internal refugees in Guatemala also were "produced" through an escalation of the armed forces' operations, there is a tragic difference from Vietnamese military operations. Guatemalan internal refugees not only fled their communities due to the increased artillery and aircraft fire power; a far more vicious cause of their plight is found in the tactics employed by the Guatemalan armed forces, especially the elite counterinsurgency Kaibiles. It is not an exaggeration to state that the armed forces and their paramilitary units have unleashed a campaign of generalized terror, which must be recognized as genocide.

The objective of standard counterinsurgency operations is to attack the guerrillas and their infrastructure, the killing of noncombatant civilians being only a collateral activity of the government forces; as the standard military wisdom conveniently rationalizes, "You have to break a few eggs to make an omelet."

But under the new, more "scientific" counterinsurgency warfare methods initiated by Ríos Montt, even the veneer of justification is cast aside, making the indefensible, predominately Indian, civilian rural population the primary target of military operations. As Amnesty International reported in July 1982, the "Guatemalan security services continue to attempt to control opposition, both violent and nonviolent, through widespread killings including the extrajudicial executions of large numbers of rural noncombatants, including entire families, as well as persons suspected of sympathy with violent or nonviolent opposition groups."[13]

It is little wonder that this onslaught of persecution generated as many as one million internal refugees[14]—that is to say, one out of every seven Guatemalans. Another 70,000 to 100,000 sought refuge in neighboring Mexico, with still others fleeing to makeshift encampments in Honduras.[15] Nearly all of the refugees come from Guatemala's Indians, who compose 55 percent of the population and historically have occupied the nation's lowest socioeconomic strata. The overall make-up of the rural class structure can be seen in the striking statistic that two thirds of all arable land is owned by a mere 2 percent of the population.[16]

A most dramatic case of Ríos Montt's new counterinsurgency strategy involved the approximately 5,100 Cackchiquel Indians, originally from about fifteen villages in the area of San Martín Jilotepeque, in the province of Chimaltenango.[17] After fleeing massacres by government forces, these villagers spent several months roaming the mountains. Finally forced by hunger and disease to return to their region, the prostrate Indians were surrounded by government armed forces and threatened with death unless they denounced the guerrillas as responsible for the massacres. Some 300 people were killed by the soldiers, but after strong international pressure, the lives of this large group of Indians were spared. First herded to the village of Coatalum, and then in most cases to the areas of their original villages, they were incarcerated in army run and guarded "relocation centers." Yet another example of this same tactic involved the nearly 2,000 refugee Indians captured and surrounded by the

Guatemalan army in the province of El Quiché; after months of hiding in the woods they also found themselves concentration camp inmates.[18]

Some observers have tried to call these Guatemalan "relocation centers" strategic hamlets. But this is in no way accurate, for they are neither strategic nor are they hamlets. Made up of agglomerations of mostly women, children, and old people suffering from hunger, sickness, and malnutrition, these Indians are kept in tents or improvised huts—their villages in most cases have been destroyed—and guarded by heavily armed soldiers who force them to labor on government-run counterinsurgency building projects. (Their situation is akin to the concentration camps that the Indonesian government constructed for the natives of East Timor, after slaughtering as many as 100,000 of them since the mid-1970s in order to "protect" them from the leftist insurgents of the Revolutionary Front for an Independent East Timor.[19]) In fact, the Guatemalan concentration camps represent a transition in the ambitious counterinsurgency program of forced relocation and the creation of strategic hamlets throughout the troubled countryside.

To facilitate such a pacification plan, the people were first terrorized into at least apparently accepting their new fate. Attempts to systematize Ríos Montt's policy of state terrorism, as outlined below, shed some light on the violence in rural Guatemala.[20]

The actions of the military and paramilitary forces are categorized along an escalating scale of terror, and utilized according to the degree of sympathy in the rural population for the insurgents. In so-called "preventive terror" actions, villagers are executed at random from communities about which little or no information exists concerning feelings for the guerrillas. The purpose is to frighten the population so badly that it will shun any possible future collaboration with the insurgents. Next along the scale is the "selective assassination" of community leaders suspected of collaboration with the opposition; the objective is not only to destroy the rebels' infrastructure, but also to prevent others from joining. Finally, there are the "massive killings" of whole communities believed to have supported the guerrillas. These massacres, carried out in an indiscriminate and generalized manner, effectively eliminate the popular base and send a message to surrounding villages.

While this categorization accurately describes individual cases of violence employed by Ríos Montt's National Plan, actually state terrorism has been part of the system for the past thirty years. Claiming at least 80,000 lives since the 1954 CIA-sponsored coup that overthrew the populist President Jacobo Arbenz, extrajudicial executions have been routinely utilized as state policy by all successive Guatemalan governments.[21]

The first instance of organized armed resistance, however, did not appear until November 1960 when a handful of nationalistic officers, who objected to their country being used as a staging ground to invade Cuba, formed a rural guerrilla *foco* after a failed revolt. Taking a break from their training for the Bay of Pigs invasion, U.S. and Cuban pilots ran a few bombing runs to help crush the attempted barracks coup from their secret CIA air base and training centers in Guatemala.[22] In fact, the small band that formed around the dissident officers never numbered more than a few hundred. Brian Jenkins, who in post-Vietnam years has studied Guatemalan insurgency, pointed out that for the government, "the guerrillas represented only a minor problem and possibly were an asset."[23] Certainly they provided the pretext for the U.S. and Guatemalan governments to build up the military, police, and an impressive network of informers,[24] whose function was to "exercise complete control and surveillance in towns and villages."[25] Furthermore, beginning in the early 1960s the infamous police *judiciales,* trained and armed by the U.S. Agency for International Development's Office of Public Safety program, steadily raised the grim statistics of extrajudicial executions.[26]

Not until the presidency of Julio César Méndez Montenegro (1966–1970), however, did the armed forces and the National Liberation Movement (the MLN is Guatemala's powerful extreme-right political party) unleash the nation's first wave of mass murder. In 1966 the MLN, together with the army and police, organized the White Hand death squads, a gang of rightist terrorists who regularly issued press releases claiming credit for their good work and insisting that to oppose the army was

"treason to the Fatherland."[27] The following year, the army—
and its paramilitary units, including the White Hand—itself became busy in the provinces of Zacapa and Izabal where the
guerrillas had become strong enough to freely move about
among the local population. Directed by U.S. Green Beret advisers, a massive force was dispatched to eliminate the insurgents
and their supporters. They were well prepared for the task, since
the U.S. Military Assistance Program under the Johnson Administration had already provided the army with weapons, communications apparatus, transportation, and other military equipment. An additional similarity to the U.S. role in El Salvador
today, at that time military advisers helped reorganize the armed
forces, including the "creation of a 'rapid reaction force,' made
up of airborne companies, which first implemented the tactics of
airmobile counterinsurgency warfare in Guatemala."[28]

While the several hundred guerrillas were virtually annihilated, estimates of noncombatant deaths during the short
Zacapa–Izabal campaign range from 3,000 to 10,000.[29] One of
the basic reasons for this extraordinarily high civilian death toll
was revealed by the U. S. military attaché to Guatemala, Colonel
John Weber, who was responsible for the U.S. participation in
the offensive. Explaining that the counterinsurgency operation
employed "armed local bands of 'civilian collaborators' licensed
to kill peasants whom they considered guerrillas or 'political
guerrillas,'" the Colonel went on to justify the slaughter of noncombatant civilians because "the Communists are using
everything they have, including terror. And it must be met."[30]

In more traditional counterinsurgency terminology, Jenkins
outlines the reform and repression aspects of the 1960s campaign: "A conspicuous part of the counterinsurgency in Guatemala was the civic action and public relations project that was
heavily funded by the U.S. Military Assistance Program."
Jenkins is even more candid about the 2,000 or so vigilantes that
assisted the armed forces. "Another element in the destruction of
the guerrillas was the employment of terror. Military authorities
in the early stages of their counterinsurgency operations permitted clandestine anti-communist groups to wage a campaign of
violence as the 'counter-terror' to frighten possible guerrilla
collaborators."[31]

Of course, with congressional concern about human rights, and the Carter Administration's highly publicized but basically ineffectual emphasis on them, it is no longer prudent to use such graphic, although precise, terms as "counter-terror," which is standard terminology in all of the Vietnam-era literature on counterinsurgency. These days, "civilian collaborators" have been euphemistically renamed the Civil Defense Corps; even the word "counterinsurgency" has been banned from the official vocabulary. As a senior U.S. military adviser in El Salvador inarticulately tried to explain, it is now called "low intensity conflict, the name being changed. Counterinsurgency no longer being, ah, having conjured up memories of Vietnam and evidently people no longer, ah, don't want to stay worrying about it."[32]

Semantic slight of mouth notwithstanding, counterinsurgency doctrine remains fundamentally the same. In Guatemala, however, the weight has always fallen heavily on the repression side of the equation. The military solidified its base even further during the reign of Guatemala's dictator-president, Carlos Arana Osorio (1970–1974), whose dedicated leadership of the 1960s counterinsurgency campaign had won him international notoriety as the "butcher of Zacapa." President Arana accomplished this through large subsidies to the Bank of the Army, establishing army businesses and, more important, setting the pattern for senior officers to expropriate or buy up peasant land at giveaway prices. This development goes a long way in explaining the resistance within the army to cede to U.S. pressures to implement reform and adhere to human rights standards—like the Salvadoran oligarchy, they perceive such reforms as directly jeopardizing their privileges. Unlike other Latin American armed forces, who are basically the elite's hired help, the Guatemalan military occupy the position of full-fledged members of the upper class.

With the insurgents nearly wiped out, Arana more than lived up to his inauguration-day promise that "anyone who does not abide by the law will be broken in two."[33] Through a policy of state terrorism, at least 15,000 people "disappeared" from 1970 to 1975.[34] The policy of selective assassination under President Kjell Laugerud (1974–1978), while relatively mild by Guatemalan standards, was an affront to the developing human rights consciousness. The Carter Administration, with the threat of cutting off U.S. aid, pressured the General to curb these crimes, a demand that he and the high command considered an unreasonable infringement on Guatemala's sovereignty; they flatly refused to comply. Consequently, the U.S. government suspended new assistance in 1977, but the funds and weapons already authorized conveniently continued to flow until 1980.[35]

With the regime of Ríos Montt's predecessor, President Romeo Lucas García (1978–1982), Guatemalan state terrorism returned to normal. Amnesty International reported on the General's policy:

People who oppose or are imagined to oppose the government are systematically seized without warrant, tortured, and murdered. . . . The bodies of the victims have been found piled up in ravines, dumped at roadsides or buried in mass graves. Thousands bore the scars of torture. Most had been murdered by strangling with a garrote, by being smothered in rubber hoods or by being shot in the head. Amnesty International holds the Government of Guatemala responsible for their fate.[36]

Lucas García will also be remembered by history for another aspect of his iron-fisted rule—the reintroduction of widespread massacres by the army. The resurgence of armed rebel activities since the May 1978 massacre of over a hundred Kekchi Indians from the village of Panzós in the province of Alta Verapaz coincided with the increasing frequency with which many Indian communities in the northern and western highlands of Guatemala were randomly destroyed, their inhabitants raped, tortured, mutilated, and slaughtered. In 1979 there were two documented massacres; in 1980 there were three. In 1981 the number skyrocketed to at least two dozen mass killings.[37]

As shocking as the magnitude of the 1981 killings is, 1982 was even worse. In the first nine months alone, several hundred massacres were documented.[38] Moreover, compared to 1981, the total number of those killed in each massacre increased dramatically. During the first six months of Ríos Montt's rule, reliable sources recorded at least 500 murders per month.[39] The explanation lies in the National Plan's employment of massacres as a counterinsurgency tool. While for the January–February 1982 period there were numerous cases reported of whole families being killed, by the March–April 1982 period entire communities were being systematically massacred. Between March 24 and the last week of June 1982, Amnesty International, in an impeccably documented report, included a partial listing of 2,186 extrajudicial executions in rural Guatemala.[40] By the end of July, the pattern of military violence had reached an even greater degree: Entire groups of neighboring villages were being destroyed.[41] A figure accepted as minimal by people living in these areas is in excess of 10,000 people massacred by the end of 1982.*

In a cynical rationalization of the massacres, Ríos Montt candidly admitted that he had declared the July 1 State of Siege "so we could kill legally."[42] The counterinsurgency logic behind the increase in the frequency and magnitude of the 1982 massacres is best revealed in the following declarations by General Ríos Montt and his coreligionist, then the press secretary, Francisco Bianchi. When asked about army killings of unarmed civilians, the president, in an obvious reference to the insurgents' infrastructure, replied: "Look, the problem of the war is not just a question of who is shooting; for each one that is shooting there are ten working behind him." His press secretary went to the heart of the matter—the destruction of the rebel's popular base—when he elaborated upon the policy of systematic massacres: "The guerrillas won over many Indian collaborators. Therefore, the Indians were subversives, right? And how do you fight subversion? Clearly, you had to kill Indians because they were collaborating with subversion. And then they would say, you are massacring innocent people. But they weren't innocent. They had sold out to subversion."[43]

A soldier in one of these "subversive" villages described what all this means, when put into practice, by complaining that "It is very hard. There are so many of them, they are more popular

*An informal poll of dozens of residents from all social classes in January and February 1983, showed that the vast majority would place the death toll above 15,000 while virtually everyone agreed that 10,000 dead was an absolute minimum estimate.

than we are. . . . Although very few of the guerrillas were armed," he dryly added, "we have to kill them."[44] For all intents and purposes the Indians have been identified as the enemy. In the eyes of the common soldier, no distinction is made between the unarmed civilian rural population and the actual guerrilla combatants. Moreover, deep-rooted racism characterizes Guatemalan "civilized" society, and the strategically important mineral and petroleum deposits are in the northern and western parts of the country, where the population is overwhelmingly Indian and where senior military officers own a disproportionately large amount of the land. Thus the seemingly pathological nature of the army's almost daily massacres in the countryside becomes, if not justifiable, at least more understandable.

SCORCHED EARTH AND GENOCIDE

Beginning in July 1982, the Guatemalan armed forces started to implement a *cordon sanitaire* along the northwestern border with Mexico in an attempt to resolve two major problems. Stemming the flow of refugees to Mexico, the living evidence of the genocidal campaign in the countryside, a militarized frontier would also help to cut the guerrillas' supply lines, which, Guatemalan military assume, pass through Mexico. In the province of Huehuetenango alone, twenty-six villages were destroyed, their inhabitants either massacred or forced to flee, their dwellings and crops burned and their livestock slaughtered.[45] In search of historical parallels to explain these operations, numerous analyses have referred to the Vietnamese scorched earth tactic. Guatemalan reality, however, presents a much bloodier face.

There is no doubt that the Guatemalan insurgents—particularly the Guerrilla Army of the Poor and the Revolutionary Organization of the People in Arms—include large numbers of combatants drawn from the country's twenty-three ethnic groups. Significantly, however, there are no official claims that guerrilla fortifications or storage facilities existed in any of the destroyed villages. Neither are there any cases of guerrillas fighting the government forces from within a village or hamlet that was subsequently leveled. At most, the government reported that insurgent encampments had been found in the regions where massacres later occurred.

These facts are important, because the so-called scorched earth tactic employed by the Guatemalan military is occurring within a totally different context than that of Vietnam. Then, U.S. and South Vietnamese forces customarily counted as Viet Cong all the dead found in the destroyed hamlets only when these villages had been defended by the insurgents; that is, only when the fire was directed at the allied troops from within the hamlets.[46] Although the laws of war forbid the destruction of personal property "except where such destruction is rendered absolutely necessary by military operations,"[47] it clearly does allow for the destruction of fortifications. United States and allied military strategists found that the Viet Cong often built their trenches, bunkers, and escape tunnels within the hamlets, thereby in their opinion making necessary the destruction of entire villages. Moreover, since these circumstances did not permit any distinction between willing supporters of the Viet Cong and the uncommitted villagers, it was impossible to spare the people of these villages. One apologist attempted to justify these inevitable civilian deaths caused by the scorched earth tactic in Vietnam: "in the special conditions of modern insurgency warfare . . . the distinction between 'members of the armed forces' and 'persons taking no active part in the hostilities' is distinctly hazy."[48]

What has occurred in Guatemala is much worse than the "inevitable" application of the scorched earth method in Vietnam. The mass murders being carried out by the Guatemalan armed forces have all the characteristics of genocide in its strictest sense. The Convention on the Prevention and Punishment of the Crime of Genocide, of which Guatemala is a signatory,* was adopted unanimously by the United Nations General Assembly on December 9, 1948.† Article 2 of the Convention defines the crime of genocide as committing acts "with intent to destroy, in whole or in part, a national, ethnical, racial or religious group." This includes (1) "Killing members of the group"; (2) "Causing

---

*As of June 22, 1949; Guatemala ratified the Convention on January 13, 1950.
†By Resolution 260 (III) A.

serious bodily or mental harm to members of the group"; (3) "Deliberately inflicting on the group conditions of life calculated to bring about its physical destruction in whole or in part. . . ."[49] Furthermore, in order to establish the crime of genocide, it is imperative to demonstrate the intent to destroy a particular people, in whole or in part.

The critical difference here is that, unlike civilian deaths inflicted by the Vietnamese scorched earth tactic, the Guatemalan massacres are not caused by acts of war in the legal sense, because they do not involve any enemy combatants. Consequently, the actions of the Guatemalan military must be recognized as genocide, in that the intention behind the massacres is to exterminate the Guatemalan Indians, who are considered actual or potential supporters of the insurgents.

CIVIL DEFENSE CORPS

Another important aspect of Guatemala's National Plan is the so-called Civil Defense Corps. During 1982, in both Guatemala and El Salvador, Civil Defense Corps units increasingly have come to be utilized as adjuncts of the armed forces in their pacification programs, though they are organized in somewhat different ways. As support personnel for the counterinsurgency campaigns, these paramilitary organizations have as their primary purpose the gathering of intelligence; they also provide an armed government presence in the countryside and outlying villages where it is not feasible to deploy regular troops.

In Guatemala, a good example of how the Civil Defense operate can be seen in the village of Las Pacayas, located some twenty-five miles from Cobán, the provincial capital of Alta Verapaz. It is not accidental that Las Pacayas was chosen as a site for this model Guatemalan version of a strategic hamlet: For generations it has been a pro-government village which has traditionally provided the army with some of its most fierce recruits, many of whom take pride in being selected to serve in the elite counterinsurgency Kaibile units. Because of Ríos Montt's strategy of depopulating the remote hamlets, between November 1982 and January 1983 the population of this showpiece of the government's pacification program had doubled to about 450 people. The new arrivals, largely rightist peasants from the surrounding hamlets, also included a minority of "depoliticized" peasants who "perhaps had been deceived into supporting the subversives."[50]

Organized by the army, all males between the ages of 15 and 60 years old had "volunteered" to participate as active members of the Civil Defense Corps. Their leaders, chosen from among former soldiers who had already fulfilled their military service, were provided with World War II M-1 rifles and ammunition, while others carried shotguns and small caliber rifles. Most, however, were armed only with machetes and long wooden clubs. The overall organization was divided into squads of about a dozen men, who were required to spend every third day on duty patrolling the surrounding countryside. Moreover, just as with all the other civil patrols throughout Guatemala—even, or perhaps especially, those whose loyalty is not so clearly established—they had to participate in periodic sweeping operations that lasted from two to six days. It was embarrassingly obvious that such ill-equipped and poorly trained militia presented no match in combat with experienced guerrillas. Further investigation showed that combat was not their real purpose.

An insight into this apparent contradiction came from a high-ranking Western military analyst, who asked not to be identified.

One of the problems is the ability of the army to stay. Once they sweep through an area, is there still a presence? And unfortunately that is not normal. They will sweep through and leave the bodies on the other end, and keep on going. When I was teaching at Fort Leavenworth, I used to say that the first line in any counterinsurgency is the cop on the beat. He knows the population. He knows what the ambient level of violence is. He knows who the players are, the changes in behavior patterns and the way things are going on. He is the first guy to know. You cannot beat that kind of intelligence. Because, you know, the three most important things in a counterinsurgency exercise is intelligence, intelligence and intelligence.[51]

To garrison combat troops in the numerous villages for the constant patrol of such vast areas is simply beyond the physical capabilities of the Guatemalan army. So, the Civil Defense units are assigned the tasks of finding rebel camps, detecting insurgent movements, and locating groups of "subversive" refugees. Once such information is reported by radio to the nearest army garrison, combat troops are sent to deal with the situation. An example of this occurred on February 22, 1983, when patrolmen from the town of Nueva Concepción, Escuintla, reported suspicious movements of strangers in their vicinity. According to the armed forces, these people "who want to live in peace, free from all kinds of problems" promptly notified the army, who then discovered a large cache of rebel arms buried at the outskirts of the town.[52]

Another way the Civil Defense units provide intelligence is through their policing activities. Living in these small communities, they inevitably come to know which citizens are less than loyal to the government, and are in a position to quickly detect any questionable activity, such as organizing efforts or contacts with the insurgents. Certainly these untrained vigilante squads, toting a few old guns, machetes, and clubs, shun any contact with the guerrillas, but these paramilitary bands have no problem bullying unarmed civilians. When they get in over their heads, such as in the event of insurgent infiltration, they quickly call in regular army units to come to the rescue.

Needless to say, very few of the civil patrols are as loyal as those of Las Pacayas and Nueva Concepción. In fact, because all men are forced to serve, most of the civil patrols are assumed to be untrustworthy, and therefore must be "conditioned" and "disciplined."

The most superficial level of conditioning can be illustrated by a loose analogy to the literacy campaign in Cuba and Nicaragua that immediately followed the triumph of the revolutionary forces. During these mobilizations, the participants not only learned how to read and write, but their daily involvement in the government literacy programs also served as a personal investment that helped bring them into the revolutionary process. The structure of the Civil Defense program reveals a similar, if counterrevolutionary, dynamic. As the commander of the province of El Quiché, Colonel Roberto Matta, put it: "The Civil Defense members are very proud of themselves. They no longer only depend on the Army to protect them. Now they feel that they are defending themselves against the subversives. This is a commitment because they have actively chosen sides. For the first time in history they have been brought into the national life. This is the true revolution."[53]

But what Colonel Matta neglected to talk about was the comprehensive conditioning and disciplining program that the patrolmen undergo. That was discovered only through extensive and in-depth interviews with many of these men in three different provinces. Stories, or perhaps more accurately they should be called confessions, were repeatedly related about how during sweeping operations the men were forced to torture and kill suspected insurgent sympathizers. It turns out that the army has this aspect of the conditioning process down almost to a science. When civil patrols are first organized in an area and sent on these sweeps, they are always led by large army units. An initial ratio normally would be 80 percent army and 20 percent civil patrol. In order to prove their loyalty, and manhood, the army requires them to torture and kill "passive guerrillas."

By forcing the men of the civil patrols to commit these atrocities, the army believes that it is winning the peasants' allegiance. The idea seems to be that, once these people become involved in the crimes, they become accomplices and allies in the government's counterinsurgency campaign. Testimony given to the Guatemalan Peace and Justice Committee by a person who participated in one such massacre graphically depicts the effectiveness of this diabolical "civilian collaboration of counterterror." On December 22, 1982, all the men from Chiul, El Quiché, forcibly led by the local army commander, surrounded the neighboring village of Parraxut. After separating the inhabitants by sex and age, the officer ordered the villagers from Chiul to massacre all the men. Those who refused were executed by the soldiers. Next, all the women who refused to be raped were killed; the following morning the rest met the same fate. Most of the children, who had been locked up in the schoolhouse, escaped in the melee—but the entire adult population of Parraxut, about 350 men and women, was massacred. On the way back to Chiul, the patrolmen, in the words of the witness, "didn't say a word; they walked in complete silence and when they reached their homes, they broke down in tears. They cried for several hours." Some, feeling deep remorse, returned to Parraxut to try to help the children, but seeing the men who had killed their parents they hid by running off into the jungle.[54]

The Parraxut massacre also provides insight into the fear and collective guilt that blocks the flow of information about Guatemala's genocidal counterinsurgency campaign. News of the killings did not reach the international press for a couple of weeks, at which time several journalists, taking advantage of Ríos Montt's standing invitation to investigate any such reports, asked the president about the "Chiul massacre." In an apparently open and sincere manner, the General denied that it had occurred, and provided them with a helicopter to visit the village. Upon arrival in Chiul everything seemed normal and the people claimed to know nothing about any massacre. Had the journalists continued on to Parraxut they may have uncovered the truth, but their information had incorrectly placed the killings in Chiul. The result was a coup for the Guatemalan propaganda machine, which repeated the story to arriving journalists as proof that "there is a false campaign about government atrocities," while assuring them that "we will do everything in our power to show you that such atrocities do not take place, as was the case with the false reports of the Chiul massacre."[55]

Gradually, as the conditioning process makes "real men" of the civil patrol members, the proportion of regular army troops accompanying them on sweeps and other functions is reduced, while the process of instilling discipline continues. In this context, discipline does not mean military training, but rather, following orders: shoot only in self-defense if attacked by the insurgents; propagate the image of the "good army" and a concerned government; capture, torture, and hand over to the military authorities those suspected of being guerrillas or insurgent sympathizers; and follow to the letter regulations about manning roadblocks or guarding bridges, electric power transformers, and other static positions considered vulnerable to rebel attacks.

Any sign of lukewarm attitudes, individual or collective, is enough to cast suspicion upon the patrolmen as "passive guerrillas," especially since the army believes that the insurgents follow a tactic of infiltrating the civil patrols. Commonly, patrolmen disappear or are murdered outright, as occurred on February 28, 1983, at the Cabel Bridge, situated about thirty miles from the Mexican border on the Pan American Highway. That day, the bridge was being watched by a patrol that was considered notoriously undisciplined. According to the survivors, rather than spacing themselves the regulation five paces apart the men had broken yet another rule by huddling together around a fire under a plastic awning to keep out of the rain. At two o'clock in the morning, someone threw a hand grenade into the group, killing one and seriously injuring three others. As the attackers approached, the remaining nine jumped over the bridge into the shallow water below, from where they heard the shots executing the three wounded patrolmen who were unable to escape.

When the guerrillas attack, it is normal procedure for the army to immediately organize a search operation. This time it did nothing. For this reason, and because of that particular patrol's "bad reputation," there is no doubt in the minds of the local people that the army perpetrated the attack and executions as a disciplinary measure.

STRATEGIC HAMLETS

The history of strategic hamlets begins in the Malay peninsula in the early 1950s. Under the leadership of Lieutenant-General Sir Harold Briggs, the British authorities devised an embryonic form of the strategic hamlet concept to root out the Malay Communist Party–led insurgency. The first step of the Briggs plan consisted in the creation of a physical separation between the guerrillas and their popular base. The scheme called for the resettlement of the large squatter settlements, which, like the Malay Communist Party, was almost entirely Chinese. The Chinese made up almost half the population and were bitterly resented by the original indigenous population, the Malays. Between 1950 and 1952, the British built 410 so-called "new villages"—actually compounds surrounded with barbed wire and fully under police control—that held more than 420,000 people.[56] Unques-

114

tionably, this strategy dealt a major blow to the insurgent movement, and when coordinated with complementary administrative, police, and military measures, it proved to be the counterinsurgency formula that turned the tide in favor of the government. By 1966, the year that the Emergency formally ended, the insurgent movement had been virtually defeated.

Vietnamese strategic hamlets were only one of the "rural development" programs that attempted to "pacify" the rural population. Their immediate predecessor, the Agroville program (1959–1960), resettled several hundred thousand peasants into new "rural towns." Accompanied by intensified military and police operations, as well as civic action projects, the Agroville program proved too ambitious for the corrupt and inefficient Diem regime.

In 1962, the concept was transplanted from Malaya to South Vietnam, and many of the elements of the Briggs plan were revived with large-scale U.S. support. The scheme intended first to secure a firm base, and then to gradually expand the strategic hamlets outward into disputed areas, and finally into the insurgent-controlled territory. Instead of placing the emphasis on eliminating the Viet Cong through conventional military means, moreover, the program in General Sir Robert Thompson's words,[57] aimed to "protect" the villagers from contact with the insurgents: Strategic and defended hamlets, it was expected, would prevent both overt attack[58] and covert infiltration.[59]

In order to prevent the peasants from being contaminated by alien ideologies, the strategic hamlet concept necessitated their "political isolation" as well as physical isolation. For as a 1963 U.S. Agency for International Development study put it: "the ultimate target is the human mind. It may be 'changed,' it may be rendered impotent for expression or it may be extinguished, but it still remains the critical target."[60] According to strategic hamlet theoreticians, peasants' "hearts and minds" would be won over through the rigorous implementation of civic action programs in the hamlets and through more responsive government attitudes toward the "felt" needs of the resettled population. This "improvement" in the peasants' lives, however, must be accompanied by strict security and control measures. Security

would be achieved by coordinating the activity of the hamlet
militias, the paramilitary squads, and regular military units;
dusk to dawn curfews and checkpoints—together with a good
radio and communications network linking the hamlets, villages,
and the municipal or district capital—would control the flow of
people and supplies.

The official theory contends that only after isolating the insurgents from the rural population through these coordinated measures can military operations by the government forces achieve
lasting results. After the government forces had recovered all the
densely populated areas (including those in disputed territory),
attacks on guerrilla-held areas would be conducted in an outward movement from the strongest area of control. Whole areas
are cordoned off, and free-fire zones are established; then the
encircled villages are saturated by artillery and aircraft bombing
to drive as many of the surviving villages as possible to the nearest strategic hamlet. Consequently, the ever-shrinking popular
bases will suffer a devastating logistical strain because the insurgent combatants must be fed and supplied by a decreasing base
of popular support.

The dispersed guerrilla units are then aggressively attacked by
conventional search-and-destroy operations and saturation patrolling by hunter killer units. Since such casualties cannot be
replaced by fresh recruits—in theory by this point the population
is virtually imprisoned in strategic hamlets—a process of attrition will result in the gradual decimation of the insurgents.
Those small groups of guerrillas who survive find themselves
forced to retreat to the most inhospitable mountainous, swamp,
or jungle area, where they are then simply mopped-up by the
government's small-unit special counterinsurgent forces or fin-
ished off by hunger and disease.

So much for the elaborately conceived theory behind strategic
hamlets; the reality of the program in South Vietnam proved
quite different.

In January 1962, the South Vietnamese government announced that it intended to include the entire rural population in
the program.[61] An Inter-Ministerial Committee was set up and
by the next month some 1,500 civil servants had received train-

ing in special courses. Even so, the program did not get off to an auspicious start.

The first attempt to establish strategic hamlets, code-named Operation Sunrise, centered upon a Viet Cong–controlled location in Binh Duong province. Preceding the operation, government military units duly swept the area, burned the people's homes and belongings and then forcibly relocated the survivors (among whom they encountered virtually no able-bodied men) into five rebuilt hamlets. Other than alienating the local population even further, Operation Sunrise accomplished little; insurgent activities in Binh Duong province were not affected in any appreciable way because the Viet Cong had stopped using those particular villages as active bases some time before.

By August 1962, the inevitable National Plan was finally formulated. It divided the country into four zones, marking as priority areas the Mekong Delta and the provinces around Saigon. By October 1962, only two months later, the South Vietnamese government boasted the construction of 3,225 hamlets, holding over four million people.[62] Technically, a "completed hamlet" had to meet six criteria: 1) the clearing of the Viet Cong from the area; 2) the organization and indoctrination of the population; 3) the establishment of a work and disaster plan that assigned specific duties to all inhabitants; 4) the completion of a static defense and security system to protect the overall compounds; 5) the formation of special commando cells, and 6) the election of an advisory council.[63] In April 1963, claiming the establishment of 5,900 strategic hamlets, the government news agency, Vietnam Press, proudly announced that "this movement has upset all the subversive maneuvers of the enemies of the nation, and it has, in addition, strongly shaken the foundations of their very organizations."[64] By October 1963, furthermore, the government boasted the spectacular completion of nearly 9,000 hamlets "protecting" 8,737,000 people.[65] Had this figure been true, it would have represented more than half of the nation's people, since the population of South Vietnam reached the 16 million mark only in 1965.[66] In any event, all came to naught when the Diem regime collapsed, putting an abrupt end to the strategic hamlet program in South Vietnam after only twenty-one months of operation.

In their evaluations of the program, advocates of this counter-insurgency measure have largely concentrated on the failures of the Diem regime to implement properly the proscribed formula for successful strategic hamlets. According to Sir Robert Thompson, the program had moved much too quickly, resulting in the falsification of statistics; in many cases claims were made that the criteria for a completed hamlet had been met when in fact all that had been done was to put up a fence.[67] Neither had the principle of building outward from already secure areas been followed: Subsequent critics of the Vietnamese program observed that the hamlets never constituted a front line against Viet Cong advance. Instead, they were built haphazardly all over the country.

Another major problem was the configuration of the South Vietnamese villages. For example, in the Mekong Delta, where most of the rural population lived, villages were strung out for miles along the canals. The construction of dependable defenses around each hamlet was at best impractical, and more often simply impossible, without moving most inhabitants to a central point. But given the distances and the imposition of curfews after nightfall, where such regrouping was tried, agricultural production fell drastically. In other words, the critical self-sufficiency requirement could not be met by the hamlets. On the contrary, a grave syndrome of dependency upon the government and other sources developed among the resettled population. To make things worse, the great majority of financial and other resources supplied by Washington and Saigon never reached the intended beneficiaries, but evaporated through inefficiency and corruption, much of it falling into the hands of the rebels.[68]

But by far the most serious defect of the Vietnamese program, according to the supporters of this strategy, was that it never successfully combined the reformist and the repressive aspects of the counterinsurgency doctrine. The failure of the strategic hamlet program in Vietnam was not only caused by its own inherent problems, but also reflected a shift in U.S. military strategy. With the assassination of President Kennedy in November 1963, military traditionalists came to dominate the nature of U.S. intervention. Without presidential patronage to insure the enactment of the full counterinsurgency program, the U.S. armed forces imposed their conventional concepts, while neglecting the other aspects of counterinsurgency.

Thus, unconventional warfare methods and the strategic hamlet programs were deemphasized, underfunded, and never adequately supported. Consequently, as far as U.S. military operations in Southeast Asia were concerned, they were never fully tested, and their effectiveness or ineffectiveness remains unproven.

The Guatemalan National Plan also includes a central component that closely approximates the strategic hamlet concept. Even more so than in South Vietnam, its emphasis falls heavily upon repression, with only minimal efforts at reform. This counterinsurgency campaign has been distinguished by its genocidal core: leaving thousands dead and as many as a million internal refugees. After months of hiding in the mountains or jungles, without regular access to food or medicine and hunted by the military and the civil patrols under the "rifles" part of the National Plan, these prostrate people are often forced into "relocation centers," becoming recipients of the "beans" component: In return for manual labor on road construction crews and other civic action projects, they receive a minimal quota of basic foodstuffs. Smaller groups also regularly arrive at the larger towns and cities where they are most often accorded remarkable hospitality by the local population, who have proved their humanitarian generosity by sharing their homes and meager food supplies with the refugees.[69]

The next step in the creation of Guatemalan strategic hamlets is to repopulate the abandoned communities: first the larger rural towns, usually the county seats, then the surrounding villages and hamlets. The examples of Joyabaj in El Quiché and San Miguel Acatán in Huehuetenango serve to illustrate how this aspect of the counterinsurgency campaign functions. The residents of both towns, subjected to vicious army attacks, abandoned their communities by mid-1982. After establishing new garrisons in September and October, the military ordered the former inhabitants back to the towns. Failure to return resulted in the forfeiture of house and land, which were given to other refugees. (This sanction serves the dual purpose of inducing people to return, often even at the risk of being denounced as "passive guerrillas" because of their former activities, and of breaking up traditional community solidarity through the forced introduction of people from other areas.) Once the civil patrols had been formed, conditioned, and disciplined, sweeps of surrounding hamlets were conducted to clear out suspected subversive elements and to control the repopulation of outlying strategic villages. Those hamlets considered "beyond rescue" because of their support of the insurgents were routinely burned to prevent their uncontrolled repopulation. Under forced labor drafts imposed by the armed forces, the people are required to harvest the crops on abandoned land. The proceeds are appropriated by the government for civic action projects such as the rebuilding of municipal buildings and repairing damaged infrastructure. This aspect of Guatemala's National Plan has been widely implemented throughout the countryside, as demonstrated in the case of Chuatalúm, Chimaltenango, and fourteen neighboring hamlets in October 1982.[70]

The town of Nentón, Huehuetenango, one of the first places to be "repopulated," provides a less successful example. The town was completely abandoned in early 1982 after suffering repeated army sweeps and aerial attacks from air force helicopters and A-37B Dragonfly light bombers. In August, the military ordered the former inhabitants to return within three days; failing to do so, of course, was considered proof of subversion and punished accordingly. On August 24, the government flew in by helicopter a dozen Guatemalan newspaper, radio, and television correspondents to witness the "successful repopulation" of Nentón. But even with such elaborate preparations, the journalists could report that only 172 out of the original 700 families had returned to their former community.[71] Because of continued insurgent activity, the military resumed its attacks and bombing of Nentón, once again sending the residents fleeing. Only in January 1983, after establishing an army garrison to back up the national police, were the people once gain ordered back. Even though the government has appointed functionaries, such as municipal authorities, school teachers, and health workers, the people are extremely reluctant to return. According to local sources, by late February, Nentón was still only about 25 percent repopulated.

120

THE MORASS

The civil patrols, through their defense of static positions, patrolling, sweeping, and policing activities, fulfill the strategic hamlet military requirements. Furthermore, they are used as a source of preselection and conscription of men for the buildup of the army, so that it will have sufficient manpower to deploy new garrisons throughout the conflictive areas of the country. Each civil patrol must choose two of its best members to serve the mandatory 30-month army tour of duty. Needless to say, this preselection is far more efficient than the old quota system—especially since the army fears insurgent infiltration into its ranks—under which eligible-looking young men, of undetermined loyalty, would simply be picked up off of the city streets or in the villages.

Although the exact size of the army's expansion is secret information, judging from the large number of conscripts, it certainly is substantial. A concrete gauge is the conditions and a revealing statement made by the commander of the army base at Cobán in Alta Verapaz, in late January 1983. When questioned about the large number of recruits, Colonel Juan Marrorquín complained about the crowded conditions, saying "this base was built for one battalion, now we have more than three."[72] Guatemala's "secret" military buildup also sheds light on the apparent contradiction between the government's claim of crushing the insurgent movement and the simultaneous resumption of U.S. military aid during this same month.* Part of the buildup, and the reasons behind it, became public in mid-1983 when Army Chief of Staff General Héctor Mario López Fuentes announced the establishment of twenty-two new military bases strategically situated throughout Guatemala. General López Fuentes went on to underscore the importance of this new development as he elaborated upon the function of the bases: "By establishing a military presence throughout the Republic, there will not be any subversive presence. . . . We need to reinforce control, not only of territory but also of the population."[73]

The forced participation and control of the civilian population

*The resumption of U.S. military aid to Guatemala in January 1983, after being suspended since 1977 because of the country's persistent violations of basic human rights, will be discussed in detail later.

within the National Plan is further met through the creation of a corporatist structure: the local, municipal, provincial, and national councils. At the hamlet level they are known as the Communal Institutional Coordinators (CIC). Each CIC is made up of local community leaders selected by the nearest military authority and usually includes the mayor and other civil servants (who, since the declaration of the state of siege on July 1, 1982, are appointed by the executive) as well as the leaders of the civil patrols, school teachers, health workers, large landowners, and directors of any local cooperatives. Appointment to the CIC is compulsory, and attendance at all meetings is obligatory. Their function is to assess the community's needs and to allocate available resources according to the military's overall priorities. The highest ranking army officer from the nearest garrison enforces discipline over the CICs, and holds veto power over all of its decisions. Through this mechanism, which has replaced the banned traditional Indian communal councils, the military maintains strict control over community life, from the granting of permission to hold dances to any other congregation of people, from the establishment of a cottage industry to the mandatory participation in public works projects.

The CICs in turn depend on similar organizations at the municipal level, usually located in their county seat, known as Municipal Institutional Coordinators (CIM). The structure and composition of the CIMs are similar to the CICs, although they include some personalities not usually found in the hamlets, such as the chiefs of the national and treasury police, Catholic priests and Protestant pastors, and leader of civic, cultural, and even sports organizations. The next step in this corporatist structure is the Regional Institutional Coordinators (CIR), which operate on the provincial level. Commensurate with their higher status, in addition to those categories of people already mentioned, the CIRs also include heads of the regional health, educational, and commercial institutions, such as university administrators and professors, directors of the Coffee Growers Association and even the president of the Lions club. In all cases, the highest local military officer holds veto power. The overall coordinating body is the National Committee for Reconstruction, based in Guatemala City and composed of the nation's notables. Of course, as with the three lesser levels, its decisions are subject to approval of the military, which in general has the last word on all matters it considers to be of interest, in practice meaning everything.

Through this structure of CIC, CIM, and CIR civilians are forcibly integrated into the counterinsurgency campaign, because they function as an extension of the military government and its efforts to pacify the country. Through them, the government is able to analyze the overall workings of society down to the most isolated hamlet, and to allocate resources, which it channels in the most useful fashion to complement the objective of the National Plan. Towns and hamlets that are considered loyal may receive a waterworks project funded by regional or national sources, whereas others may find themselves required to construct and maintain roads so that the army can more rapidly send in troops in the event of trouble. Unions and other labor, peasant, and community organizations are outlawed, while the private enterprise sector is further helped by the absence of a minimum wage and the routine granting of its petitions to the councils. Catholics, who are suspected because of their "developmentalist" and "human promotion" orientation, invariably find restraints placed upon their communal and missionary works: Their catechists are in constant danger of denunciation; supplies and equipment sent from abroad are heavily taxed; and their petitions to engage in community work are rarely granted. In contrast, evangelical Protestants—who preach a personal relation with God (rather than community solidarity), and the obligation to obey all authority, even to the point of informing the authorities of suspicious activity among their families and neighbors—were accorded every advantage while Ríos Montt was in power. Their missionary supplies regularly entered Guatemala duty free and were often shipped to outlying places in air force transport; and the rapidly growing numbers of their missionaries and projects received a sympathetic hearing at all levels of the councils, even to preferential permission to teach their doctrine in the public schools.

The long-term effects upon the Guatemalan economy of extracting approximately half the male working hours because of their civil patrol duties is still unknown. In the areas of conflict, the fall 1982 harvest was lost, whereas the winter 1983 coffee crop was partially salvaged by government-organized work gangs. The short-term scarcity is being met by army distribution of food and other necessities in return for forced counterinsurgency-related labor. Although a small portion of the food and medicine did arrive from different evangelical Protestant groups, such as Ríos Montt's California-based Gospel Outreach project, by far most of these goods come from the Roman Catholic charitable organization Caritas and the United Nations' World Food Program.[74]

Guatemala's economy cannot support any real welfare program, nor does the political will or moral inclination exist to better the lives of the Indians or change the centuries-old patterns of domination and repression of the country's ethnic groups. The nature of the military's distribution program was described in a report by a private U.S. development corporation when it flatly stated that "the food is being used as a tool. . . . There is no neutrality whatsoever regarding its use."[75] Indeed, the military's guiding philosophy, according to an army officer directly involved in distributing food to refugees in the Quiché village of Cunén, is even more clear cut: "If you are with us, we will feed you, if not, we will kill you."[76]

THE FALL OF RÍOS MONTT

Initial coverage of the August 8, 1983, barracks revolt that toppled the Guatemalan dictator Ríos Montt attributed little significance to the event, blithely writing it off as little more than another of the interminable rounds of military musical chairs played by Latin American dictators. On the surface it did appear to be just one more palace coup, a changing of the guard that replaced General Ríos Montt with his Minister of Defense, General Oscar Humberto Mejía Víctores; a mere power shift within cliques of the ruling elites that meant nothing to the basic structure of Guatemalan society.

Certainly the counterinsurgency National Plan will continue

unaffected by the hard-line Mejía Víctores, for it is the brain child of the army; Ríos Montt was only its adoptive parent entrusted with custody over its growth. Indeed, reflecting the pragmatic truism that no matter how bad things are, they can always get worse, a disgruntled junior member of the U.S. diplomatic corps in Guatemala privately remarked a month before the coup: "Ríos Montt is actually the best of the lot, when he goes things are really going to get tough."

The more superficial explanations of Ríos Montt's fall stress his ardent proselytising of evangelical Protestantism in overwhelmingly Catholic Guatemala. None fail to cite the military's communiqué justifying their decision to depose the General, which claimed that "a fanatic and aggressive religious group, taking advantage of the positions of power of its highest members, has used and abused the Government for its own benefit."[77] Surely Ríos Montt's religious zealousness did not sit well with the nation's elite, particularly the Catholic hierarchy. Upon coming to power, for example, the General proclaimed that "God has decided that I'd become President of this Nation."[78] Moreover, the patronizing tones of his Sunday night televised sermons no doubt were as irritating as his attempt to forbid the keeping of mistresses. But even for the macho military, such antagonistic behavior clearly could not have provided sufficient cause to forge the unity required to organize a successful revolt. Guatemalan coups just do not happen that way.

True, Ríos Montt was not the run-of-the-mill Latin dictator. Similar to other fascist mystics, behind his brutal rule was a pseudospiritual vision of an orderly, moral, and law-abiding society. While his fundamentalist fanaticism served as a contributing factor, the full explanation of his downfall lies in his drive to fulfill these goals, an obsession that ultimately alienated the nation's elite—the business community, the large landowners, and the senior military officers and the far-right ideologues within the Reagan Administration.

Already suffering the effects of world recession, the virtual end of tourism, and decreased coffee and cotton exports, the nation's agro-commercial elite found Ríos Montt's other measures intolerable. Among the most objectionable were his policies of keeping private enterprise out of oil development and enforcing strict government currency controls. For the first time in Guatemala's modern history, a thriving black market for dollars developed, while foreign investment dried up and international trade all but came to a standstill. Reflecting the gravity of the nation's economy, the gross domestic product fell from a 1 percent growth in 1981 to a devastating minus 3.5 percent decline in 1982,[79] while according to official figures, unemployment soared to over 40 percent.[80] By April, the Minister of Finance admitted that the economic crisis "was the worst in the country's history."[81] The straw that broke the businessmen's back—a group that President Ríos Montt likened to "greedy merchants, who like the conquistadors, still seek only gold"[82]—seems to be the 10 percent sales tax that he announced would take effect on the first of August to help pay for the extraordinary costs of the counterinsurgency campaign.

Further, the president's frequent references to enforcement of a land reform program to complement the counterinsurgency effort raised the ire of the large landowners, many of whom are senior military officers who over the years have become an integral part of the landed oligarchy. But the generals and colonels found even greater cause for concern in their commander in chief's policy of rapidly promoting to strategic positions junior officers, who were crucial in bringing him to power. Moreover, the heavy reliance upon a small group of about sixty young officers appointed to high-level government posts, along with his ambitious campaign to root out corruption in the armed forces, provided reason enough for the senior officers to worry about the institutional survival of the traditional army, to say nothing about their own positions.

Leaders in the powerful right-wing political parties, especially the National Liberation Movement that for decades has controlled Guatemala's politics, began to fear that they might never regain their former status. After a year of failing to announce elections, they were shocked by the March 1983 "political opening" that encouraged the creation of multiple rival parties. Worst of all, the president continued stalling to set a date for elections. Primarily they feared that he might indefinitely stay in power or, nearly as bad, schedule elections so far in the future that they would lose the almost certain prospect of victory that quick elections assured them, since the new parties could not possibly match their well-organized and experienced party machines.[83] In May, the politicos received another shock when Ríos Montt unexpectedly declared that the nation was not prepared for elections, and that he did not intend to schedule them until he had created a new party system.[84]

Failure to enact this political reform and hold elections also played a role in determining U.S. support, since at least the veneer of democracy is vital to Washington's Central American policy in two important ways. First, holding elections would help convince Congress to keep open the renewed aid channels engineered by the Reagan Administration. Since 1977, when President Carter ceased assistance because of Guatemala's insistence upon employing extrajudicial executions as state policy, no new U.S. military aid was permitted until 1983. In January of that year, President Reagan opened a crack in the wall by approving the sale of 6.3 million dollars' worth of badly needed spare parts for the air force's U.S.-made helicopters, a move that bypassed congressional oversight.[85] For fiscal year 1984 (which began on October 1, 1983), the Administration felt it opportune to deepen the wedge and asked Congress for 10.25 million dollars in military aid on top of a whopping 66.5 million dollars in economic assistance.[86] The timing was right and the funds were authorized;[87] once again the United States was on the verge of financing counterinsurgency in Guatemala.

Needless to say, such largess gave Washington enormous leverage; not so much with the independent-minded Ríos Montt, but with the military and the rest of the nation's tiny elite. Still, without at least some cosmetic reforms—in particular, quick elections and the abolition of the secret tribunals that had gained world condemnation—the Reagan Administration faced formidable opposition in obtaining final congressional appropriations for U.S. military assistance to Guatemala. Indeed, in early August Congress refused to resume military aid to Guatemala, underscoring Ríos Montt's failure to win over this crucial support, and certainly contributing another reason to oust him in the minds of the Guatemalan officer corps and the Pentagon.[88]

The other objective hindered by Ríos Montt's refusal to call quick elections was the Administration's long-standing desire to involve Guatemala in a more active regional role in its Central American crusade. The erratic and inward-looking president, while not an outspoken critic of the United States, was neither a reliable nor a pliable ally. For example, he quietly looked with sympathy upon the Contadora Group's efforts at devising a negotiated peace proposal for the Isthmus's convulsions, while he shunned any military collaboration with neighboring El Salvador, and steadfastly refused to allow Guatemala to be used as a base for U.S. espionage activities.[89] Another stumbling block to Washington's adventure in the region was that without at least the charade of democratic elections, Guatemala could not possibly join the Central American Democratic Community—the U.S.-forged military alliance among El Salvador, Honduras, and Costa Rica. Without the intervention of the powerful and efficient Guatemalan army in the Salvadoran civil war, and its commitment to a regional military pact, the Reagan Administration's plans to forge a solid Central American counterrevolutionary block remained unfulfilled.

In June 1983, when the right wing twice attempted to oust Ríos Montt, these factors started to gel into widespread opposition among the elite, which seriously threatened the president's position. He reacted by clamping down even harder on civil liberties, while at the same time making a series of concessions in a futile attempt to placate the growing opposition.[90] After officially launching the long-promised democratic process by swearing in the Electoral Tribunal, he announced that elections for a Constituent Assembly would take place on July 29, 1984.[91] Moreover, he dismissed nearly all of the junior officers who surrounded him in the government and replaced them with civilians, although he insisted upon retaining his top two religious advisers.[92]

But the forces set in motion already had gained too strong a momentum to be so easily appeased, and on the morning of August 8, General Mejía Víctores led a superbly coordinated revolt that smoothly ousted Ríos Montt. The new head of state immediately made all the right moves: He lifted the state of siege, abolished the secret tribunals, promised a fast restoration of "social, economic, and political democracy," pledged to continue eradicating "the virus of Marxist-Leninism," and requested a "close dialogue" with the United States.

The intriguing events surrounding the coup provide more than sufficient cause to question the extent of Washington's involvement in Ríos Montt's fall. While Mejía Víctores is hardly a puppet whose strings the State Department can pull, neither is it likely that he or anyone else could impose a change of government without at least the tacit approval of the United States. As in the 1963 overthrow of the Diem regime in Vietnam, given the powerful elements already set to depose the Guatemalan dictator, all that would be needed was a signal that the United States would not resist the change. It was just such opposition that thwarted at least ten previous plots to topple Ríos Montt,[93] including the June 29th attempt that failed in large part because State Department officials made their strong disapproval clear.[94] Obviously, the leaders of this plot did not have Washington's endorsement. In a parallel with the Diem coup, in the days preceding the successful Guatemalan revolt, there was a significant shift in the U.S. Embassy's attitude when it refrained from any such display of opposition. As the secretary general of the Christian Democratic Party, Venicio Cerezo Arévalo, explained: "An important obstacle [to previous attempts to oust Ríos Montt] had been the U.S. Embassy attitude, which had impeded the possibility of a coup." The Guatemalan politician went on to say that prior to Mejía Víctores's successful revolt, "the embassy had neutralized itself—they may not have supported the coup, but they didn't oppose it, either."[95]

Further evidence indicates that the United States may very well have encouraged the generals' revolt through more than passive acquiescence. Two days before the coup, on August 6, then Minister of Defense Mejía Víctores flew to the U.S. aircraft carrier *Ranger* off the Nicaraguan coast for what later was officially described as a "courtesy call."[96] While this may be so, the *Ranger* did provide the ideal place for a secret meeting with any Washington-based policymakers wishing to avoid recognition by a snoopy press. On the way home the next day, the General stopped off in Honduras where he conferred with his counterparts—the ministers of defense of El Salvador and Honduras—as well as with the head of the U.S. Southern Command in Panama, General Paul F. Gorman.[97] While the State Department dismissed as "ridiculous" the notion that Mejía Víctores's weekend activities were a plotting session, it should be kept in mind that they do not enjoy a reputation as honest people.[98]

The next day, as two U.S. Navy jets remained stationed at the Guatemala City airport,[99] the U.S. deputy military attaché, Major William Mercado, encountered the misfortune of being caught on film by two Guatemalan television stations inside the National Palace as he spoke into a walkie-talkie during the actual coup.[100] The following day, U.S. Ambassador Frederic L. Chapin paid a visit to the National Palace himself to greet the new dictator—an unusual act, in that protocol normally requires a decent interval before the recognition of a head of state who comes to power by violent means, such as the several weeks that Ríos Montt had to wait to receive this honor.[101] That same day, statements out of Washington did little to allay suspicions of U.S. complicity in the change of governments: The State Department hailed Mejía Víctores's "positive steps" while Pentagon and CIA officials aired their hopes that the new Guatemalan regime would prove more cooperative with U.S. initiatives in Central America.[102]

The General hurried to fulfill their hopes. Two days later, on August 11 during a nationwide radio speech, Mejía Víctores berated the Nicaraguan Sandinistas as "not only a threat to Guatemala but to the whole continent," and even went so far as to proclaim that the "United States is the only country that can help to combat the guerrillas in the region."[103] Still better news for the Reagan Administration arrived on August 14, when Guatemalan and Salvadoran authorities made a delayed announcement that their two nations had concluded an agreement for closer military collaboration: In return for Salvadoran supplies of arms and ammunition from its U.S.–stocked arsenal, the Guatemalans would set up training camps and programs in their country to instruct El Salvador's army in counterinsurgency warfare.[104]

To top all this off, Washington enjoyed another stroke of incredibly good luck several months later, after a weekend meeting of the defense ministers of Guatemala, El Salvador, Honduras, and the head of the U.S Army Southern Command in Guatemala City. On October 3, parroting the threat of Marxist-Leninist aggression, the ministers issued a joint statement announcing the resurrection of the Central American Defense Council, thereby reviving the military alliance among the armed forces of their three nations.[105]

Certainly the evidence of direct U.S. intervention in the Guatemalan coup plot is circumstantial. Only some extraordinary breach of security—such as the Pentagon Papers provided for evidence of U.S. duplicity in South Vietnam—would give the public and historians the hard documentation of a smoking gun; but the chronology of events stretch the bounds of coincidence and Washington's ability to deny involvement. While no serious scholar subscribes to the conspiracy theory of history, to think that history proceeds without conspiracies is simple fantasy.

SIX

EL SALVADOR

The misery caused by the Great Depression swept Latin America like a hurricane, generating a tidal wave of political unrest. In its wake, the military, in keeping with its historic role as the guardian of the status quo, toppled civilian governments throughout Central and South America, frustrating popular attempts to bring about democratic changes. El Salvador, far from being among the few exceptions to this historical rule, provides one of its more violent examples. Moreover, the Salvadoran military, instead of retreating from center stage once the crisis had passed as was customary, cut out a special place for itself; for almost half a century, it functioned as a virtual fourth section of the nation's government, overshadowing by far the combined strength of the judicial, legislative, and executive branches.

Culminating a decade of political and labor organizing, in 1931 a center-left coalition elected Arturo Araujo as president under the banner of the Salvadoran Labor Party, the last indisputably honest election seen in El Salvador. Within months, Araujo's populist government fell to a military coup led by General Maximiliano Hernández Martínez, who promptly declared himself president, a position that he held for the next thirteen years. Right from the beginning, the General left no doubt about the nature of his regime. As one of his first acts, the dictator nullified all of the municipal elections won by the Salvadoran Communist Party, thereby putting an end to any hopes of bringing about even minimal changes through the democratic process. With all legal avenues to gain better wages and living conditions blocked by the indurate Hernández Martínez, and encouraged by the example already set in neighboring Nicaragua by Augusto

Sandino's revolutionary movement, the frustrated Salvadoran peasantry rose up in the first Communist Party–organized rebellion in the Western hemisphere. But unlike events in Nicaragua, the revolt in El Salvador—led by the nationalistic socialist Farabundo Martí, from whom the current-day revolutionary front takes its name—was less of a guerrilla-style insurrection than a spontaneous popular uprising. Reflecting this vital difference is the fact that while it took U.S. Marines and the first of the Somoza dictators years to defeat the Sandinistas, Hernández Martínez crushed the Salvadoran revolt in a vicious one-month campaign. During January 1932, in what is known simply as *La Matanza* (The Killing), a massive army force rampaged through the western part of the country slaughtering up to 30,000 people, most of them after the rebels had ceased all armed resistance.

Institutionalizing their power in the National Conciliation Party, the army established itself as a governing caste; not only did it determine who would be president, most of the time it selected one of its own senior officers to fill the job. The arrangement proved more than satisfactory for both the military and the oligarchy, the so-called "fourteen families" (the anachronistic name by which the Salvadoran elite is still known comes from the initial agreement made with the military following *La Matanza,* which supposedly designated one prominent family to reign in each of the nation's fourteen provinces) that now number closer to a couple hundred notable families. Through corruption and their power brokering, the military provided a certain means of upward social mobility for its ambitious officer corps, who traditionally come from the small middle or even lower classes. In return, they loyally have served the elite's interests by protecting them from any upstarts among the remaining 95 percent of Salvadorans who might dare to threaten their privileges.

During the early 1960s, under the influence of the U.S. counterinsurgency doctrine that provided training for the armed forces, the infamous rural vigilante Democratic National Organization (ORDEN) was created in order to further control the countryside. As its founder, General José Alberto Medrano (Ret.) proudly explained in a 1980 interview, ORDEN (which is the Spanish word for "order") was founded in 1961 "in order to indoctrinate the peasants, making them the backbone of the ideological campaign supporting the free-world system against the inroads of international Communism."[1] During the following years, ORDEN joined the armed forces in waging a bloody campaign attacking organizations suspected of "Communist subversion," raping the women, executing the leaders, and pillaging and burning their homes. So despicable had ORDEN become that one of the first steps taken by the new government following the 1979 coup was to officially "outlaw" the organization; although it quickly regained and even surpassed its former role as the civilian adjunct of the military as they stepped up their counterinsurgency campaign. Today, its members form the core of the newly organized Civil Defense Corps.

As the 1970s progressed, so did the awakening demands for social change. Although the first guerrilla groups formed at the beginning of the decade, these small bands remained politically and militarily marginal until the late 1970s. Even at this late date, the most powerful forces for social change still rested in the popular organizations—the peasant leagues, labor unions, and slum-dweller organizations, such as the socialist-oriented Revolutionary Popular Bloc and the Catholic-affiliated Union of Rural Workers, to mention but two of the dozen or so that mushroomed from 1975 on. As their efforts consistently met with the most brutal repression from the army and ORDEN, some of these mass organizations began making contacts with the armed insurgents, and the increased volatility of the situation became clear to everyone. Again, as a half century before, events in Nicaragua exercised a strong influence upon Salvadoran history. The July 1979 Sandinista-led victory in the civil war, while encouraging the opposition, sent quite another message to the beneficiaries of the Salvadoran establishment.

The Carter Administration's half-hearted measures to influence Nicaragua's revolution, when compared to its adamant stance against the Salvadoran opposition movement coming to power, serves as a good indicator of the fundamental differences between the revolutionary process in the two nations. The insurgency against the Somoza dictatorship, involving widespread participation from all social classes, presented an almost storybook scene of the people rising up in unison against the wicked tyrant. Washington's soft-line approach reflected its liberal foreign-policy priorities and its hopes that a pluralistic society would ultimately emerge in Nicaragua, which it could more easily live with than the internationally loathed Somoza dictatorship. To the contrary, in Washington's opinion the developing Salvadoran revolution ruled out the possibility of any such accommodation. From the beginning, the battle lines were unequivocally drawn in a classic confrontation of the poor against the rich. It could hardly be interpreted as a multi-class rebellion, but rather, a clear-cut class conflict whose goal was the establishment of a socialist society.

Such fine distinctions were lost on the Salvadorans, although they did make other vital differentiations. Both the oligarchs and the military agreed on their determination to prevent the opposition from coming to power, but while the "fourteen families" unanimously saw their interests best preserved by continuing a stone wall of resistance to change, some of the more enlightened officers analyzed the growing civil unrest from a significantly different perspective. From their point of view, Somoza's fall and especially the total destruction of the Nicaraguan National Guard with at least the tacit approval of Washington, impressed them as an extremely sobering development. Their unique solution to the crisis stemmed from the shock that nothing like this had ever happened before. Always when things got so far out of hand that the local military could not maintain control, the United States sent in its marines, or at least emergency military and economic assistance, together with experts in counterinsurgency to put it to its best use. But now the Carter Administration apparently had changed the rules of the game; just as it let their Nicaraguan colleagues be mauled by the revolutionaries, powerful sectors of the Salvadoran military came to believe that the same could happen to them.

Sure enough, on October 15, 1979, just a little less than three months after the Sandinista victory, it happened. With the undisguised approval of the United States, a group of liberal and "pragmatic" army officers carried out a preemptive coup, over-throwing President General Carlos Humberto Romero and forcibly retiring all but a third of the most senior officer corps. In a masterful counterinsurgency stroke, following the Carter Administration's "suggestions," the first five-man governmental "revolutionary junta" created by the military consisted of three civilian Social Democrats. Of course, the real power remained in the hands of the two military junta members—and, as always, ultimately with the army high command. Less than three months later, in early January 1980, the leftist Social Democrats all resigned in protest over the military's refusal to halt the upsurge in extrajudicial executions carried out by their own security forces, ORDEN and "independent" death squads. Within the polarizing context of Salvadoran politics at this time, little hope was held out for the second junta, made up of left-leaning Christian Democrats who replaced their Social Democratic colleagues in the government. During March, in a complex sequence of events, it all fell apart.

Early in the month, the junta's leading member, Dr. Hector Dada, resigned in protest over the continuing, and increasing, murders. Two days later, the counterinsurgency campaign began to take official form. The nationalization of the banking system and foreign commerce was announced; and on March 6, the U.S.–sponsored Agrarian Reform Law was instituted, along with a state of siege that legally repressed all civil liberties. Replacing Dr. Dada, the more conservative José Napoleón Duarte joined the junta three days later, touching off not only mass resignations among the Christian Democratic officials in the government but also a stampede of defections from the Christian Democratic Party itself—leaving a shell of its former stature. The March 24 assassination of Archbishop Oscar Romero (the day after he ordered all soldiers to stop the killing) and the massacre at his funeral a week later marks the utter failure of the U.S. experiment to control social change in El Salvador.

As the sequence of events demonstrates, from this point on the name of the game was undisguised counterinsurgency. On March 27 the U.S. Agency for International Development pumped in the first 13 million dollars to begin financing the reforms, and on April 1, acting on the White House's request, Congress rescinded its 1977 ban and appropriated the first 5.7 million dollars in military aid. Under the leadership of Defense Minister García, the Salvadoran military regained confidence from the strong support of the United States and began purging its liberal officers, slowing down the enactment of reforms to a snail's pace and stepping up its repression throughout the country. Lionel Gomez, a former high-ranking Salvadoran government functionary and civilian expert on his nation's military, succinctly stated: "The army staged the 1979 coup because it was horrified to see the Nicaraguan National Guard being jailed or forced into exile. But it was even more horrified when it saw what the Salvadoran left was doing in the junta."[2]

The election of Ronald Reagan in November was interpreted by the Salvadoran army as nothing less than a green light. On November 27 the Maximiliano Hernández Martínez death squad, with the brazen participation of uniformed soldiers, kidnapped and tortured to death almost the entire directorate of the legal Democratic Revolutionary Front (FDR). Less than a week later, National Guardsmen raped, tortured, and executed four North American churchwomen; three days later, on December 6, the last liberal military member of the junta, Colonel Adolfo Majano, was thrown out of office. The following week, dissolving the third junta and forming a new one, the military selected Duarte to be its figurehead president; and before another week had passed, an astounding 45 million dollars in new aid poured in, bringing total U.S. assistance for 1980 to a staggering 150 million dollars.

The last weeks of the Carter Administration continued in the same vein. On January 3, two U.S. land reform advisers and the head of the Salvadoran agrarian reform program were machine-gunned to death in the coffee shop of the Sheraton Hotel by "off-duty" soldiers on the orders of two members of the "fourteen families." Six days later the insurgent Farabundo Martí National Liberation Front (FMLN) launched its first major offensive, followed by an FDR call the next day for a general strike. Reacting to this dramatic FMLN–FDR political–military initiative, President Carter granted another 10 million dollars in military aid just days before the end of his term. Since the actual weapons and ammunition did not arrive until months after the offensive was over, its primary usefulness to the Salvadoran military was to bolster its capacity to attack the insurgents' infrastracture through massacres of civilian noncombatants and yet more murders of "suspected subversives." Then President Reagan took office and things got really bad.

THE INFLUENCE OF U.S. MILITARY DOCTRINE

Once again secure in their position as El Salvador's key institution, the military reverted to many of its old ways. As one patently false Reagan Administration certification followed another and as a complacent Congress accepted each of these shams every six months, it became obvious that only the most cosmetic gestures were necessary to satisfy U.S. military aid "conditions" of improving human rights, making progress in bringing to justice the murders of U.S. citizens, implementing political and economic reforms, and reaching a political settlement with the opposition.

Sliding back to a more comfortable relationship with the oligarchy, the Salvadoran armed forces fell back on their traditional formula of arbitrary repression and total disregard for human life (Tables 2 and 3, page 44). Seeking a quick victory over the insurgents in the merciless civil war, they resumed routine massacres in the countryside, where monitoring their actions is nearly impossible. Meanwhile, their "off-duty" colleagues organized and led death squads that slaughtered more people in the relatively closely watched cities. In sharp contrast to the court-martial of Lieutenant William Calley, Jr., for the 1968 massacre of a mere 102 villagers in My Lai, the impunity with which the Salvadoran military operates can be seen in their flawless record of lawlessness: Not a single Salvadoran officer has been convicted for killing a civilian.

Since the Reagan Administration has failed even to use its leverage to discipline the murderers in Salvadoran ranks, it is little wonder that the military realizes that Washington does not consider as a real option applying the ultimate sanction of withdrawing support. Consequently, with the arrogance of petty despots, the Salvadoran elite, while accepting massive economic and military assistance as their due, disdainfully rejected U.S. proposals on how best to use it in countering the insurgents. Only after three years of humiliating military defeats at the hands of the ever-more powerful FMLN guerrillas and constant pressure from the U.S. military advisers did it finally dawn on the complacent officer corps that their conventional warfare tactics and policy of state terrorism no longer constituted an adequate solution. Much of the elite's resistance to change must be attributed to the inherent problems of enacting reforms during crisis, but there is a purely military side that illuminates other major obstacles which must be overcome when the United States attempts to implement counterinsurgency as foreign policy.

Since the beginning of the war in El Salvador, Washington has been trying to reorganize its military apparatus according to a two-pronged plan. While encouraging the armed forces to adopt unconventional warfare methods on a generalized scale, at the same time it is also modernizing its military technology. By the Pentagon's February 1981 assessment, the situation was dismal, since the Salvadoran army was "not organized to fight a counterinsurgency war"; and because of its limited resources, it held out "no hope" of defeating the insurgents.[3] Of course, the essential element in the Pentagon's plans to upgrade the Salvadoran military is widespread and intensive training since, in their words, such instruction is necessary to "expose key military personnel to U.S. military doctrine and practice, provide training in internal security and interdiction, and assist . . . in the use of U.S.-supplied equipment."[4]

By the time President Carter left office in January 1981, 19 U.S. military training personnel were already stationed in El Salvador.[5] Within two months, however, the Reagan Administration had reached a "gentlemen's agreement" with congressional leaders to increase the allowable number of personnel in El Salvador to a maximum 55.[6] As their deployment shows, the task of the advisers was to revamp the tradition-bound Salvadoran armed forces: fourteen were assigned to train military personnel in the use and maintenance of helicopters; one advised each of the five regional commanders in improving their intelligence, communications, and logistical capabilities; another five served as liaison officers between the regional and national commands.

Most significant, this group of U.S. military advisers included 15 army Special Forces counterinsurgency experts, their responsibility being in-garrison training for the first of five "rapid reaction battalions."[7] The three-month course for the 2,000-man Atlacátl Battalion, named after a legendary Indian warrior chief, consisted of the regular counterinsurgency skills: hand-to-hand combat, small-unit patroling and ambushes, air mobile exercises, and other counterguerrilla operations.

The principal innovation in the Salvadoran military's mode of warfare, moreover, centered upon correcting the infantry's major operational deficiency. This was to be accomplished by increasing its mobility through the use of U.S.–supplied helicopters to transport the elite fighting troops rapidly to various combat zones throughout the small country. As described by a high-ranking Reagan Administration official in May 1981, the problem was that "right now, the government army is ineffectual. It can sweep rebel-held areas, but it can't close in on the enemy and destroy its forces."[8] Just as in the early days of the Vietnam war, Washington analyzed the situation in terms of tangible and manageable problems that would be solved by U.S. know-how and technology. According to Pentagon counterinsurgency specialists, the mobility of the rapid reaction battalion would enable government forces to encircle guerrilla units and wipe them out, thus making a transition in tactics from ineffectual large-scale sweeps to the far more efficient contemporary version of search-and-destroy operations. In July 1981, the Atlacátl Battalion was ready. But so were the insurgents.

Three months before, the FMLN rebels had established eight defined military fronts and de facto control over a broad strip of land spanning the nation's northern border. In these zones of control, the guerrillas consolidated their strategic rearguard areas by building training camps, developing logistical support systems, and creating embryonic forms of popular governments. The limited military operations conducted by the FMLN immediately following the January 1981 offensive took the form of classic guerrilla tactics: hit-and-run raids, ambushes, attacks against outlying military posts and garrisons, and, to a lesser degree, the temporary occupation of small towns and villages. Stepping up their economic sabotage campaign, during this period the insurgents carefully avoided major clashes with the Salvadoran armed forces; their objective was not to inflict heavy casualties but rather to capture as many arms as possible, while gaining combat experience and recruiting new troops. By July, the FMLN felt strong enough to launch its second largest offensive of 1981.

During this early stage of the war, both the U.S. and Salvadoran military planned on a fast knock-out punch victory against the insurgents: to some, a full-fledged counterinsurgency campaign seemed unnecessary; to others, the failure of the South Vietnamese army—a far more sophisticated fighting machine than the notorious Salvadoran armed forces—to hold swept areas indicated that such a long-term strategy would also prove futile in El Salvador. The first combat tests of the elite Atlacátl Battalion soldiers against the insurgents came in July. The beating they took in the provinces of Cabañas[9] and Chalatenango[10] served only to reinforce the military's tendency to try to overwhelm the rebels with superior strength. These elite troops turned out to be no match for the guerrilla fighters operating in the very terrain where they grew up. As their ambushes backfired and their small-unit patrols consistently failed to return, the Atlacátl soldiers quickly adopted the customary "search-and-evade" missions of the rest of the army.

Faced with the insurgent offensive, the Salvadoran army countered with large-scale operations of their own against FMLN strongholds in guerrilla zones of control. Reflecting the continuing domination of the traditionalists' predilection for concentrating fire power, in 1981 the armed forces conducted a total of 42 major operations, each involving from between 2,000 to 7,000 government soldiers, the majority being carried out during the second half of the year.[11] The Salvadorans' four-phase plan outlined below bears such a striking resemblance to U.S. strategy in Vietnam, it will come as no surprise to learn that it stems from the Pentagon's begrudging attitude toward engaging in counter-insurgency warfare.

Demonstrating the U.S. obsession with finding and eliminating the channels through which the Salvadoran guerrillas presumably received arms and ammunition from abroad, the objective of the first phase was to destroy FMLN logistical support—that is, cut their supply and communications lines. The military principle behind the Pentagon's preoccupation was confidently explained by an unnamed U.S. general "in making war, amateurs talk about tactic. The real professionals talk about logistics and sustainability, because that's where wars are won."[12] While certainly a sound concept regarding conventional warfare, steady outside logistical support, as events have subsequently shown, does not constitute the top priority in counterinsurgency warfare, since guerrillas by and large live off the land and capture or buy most of their supplies from the enemy.

The second phase of the plan—depopulating large areas to "isolate" the guerrilla forces from the rural population—is, of course, another favorite Vietnam illusion. Upon returning from El Salvador, a U.S. congressional delegation reported the graphic description offered by Salvadoran officers of this tactic: "the subversives like to say that they are the fish and the people the ocean. What we have done in the north is to dry up the ocean so we can catch the fish easily."[13] According to this same source, "the Salvadoran method of 'drying up the ocean' is to eliminate entire villages from the map."[14]

The third phase of the plan—a standard fantasy of the traditional-minded soldier dragged into the demeaning task of counterinsurgency—was to wear down the insurgents by forcing them to confront and fight head-on battles with superior government forces. The fourth phase completed the daydream. The plan's logic held that, following the successful application of the first three steps by the Salvadoran armed forces, the FMLN would be on its last legs, reduced to a few centers of resistance that the new rapid reaction battalion could simply mop up.

Within the overall military strategy, rather than employing the regular sweeping tactic, the government's forces would make the transition to far more effective forms of search-and-destroy operations. One of these is the piston-and-cylinder, so called for sending out large mobile units that, with the coordinated support of aircraft and artillery, would rapidly drive its deadly column of troops deep into enemy territory, catching the guerrillas off guard and destroying them before they had a chance to flee. The other innovation was the hammer-and-anvil tactic. After deploying with lightning speed an almost complete circle of soldiers around a rebel stronghold, a "hammer" of troops, bombers, and artillery would unleash their awesome fire power, forcing the guerrillas to beat a retreat through a single exit where they would encounter another government force awaiting them, the "anvil."[15]

As good as all this looked on paper, it just did not work in the field. Not only did the plan fail to seriously disrupt the FMLN's supply and communications networks, the insurgents actually ended up capturing large quantities of weapons and ammunition before abandoning the areas of operations. Certainly the armed forces' large-scale operations caused numerous noncombatant deaths and civilians did flee in their path, but as soon as the soldiers left an area, the people invariably returned to their land, even if their homes had been burned. As Salvadoran officers bemoaned at the time and during similar situations ever since: "it is like shoveling water." The efforts to inflict decisive defeats upon the guerrillas, or even to wear them down, turned out to be little more than a wasteful expenditure of the armed forces' material resources. Moreover, it did nothing to lift troop morale.

The military's grand plan that put to use U.S. advice and technology amounted to nothing more than an unqualified flop. The insurgents not only withstood the offensive, they came out of it stronger than ever. Toward the end of December 1981, demonstrating an impressive increase in the number of its combatants as well as vastly more efficient communications and supply systems, the FMLN mounted its third offensive of the year, which lasted into the next.

The first half of 1982 marked a watershed period of the war. The government clearly demonstrated its ability to defend the nation's urban centers as they turned back the insurgents' determined attempts to infiltrate the major towns and cities in order to disrupt the March elections. But its counteroffensives in the strong rebel northern and eastern provinces, lacking even the initiative shown during their late 1981 campaigns, turned out to be indecisive at best.* As the massive concentrations of advancing government forces "telegraphed" their approach, the insurgents would invariably slip away, only to return immediately after the military had passed through. Once back in familiar terrain and areas of operations, they would resume their guerrilla war against selected military positions and continue with their economic sabotage campaign of destroying the country's bridges, power lines, and communications facilities. The FMLN certainly did not constitute an imminent military threat to the Salvadoran armed forces, but neither could the army regain their former superiority in the field, to say nothing of scoring their fantasized quick victory over the rebels. In short, the war had reached a stalemate.

But in the early summer of 1982, the military's spirits once again rose. More than 500 junior combat officers returned after intensive training at Fort Benning, Georgia, along with the 960-man Ramón Belloso Battalion, the second rapid reaction unit, which had just completed a 14-week counterinsurgency course at the Green Beret headquarters in Fort Bragg, North Carolina.

Unlike the Atlacátl Battalion, the Ramón Belloso was viewed as a true elite, trained at the most prestigious U.S. counterinsurgency facility by the top U.S. Army Special Forces instructors and equipped with the best U.S. weapons and communications gear. Now, many believed that finally the Salvadoran army had a highly efficient fighting corps, which would not only gain impressive victories over the rebels, but also have a positive influence on the rest of the troops, upgrading their fighting capacity and effectiveness.[16]

In early June, during a ten-day offensive in Chalatenango, the Ramón Belloso Battalion made its debut, spearheading a force of approximately 4,000 troops, ten Huey UH-1H helicopters, two A-37B Dragonfly fighter bombers and massive artillery.[17]

*From this time onward the insurgents have been strongest in the provinces Usulután, San Miguel, San Vicente, Cabañas, Cuscalatán, and especially Morazán and Chalatenango.

Throughout the operation, however, the Salvadoran armed forces used both the new guerrilla-style and more conventional tactics, resulting in a type of hybrid military operation that came to characterize most of their subsequent operations: large concentrations of troops dislodged the insurgents, who were then pursued by the smaller elite squads. The problem with this combination approach is that while the elite troops operating in small and mobile commandos may be effective in attacking and chasing the guerrillas, this advantage is negated by the concurrent use of conventional tactics. The presence of these massive troop formations invariably alerts the rebels to an impending attack which, of course, they can evade by abandoning the area. As the record of this and subsequent operations deploying the U.S.-trained elite counterinsurgency battalions demonstrates, it is the civilian population which remains behind in its villages that suffer the wrath of the government soldiers.

The massacre of noncombatant civilians illustrates the claim by a top U.S. military analyst in El Salvador that Salvadoran counterinsurgency training offered only "one half of the equation," neglecting to instill in them the importance of winning the confidence of the people. Contrary to the widely publicized claim that these troops would only employ "surgical" force, which is used discriminately against the guerrillas, the truth is that they continued to massacre civilians who were considered insurgent sympathizers or infrastructure members. By ignoring the advice of their Green Beret instructors, the elite troops violated one of the fundamental principles of counterinsurgency warfare: In order to win the allegiance, or at least neutrality, of the civilian population, during military operations it is essential to exercise a minimal respect for their human rights.[18]

The limited effectiveness of the unconventional warfare tactics employed by the Atlacátl, the Ramón Belloso, and the Atonal (the third rapid reaction unit trained in Chalatenango by the Green Berets) battalions soon became apparent. Although these units did employ guerrilla-style tactics and were deployed rapidly to points of conflict—especially in Cabañas, where they experienced most success—the FMLN also developed effective countertactics.[19] In April 1982, the insurgent forces began regrouping and consolidating. Gaining experience in taking over villages and small towns, and in attacking and occupying small to medium-sized garrisons and military posts, they also started to use tactics involving greater maneuverability, while increasing their ability to effectively deploy much larger units of several hundred combatants at a time. These insurgent tactical advances, and the limited effectiveness of the new counterinsurgency battalions, clearly showed up in the summer 1982 guerrilla offensive in the northern province of Morazán.

On June 5, the same day that the government began a major offensive in the province of Chalatenango, the FMLN again seized and occupied the strategic town of Perquín, which they defended with a force estimated as large as 800 soldiers.[20] The Salvadoran armed forces immediately reacted by helicoptering 250 extra troops to the nearby town of San Fernando, which came under rebel siege the following day. On June 9, further reinforcements dispatched by truck—since bad weather conditions had grounded the helicopters—to the besieged towns, fell prey to guerrilla ambushes, after which the rebels took San Fernando. During the next few days, another 400 elite counterinsurgency troops began advancing toward the guerrilla-held towns. As they approached, they met the same fate: Ambushed by the FMLN forces, they were forced to beat a hasty retreat. At this point, with the world watching one government defeat follow the next, COPREFA (the Salvadoran Armed Forces Press Committee) announced the largest counterinsurgency operation since January 1981.

In preparation for the attack, between June 15 and 17, 1982, the Atlacátl, the Ramón Belloso, and the Atonal battalions, as well as several crack parachute units—comprising all of the government's approximately 3,000 best troops—massed in the town of Osicala, twenty miles south of Perquín. But the key to the counteroffensive was the arrival in El Salvador, on June 15, of six more U.S.-supplied Dragonfly fighter bombers, whose rockets, bombs, and devastating mini-guns make a deadly combination when directed at fixed targets.

To the delight of the Salvadoran armed forces, at last they could use their superior military might directly against their foe, since finally the FMLN guerrillas apparently had come out of their hideaways, taking a stand to "fight like real men." Indeed, according to both the rebels' Radio Venceremos and COPREFA, the coming battle in northern Morazán undoubtedly was the most fierce of the war up to that time.[21] Behind a screen of heavy air and artillery bombardment of the entire area between Perquín and San Fernando, government troops began their advance. But the insurgents had also called in strong reinforcements, and to the government's dismay, for nearly a week their forces proved unable to take either town or break through the two-mile-wide FMLN defense line. In an uncharacteristically frank statement during the first week of combat, a Salvadoran officer admitted that the military had already suffered "very, very heavy losses in the fighting."[22]

But the wily guerrillas hardly planned to slug it out to the suicidal end. After setting up barricades and ambushes on the main road linking the provincial capital of San Francisco Gotera with the contested towns, on June 21 the main insurgent forces quietly withdrew from the combat zone. Alarmed by their inability to dislodge the rebels, the high command called in massive reinforcements: Two days later, an additional 2,000 Salvadoran soldiers arrived from the south while at the same time another several thousand Honduran troops marched in from the north. Even though this first instance of Honduran military collaboration with El Salvador on such a large scale was sure to cause strong domestic and international repercussions, it seemed just too good an opportunity to pass up. Through this unprecedented joint maneuver, they hoped to surprise the enemy and finally inflict a decisive blow to the FMLN by encircling and annihilating the enormous guerrilla units in a hammer-and-anvil operation.

As it turned out, it was all too good to be true. Once again heavily bombing the now virtually abandoned towns of Perquín and San Fernando, the Salvadoran troops moved in for the kill. In one of the war's classic understatements, General Wallace H. Nutting, then Commander of the U.S. Army Southern Command, dryly explained that "in the functional areas of military operations [the Salvadoran army] faced deficiencies in command and control, tactical intelligence, tactical mobility and logistics."[23]

SALVADORAN WARFARE METHODS

Perhaps one of the most revealing commentaries on the radically different philosophies influencing Salvadoran warfare methods came from Raúl, a FMLN political officer in the rebel stronghold of Guazapa.* After questioning a captured Salvadoran army lieutenant in early 1983 about his officer training curriculum, Raúl mentioned to a visiting reporter that "I told him I had read von Clausewitz, Mao, Giap and Ché Guevara. He said he had studied mostly Eisenhower and MacArthur. I wonder what war they are preparing for in the Army's officer school."[24]

Looking into the matter, one discovers that old-guard tradition is not unique to the Salvadoran armed forces, but is also deeply embedded in the mentalities of their U.S. mentors. When asked about the discrimination that allegedly existed in the U.S. Army against counterinsurgency officers, a high-ranking Special Forces officer in El Salvador exploded: "It still does. . . . Because our fucking institution is not capable of, is, is, very reluctant to dabble in this business. . . . I'm a survivor. Do you know how many colonels there are in the United States Army that have any kind of a background in the unconventional warfare/counterinsurgency business? That know what the fuck they are talking about? . . . When I came back into this business, after I was teaching at Leavenworth, my career was resurrected. I was on a terminal assignment, then they finally decided that they better not retire all of us. There may be a requirement for some of this craziness." When pressed to explain the intransigence of the Salvadoran military to accept the counterinsurgency warfare methods advocated by U.S. advisers since 1981, this same source went on to describe an institutional inertia and traditional mentality among the Salvadoran officer corps similar to the one that dominates the U.S. armed forces. Finally, he did become a bit

---

*The volcanic mountain only twenty miles from San Salvador, where despite persistent government assaults the insurgents have been dug in since the beginning of the war.

more professional, talking about the "generation gap" problem: "What you have identified is that there are retired generals and some very, very senior colonels, a few . . . who are a product of our early sixties training. Since that time, and we started in the seventies where [counterinsurgency] was a nonsubject, we cut it out of the curriculum at the School of the Americas.* And so for about a ten-year period it has been a nonsubject in the American military school system. I can attest to that, personally, having been an instructor at Leavenworth and watch the program dwindle down to something around eight hours out of a thousand hour curriculum for our mid-level staff officers." Regaining his composure, this counterinsurgency expert ended on an upbeat: "It is coming back. In fact I am going next week to a conference to take a painful look at our curriculum." [25]

Raúl's wonder and the Green Beret's bitterness are but two differing expressions of the same thing: The traditional brass's closed-minded monopoly of authority that, until at least mid-1983, only reluctantly granted minimal concessions in adopting counterinsurgency warfare methods. In spite of the recommendations of the U.S. Special Forces advisers stationed in El Salvador, the military strategy employed during this early period was almost a carbon copy of Vietnam-style operations that were proposed by the Pentagon and readily accepted by their equally traditional counterparts in the Salvadoran high command. During an interview following the series of summer 1982 fiascos, General García, then Minister of Defense, offered a classic display of the almost indestructible hold that conventional military concepts exercise upon the officer corps. Attributing the mess to a lack of sufficient ordnance, the General complained: "This is not Vietnam. You cannot use the same tactics, we do not have the bombers to wipe out large sectors and then come in with patrols." [26] From the perspective of U.S. counterinsurgency warfare strategy, the General completely missed the point. As was demonstrated during the Vietnam war, the employment of massive military power—even the extensive use of napalm and precision B-52

---

*The School of the Americas is the United States armed forces center in Panama, where enlisted men and officers from throughout Latin America are trained in the various methods of conventional and unconventional warfare.

saturation bombing, which as yet has not been used in El Salvador—simply does not inflict decisive damage against guerrillas.

The frustration of the U.S. military advisers is seen further in their condemnation of the Salvadoran army combat commanders, whom they disdainfully refer to in private as the "warlords."[27] These U.S. advisers even go so far as to attribute guerrilla successes in some provinces to the refusal to employ unconventional small-unit tactics.[28] According to a high-ranking U.S. government functionary, the effectiveness of the Salvadoran rapid-reaction battalions has been seriously undermined by these old-guard military commanders, who continue to deploy even the elite counterinsurgency units in traditional tactics such as massive sweeps.[29]

A particularly outspoken U.S. military analyst summed up these complaints when he claimed that of the fourteen combat commanders leading the fight against the FMLN, only about half were "aggressive and understand the true nature of the war. . . . The others may as well stay home. They have a garrison mentality. The only time they put troops in the field is in large numbers. They have not adapted to night operations, small patrols, ambushes. They do not believe a five-man reconnaissance patrol can have more success than a 50-man reconnaissance patrol. They are just not doing it."[30]

The other major factor determining the warfare methods employed by the Salvadoran army has been the growing ability of the insurgents to control both the tempo and scope of the civil war. This first became apparent during the July 1982 operations, but became even more pronounced since the FMLN's Heroes and Martyrs of October 1979–1982 offensive. The offensive, which without question amounted to the insurgents' most impressive military display of the war to that time, began on October 10 and continued uninterrupted well into 1983.*

Although it was still too soon to claim with absolute certainty, as the insurgents asserted, it did seem likely that the October

___

*On January 8, 1983, the FMLN announced the beginning of the "January Heroes and Revolutionaries Offensive" but in reality this was not a new insurgent offensive but rather a continuation of the guerrilla offensive that began during the summer of 1982.

offensive historically marked the FMLN's progress to the final stage of all successful insurrections—the transition from purely guerrilla-style tactics to the simultaneous employment of conventional warfare methods. The insurgents' objective, however, is not to inflict a decisive defeat upon the Salvadoran armed forces. Their strategy, more precisely, is to demonstrate that they cannot be defeated. Within this context of prolonged military stalemate, the rebels intend to increase the military, political, and economic costs of the war to an intolerable degree. In this way the FMLN–FDR expect eventually to force the Salvadoran regime, and its U.S. supporters, to enter into serious negotiations that will end the civil war and bring them a position of power with a new coalition government.

The October 1982 offensive did not represent a rupture with previous guerrilla campaigns, but more accurately (as demonstrated by the preceding military operations) a far more intensive phase in the FMLN's military strategy of continual offensive. During their summer counteroffensive "Chalatenango and Morazán, Unidos Vencerán," the insurgents surprised most observers with the impressive display of waging full-fledged campaigns simultaneously on at least two separate fronts.[31]

Following a brief period for regrouping after their Perquín–San Fernando battle in Morazán, the army on July 14 redeployed a large contingent of its forces to the province of Chalatenango.[32] The main purpose of this government operation was to recapture the villages of Ojos de Agua, El Carrizal, and Las Vueltas, which the rebels had taken on June 26. It employed between 2,500 and 3,000 Salvadoran soldiers (among which were units belonging to the elite rapid-reaction battalions), heavy artillery, and air bombardment. Following an already established tactic, the operation also counted on the collaboration of the Honduran army, which mobilized troops along the border with Chalatenango in an attempt to crush the insurgents in the hammer-and-anvil maneuver.

The FMLN responded by opening other fronts throughout the country. These served the double purpose of forcing the army to deploy units to other theaters of battle, which in turn limited the number of troops that it could commit to the Chalatenango offensive. Consequently, the army units laying siege to the three villages proved inadequate to their task. Their advance stopped by large insurgent troop concentrations, they suffered heavy casualties and lost large quantities of weapons and ammunition to the FMLN before the insurgents slipped back into the safety of the countryside.[33]

Next followed even larger-scale army sweeps in the provinces of Usulután and San Vicente beginning on July 26. This massive five-day offensive involved approximately 5,000 government soldiers, including contingents from the elite Atlacátl and Ramón Belloso battalions.[34] Evading head-on battles, the rebels surfaced again as soon as the military departed, causing them to send another 3,000-man sweep into San Vicente from August 27 to 29; particularly heavy civilian deaths resulted from the indiscriminate bombing and the savagery of the government troops.[35] Between mid-September and the beginning of October, the army launched yet another series of sweeping campaigns, in the four southern provinces of La Union, San Miguel, Usulután, and San Vicente. Conducted consecutively, with each sweep deploying between 2,000 to 3,500 troops, as on previous occasions the official purpose of these operations was to cut the FMLN supply lines from Nicaragua. But by then, since no such supplies had ever been reported captured, no one really expected that things would turn out any different this time. No surprises followed.[36]

As can be seen in this series of military offensives and counter-offensives, the pattern of operations by the FMLN leading to the October offensive points to continuous insurgent engagement in actions ranging from ambushes of military convoys, to acts of sabotage, from the taking over of small towns to large-unit confrontations against major government troop formations.

But all this paled beside the intensity of the FMLN offensive that began in October 1982. On the tenth of that month the insurgents quickly overran and occupied a number of garrison towns in Chalatenango and Morazán. Although the campaign started with these fierce battles, in at least half of the country's other provinces, the FMLN soon mounted similar military operations. In anticipation of the harvest season for El Salvador's major agricultural crops—coffee, sugar cane, and cotton—the rebels also focused upon disrupting government control of the two main highways linking the capital with the rich southeastern agricultural region, paralyzing long stretches of the commercially and logistically important Pan American and Littoral highways. Furthermore, they intensified sabotage actions against the nation's physical infrastructure, knocking out telephone terminals, bridges, and electric power pylons, and damaging hydroelectric dams (such as the one under construction on the Río Lempa near the town of San Lorenzo), and petroleum refineries (especially the one located at El Salvador's principal port of Acajutla).

The FMLN economic sabotage campaign has come under severe, if questionably sincere, criticism on humanitarian grounds by the Reagan Administration. The argument goes that the hardships it causes fall primarily upon the people, in whose name the rebels claim they are fighting. Worse yet, by destroying these enormously expensive facilities that represent decades of accumulated national investment, the insurgents condemn the country to decades more of misery because, regardless of who ends up winning the war, it will take that long for poverty-stricken El Salvador to rebuild.

The FMLN offers quite a different picture of their highly effective economic sabotage strategy, which U.S. sources estimate by mid-1983 had caused 600 million dollars in direct damages and another 400 million dollars in indirect costs such as lost production and increased security expenses.[37] (The extent and gravity of this is dramatically reflected in the skyrocketing price of a Big Mac because McDonald's, an establishment not known for its peasant clientele, must now be protected by machine gun-toting security guards from the cover of its Golden Arches.)

Other indicators further show the failing state of the Salvadoran economy: The most optimistic estimates put unemployment at over 40 percent, and in recent years hundreds of businesses have gone under.[38] The rebels do recognize that their activities have resulted in hardship and resentment among the general population, but they claim that it is not as great as might be expected. Their campaign centers on disrupting the nation's electrical system, which during 1982 and the first half of 1983 cut its capacity by about one half, badly hampering economic activity mostly in the cities. Yet since electricity reached only 18 percent of the total population to begin with, it makes little difference to the impoverished peasant who never has service whether or not the power is on or off.[39] The same is even more true for telephone and telegraph service. The rebels did concede that the destruction of buses does cause greater problems for the people, since for many it is the only form of transportation, and for years they tried to justify this tactic on the grounds that the bus lines traditionally have been a special investment opportunity for senior military officers. Under the pressure of continuing popular criticism, the guerrillas finally relented: In late 1983 they announced that their forces no longer would destroy privately owned automobiles, trucks, or buses, but that government vehicles remained prize targets for attack.[40]

Blowing up bridges also turns out far less bothersome for the people than one would think from reading the conventional press. While their destruction is newsworthy and frequently reported, their fast restoration with prefabricated U.S.–supplied replacements seldom gets into print. Driving across one of these solid angle-iron bridges, the army commander of San Miguel commented that it gets blown up two or three times a year and is replaced each time within days.[41] The most significant results of destroying bridges would appear to be a subsidy for the U.S. corporations that manufacture the prefabricated replacements and a steadily climbing Salvadoran balance of payments deficit, since most of this type of U.S. assistance comes in the forms of loans that must be repaid.

In fact, not a single dam, oil refinery, major electrical generating plant, or any port facility has been destroyed, although the insurgents have inflicted expensive operational damage on some. Adding credibility to their claim that the objective is the disruption, not the destruction, of the economy is the fact that they do possess the capability to destroy even the most heavily protected installations. For example, they completely wrecked most of the Salvadoran air force on January 27, 1982, as it sat on the ground at the Illopango military base, as well as totally demolished the strategic Golden Bridge on the Pan American Highway to kick off the October 1982 offensive. The fear that they might one day attack critical heavy infrastructure facilities has served a military purpose: During 1982, the army assigned 75 percent of its troops to guard just six such installations.[42] Moreover, the economic instability has caused rich Salvadorans to send abroad an estimated one billion dollars rather than invest it at home,[43] and dried up foreign private credit sources;[44] by the end of 1982, the nation's Gross Domestic Product had plummeted by at least 25 percent.[45]

To understand the strategy of the FMLN's economic sabotage campaign, it must be recognized that they have no desire to govern a materially devastated country suffering from a shattered economy. More reasonable is their claim that its purpose is not to destroy the nation's economic base but to so severely disrupt the normal functioning of the economy that finally the business sector, out of fatigue and self-preservation, will abandon their support of the war and throw their weight behind serious negotiations to bring about a lasting peace.

The disruption of the economy may play a critical role in the long run, but in short-term considerations the military aspects of the war exercise a far greater impact. In this respect, certainly one of the most important developments of the October 1982 offensive was the impressive demonstration that the five guerrilla factions of the FMLN could act with unprecedented coordination, displaying an enormous improvement in orchestration of tactics and cooperation among the various fronts.[46] Burying their differences over strategy, the FMLN opened the offensive by simultaneously taking the garrison towns of El Jícaro and Las Vueltas in Chalatenango as well as Perquín, San Fernando, and Torola in Morazán. Especially surprising to many observers of the Salvadoran war was the ease with which the guerrilla forces overran the strategic and strongly defended towns of Las Vueltas[47] and Perquín: In their first attacks the rebels simply annihilated the reinforced army companies.[48] Throughout the offensive, the FMLN demonstrated its superior capacity to mass attack forces, and with extraordinary proficiency employ the captured artillery pieces against garrison towns as well as fixed government troop positions. In fact, throughout the broad section of territory stretching across the northern portions of Chalatenango, San Miguel, and Morazán, the insurgents occupied during the course of the offensive about thirty government garrison towns. At the same time, moreover, the rebels launched the largest assault against San Salvador since the March elections.[49]

In response to this unexpected display of military might, the Salvadoran armed forces continued their standard operating procedure of mobilizing large numbers of troops, in general no less than 5,000 soldiers in a single operation, which they deployed under heavy artillery and air cover. After October 20, Honduran troops were once again stationed along the border, while its air force carried out bombing raids against rebel-held villages in Chalatenango and Morazán.[50] On November 11 when between 9,000 and 12,000 Salvadoran soldiers swept known guerrilla areas in Chalatenango, perhaps frustrated by the unbroken record of failure of their hammer-and-anvil tactics, as many as 1,000 troops from the Honduran army's 6th Battalion crossed the border into El Salvador to join them in the operation.[51] Proceeding province by province, in the following weeks, the Salvadoran armed forces conducted large-scale sweeps through Morazán, San Miguel, Cabañas, and Cuscalatán.[52]

The unprecedented concentration of fire power and the deployment of massive troop formations at this time reflected a clear reaffirmation of conventional warfare methods. To avoid the guerrilla "tactic of taking remote towns and villages to attract government troops and then ambush them," the U.S. advisers, in a rare consensus with the Salvadoran Minister of Defense García, temporarily abandoned their insistence upon employing unconventional counterinsurgency tactics, counseling the Salvadoran commanders to concentrate on holding towns and using only large deployments of troops.[53] The army was even forced to use some of its rapid reaction battalions to defend static positions. For example, the high command deployed the elite Atonal Battalion in the province of Usulután to protect the Littoral Highway and shepherd truck convoys transporting coffee and cotton cash crops to San Salvador.[54] In a statement that sounded suspiciously like an excuse for the inability of the army to overpower the insurgents, General García tried to explain the new tactics: "We have not fallen into the trap of the subversives. Our objective was to maintain the principal [economic activity] and leave the rest alone for the time being."[55]

Regardless of the General's self-proclaimed tactical astuteness, the FMLN stepped up their increasingly successful military campaign. After occupying several towns in Chalatenango, on January 12, 1983, the rebels moved the center of operations to Morazán, taking the city of Cacaopera (pop. 20,000), which is a mere six miles north of the provincial capital of San Francisco Gotera, the location of the Salvadoran army's Commando Training Headquarters.[56] In the following days, the insurgents continued with ambushes and other harassing tactics including a major, but unsuccessful, attempt to overrun the military garrison in La Sociedad. On January 13, however, they did occupy Jocoatique, the second most important city in Morazán.[57]

Beginning a battle that shook the foundations of the Salvadoran military and their U.S. supporters, on January 16 approximately 1,000 rebel troops captured the strategic town of Meanguera, twelve miles north of San Francisco Gotera, Morazán. The armed forces immediately sent 3,000 more soldiers, including elements from the U.S.–trained battalions, to reinforce the approximately 3,000 troops already in Morazán thus beginning one of the government's largest offensives of the war.[58] The following day, while announcing a coordinated offensive on three fronts, the rebels blew up the strategic Torola bridge, thereby cutting off the only land access to the fighting in northern Morazán.[59] On the 19th, after a fierce battle, government forces retook Meanguera. Additional units of the Atonal and Ramón Belloso battalions, attempting to reach the government-held town, encountered such overwhelming insurgent forces that they were routed, although the armed forces officially called the defeat a "strategic retreat" to protect San Francisco Gotera.[60] In five days of bitter fighting, the FMLN, employing large troop concentrations and using heavy artillery fire to cover their advance in a completely conventional warfare assault, retook Meanguera from the reinforced government troops holding the town.[61]

The second fall of Meanguera sent shock waves throughout the nation, causing the first open expressions of concern by U.S. officials over the Salvadoran armed forces defeats and their overall combat ability.[62] Adding even more concern, during the following days the insurgents captured more towns in Chalatenango, forcing the army to deploy some of its already overextended troops back to that area;[63] attacked various military posts in and around San Salvador,[64] and on January 28, while Meanguera was finally being retaken by the Salvadoran armed forces, more towns fell to the rebels, including San Agustín in the province of Usulután.[65] These victories led to widespread speculation among military experts as to how long the Salvadoran army could hold out against the increasingly effective FMLN campaign. Assuming no major changes in the military situation on either side, the conventional wisdom at the time held that the Salvadoran armed forces could be defeated in as quickly as six months.[66] In fact, General García, in a rare statement of the gravity of the military situation, announced: "We are living a decisive moment in the struggle against subversion, and for this reason the armed forces are carrying out offensives in various areas to fulfill their commitment to the people."[67]

But the worst was yet to come. Two days later, the insurgent forces began their siege of Berlín (pop. 30,000), the third largest city in the rich agricultural province of Usulután.[68] While the fighting continued in Morazán with, according to the FMLN, the participation of the Honduran elite Mariola Battalion,[69] on January 31 after thirty-six hours of battle, the rebels took the city.[70] Again the insurgents had accomplished a first; all sides recognize the "Battle of Berlín" as the most significant military victory of the FMLN to that time. For four days the rebels held off several thousand government soldiers while the city took a severe beating from what Archbishop Arturo Rivera y Damas accurately denounced as "indiscriminate bombing."[71] Finally, on February 3, claiming that they had accomplished their objective of capturing arms and diverting government forces from their offensives in Morazán and Chalatenango, the rebels abandoned Berlín.[72]

The experts' dismal predictions seemed ever more warranted as the FMLN intensified its offensive throughout the country in the coming months. Although the action was widespread, including even a lightning raid on the central army barracks in downtown San Salvador, Morazán once again became the center of attention.[73] In early February, the insurgents again captured a number of towns surrounding San Francisco Gotera, which they threatened to take. Assaulted by the most sophisticated government equipment and more than 6,000 of its best troops, as *Newsweek* begrudgingly put it, "The leftist rebels showed a surprising ability to dig in and slug it out with the Army battalions thrown against them."[74] Later in the month, not only did they drive the Ramón Belloso Battalion out of Perquín,[75] on March 30 they dealt the army its worst defeat of the war when they caught the Belloso Battalion in a devastating ambush, badly mauling its ranks before the survivors could escape in full retreat.[76]

Little doubt can remain that during their six-month campaign the FMLN made its point that it could function as a conventional army. While continuing to fight as guerrillas, they demonstrated by traditional standards their transition to also wage conventional warfare: coordinated major offensives on simultaneous fronts and the ability to concentrate massive formations of troops and fire power in both assault operations and the defense of static positions.

Although he probably did not understand all of the implications of what he saw during his January 1983 visit to El Salvador, Senator Christopher Dodd did a fair job summing it up during congressional testimony upon his return: "We've spent 748 million dollars there in three years, we are approaching one billion dollars and what do we have to show for it? It is so sick there. The military and political situation are not improving at all."[77] United States Ambassador to the U.N. Jeane Kirkpatrick, following her February fact-finding trip through the region, more accurately recognized the crisis proportions that events had reached, reporting to her superiors that drastic measures had to be taken because, from their perspective, "the situation was deteriorating."[78] Fast action followed: In rapid succession, President Reagan came out from behind the trees and placed his personal prestige on the line by asking Congress for an additional 110 million dollars in emergency military aid for El Salvador; the bumbling General García got the boot and was replaced as Minister of Defense by the coldly efficient head of the National Guard; and the United States Army Special Forces advisers finally gained the White House's full support over their traditional Pentagon antagonists to run the war according to the rules of counterinsurgency doctrine.

THE NATIONAL CAMPAIGN PLAN

After three years of fiddling around trying to beat the insurgents with "unscientific" measures like arbitrary death squad murders and repeated army rampages and massacres throughout the countryside, the time had come to let the professionals run the show. In mid-1983 El Salvador finally adopted a National Campaign Plan, to once and for all deal with the problem. The National Plan, formulated by Army Special Forces experts in El Salvador and their home base in the Panama Canal Zone,[79] is a classic counterinsurgency program virtually indistinguishable from its Vietnamese and Guatemalan predecessors. Following the book on counterinsurgency doctrine it consists of a comprehensive campaign of reform and repression, using as its overall blueprint the Vietnam-era Civil Operations and Rural Development Support program (CORDS). In fact, some of the Green Beret advisers who wrote the Salvadoran National Plan participated in the original CORDS program.[80]

Reorganizing the country into five military zones of ascending priority, the agriculturally productive province of San Vicente rated the top position while the poorer provinces of Morazán and Chalatenango, where the insurgents are the strongest, found themselves at the bottom.[81] Starting with the highest priority zone, in descending order the remaining four were to be dealt with in sequence until the entire nation was pacified, a process that U.S. military advisers estimated would take at least a couple of years.[82]

The first step in the National Plan calls for conducting a massive sweep of the target zone; but instead of just passing through, the army must remain in the area until the guerrillas have been permanently dislodged. To accomplish this, of course, the normal sweep-and-run procedure would be replaced by clear-and-hold operations, and that meant the transformation of the slovenly Salvadoran army into an aggressive fighting machine. In operational terms, once the main force army units had scattered the rebels, specially trained hunter-killer platoons would either chase them down or drive them out through around-the-clock small-unit saturation patrolling.

Protected by these counterinsurgency commandos and civilian patrols,[83] the next phase in the pacification plan called for establishing strategic hamlets, although no one dares use that loaded terminology today. Once the general population was under control, the process of "separating out" the subversives would begin.[84] What precisely "separating" means in the Salvadoran National Plan context remained undefined; but perhaps a hint may be found in the fact that the ruthless Phoenix Operation was an integral component of the CORDS program in Vietnam.[85] In any event, the criterion for identifying the insurgent infrastructure, according to a U.S. Embassy official was quite uncomplicated: "Either you are with us or against us."[86]

Since, as a U.S. counterinsurgency expert had been trying to convince the Salvadoran army for years, "The objective in this business is not to capture terrain or a city or a town . . . but to seize and maintain the support of the civilian population,"[87] the last phase of the National Plan calls for extensive civic action programs. These local health, education, agriculture, transportation, and basic reconstruction projects—together with the fledgling national agrarian, political, economic, and judicial reforms—are the counterinsurgency doctrine's carrot at the end of the stick. The importance that U.S. counterinsurgency experts like to publicly accord reform is reflected in the code name selected for the National Plan's first offensive—Operation Well-Being—and in the embassy's convincing sales pitch: With admirable consistency, beginning in the summer of 1983, visitors there heard from members of the Military Advisory Group and the USIS staff that "you don't win guerrilla wars by killing guerrillas."[88]

But somehow this new image strikes an off-key note when listening to the preparations for implementing the National Plan; because at the highest end of the scale are the radically improving El Salvador's counterinsurgency military capabilities. Even for the fabled Green Berets, shaping up the Salvadoran army that they themselves ridicule as a "fat, lazy, 9 to 5, five-day-a-week barracks-bound corrupt and undisciplined disaster," did not promise to be an easy task. Indeed, their job appears more than formidable: many of them credit the FMLN guerrillas with superior motivation, combat skills, intelligence, and communications than their adversaries.[89]

An August 1983 Salvadoran government report on combat casualties during the preceding two years discloses the vast difference between the two fighting forces.[90] According to this official report, which probably is understated, during the 1981–1982 period the 32,000-man Salvadoran armed forces[91] took an extremely high 11 percent casualty rate;[92] and for the 1982–1983 period ending on the last day of July, the figure nearly doubled to a shocking 20 percent.[93] Had the small guerrilla forces suffered these losses, the war would have been over, because about half would be dead and the survivors would be wounded a couple of times each.

With even higher casualty rates approaching 30 percent among the Salvadoran elite U.S.–trained rapid reaction battalions,[94] it is little wonder that only 15 percent of the Atlacátl Battalion reenlisted when their mandatory tour of duty was up.[95] In fact, by mid-1983 about one half of the 7,000 soldiers that the U.S. trained had left the army; the reason that the figure is not higher lies in the fact that most of the others had not as yet completed their 18-to-24 month enlistment period.[96] Consequently, the National Plan's first order of business was to train enough new elite troops to clear and hold the target zones and then to hunt down and kill the remaining guerrillas. United States political considerations inhibited such extensive training programs in El Salvador because of the gentlemen's agreement between Congress and the President to limit military advisers to a maximum of 55, and since, according to Secretary of State George P. Shultz, conducting them at U.S facilities supposedly was not cost effective, Washington looked to its good friend Honduras to obligingly provide the solution.[97] In mid-March, the Pentagon announced plans to increase the size of the Salvadoran army by 8,000 men, as well as provide intensified training for about half of this beefed-up force, which would mean enough U.S.-trained soldiers to deploy a full battalion in each of the nation's fourteen provinces.[98] As things turned out, in early June, 525 officer cadets began receiving full-spectrum instruction at Fort Benning, Georgia,[99] and a new U.S. Regional Military Training Center had been established at Puerto Castilla on the Honduran Caribbean coast.

The establishment of the Regional Military Training Center in Honduras provides another example of the Reagan Administration's policy of regionalizing the Central American turmoil against the wishes of Congress. In a report to the President, the Senate Foreign Relations Committee specified that all training of Salvadoran soldiers should be conducted either in El Salvador or in the United States. As Republican Senator Nancy L. Kassebaum complained, "That was stated to avoid embroiling other nations in the conflict. . . . I am extremely disappointed that the administration has chosen to ignore this bipartisan advice. I think it's a mistake."[100]

Staffed by an initial contingent of 120 Green Beret instructors, in its first six months of operation the Puerto Castilla center set out to create a fourth 1,000-man Salvadoran elite battalion, as well as four special 350-man light infantry battalions.[101] In keeping with today's euphemistic changes in counterinsurgency terminology, these four hunter-killer commando units are called simply *cazadores* (hunters). The semantics game notwithstanding, they are the same animal as their Vietnam-era CORDS equivalents: "special counterinsurgency units . . . trained to attack deep inside territory where the guerrillas are active, using new communications equipment, sensors, and advanced weaponry . . . to destroy the guerrillas' command and communications structure while organizing resistance to them among the peasants."[102]

Operation Well-Being began on June 11 when government troops moved into San Vicente province, and, as usual, the approximately 1,200 guerrillas operating there faded away.[103] Leading more than 5,000 of the nation's best troops, Colonel Rinaldo Golcher, an officer hand-picked for the operation by the new minister of defense, Carlos Eugenio Vides Casanova, underscored the offensive's central theme when he announced that the "troops I have, they are not going to pull them out of here for any other operation in the rest of the country. They will be here as long as necessary."[104] A month later, the zone was officially declared cleaned of rebels. On the eve of his departure after being fired as part of the new hard line adopted by the Reagan Administration, U.S. Ambassador Deane Hinton sounded a cautious note: "Right now the army has it all its way and it's damned good. Four months ago the guerrillas had it all their way, so maintaining the momentum is a problem. Troops get tired."[105]

However, by mid-August U.S. military advisers, while admitting that the FMLN rebels had not suffered any significant military defeat nor did they show any signs of demoralization, still found cause for satisfaction in the military's performance, noting that "Seventy percent of the army has been in the field almost continuously since June 11, when the National Campaign Plan operation began." Moreover, U.S. counterinsurgency experts pointed to other heartening indicators: "one encouraging sign is that second lieutenants are starting to die out there. That means they are making mistakes and their own mistakes are killing them, but they are leading the men and being aggressive"; furthermore, "Another indication of change is that you are starting to have 'friendly-fire fights,' or cases in which two army units wind up exchanging shots. That doesn't happen unless units are working at night and moving around."[106]

Three days after Operation Well-Being began, Defense Minister Vides Casanova arrived amid great publicity in San Vicente to kick off the civic action program.[107] Claiming remarkable public support for these efforts, the government shortly announced, among other accomplishments, the establishment of new medical clinics in 12 of the province's 13 largest towns and the reopening of 38 of the 123 schools shut down because of the war.[108] Official sources accorded less publicity when in late July a column of several hundred FMLN guerrillas ambushed and virtually annihilated a special hunter platoon sent to protect a civic action crew trying to rebuild electric power pylons down for more than a year.[109]

One of the National Plan's greatest weaknesses turned out to be organizing effective Civil Defense units.[110] The United States channels multimillion dollar assistance to finance them and the civic action program, such as the Agency for International Development's May 1983 11 million dollar increase over the already 13.4 million dollars specifically earmarked for rebuilding the electricity system.[111] Similar to the situation in Guatemala, Salvadoran Civil Defense functions as an armed government presence in the small villages, where it is impossible to permanently station regular forces. Rather than including all of the local men, however, their ranks are almost completely made up of members of ORDEN, the hated paramilitary organization that in past decades has served as the military's eyes and ears in the countryside, and the Rural Patrols, a more official adjunct of the armed forces that is also comprised primarily of ORDEN members but led by army reservists. Because of the massive U.S. military and economic aid, the army not only is able to pay the Civil Defense members a small stipend, but also supplies them with food, training, and complete military uniforms, including modern weapons. Yet even with these advantages, the Salvadoran Civil Defense does not approach the effectiveness of their Guatemalan counterparts.

Certainly they command sufficient strength to police their towns. Their weakness lies in the severe limitations on their intelligence-gathering capabilities. Even though the civil war had wreaked havoc upon the nation, a Guatemalan-style genocidal campaign had been avoided (primarily because of past congressional human rights conditions for U.S. military aid*); thus El Salvador's social fabric still retains much of its former structure. The general disdain for ORDEN and the Rural Patrols, together with the widespread goodwill that the insurgents enjoy, has combined to make the civilian population more defiant, and therefore less disposed to cooperate with their traditional oppressors. In recognition of this image problem, on August 24, 1983, a San Vicente court sentenced the commanding sergeant of a local Civil Defense unit to prison for the 1981 murder of a seminary student; this is the first, and so far the only, case of a military

---

*President Reagan vetoed the renewal of this legislation on November 30, 1983.

person, albeit a reservist, being punished by the courts for an extrajudicial execution.[112]

Another major factor limiting intelligence gathering is that the Salvadoran Civil Defense cannot carry out patrolling functions. Unlike in Guatemala, where the insurgents avoid attacking the patrols because all men are forced to join them, the FMLN guerrillas operate under no such compunctions. On the contrary, such patrols are easy pickings for the combat-experienced rebels. According to Colonel Jaime Flores Lima, former commander of the powerful 3rd Infantry Battalion in San Miguel province, attempts to utilize Civil Defense squads in patrolling operations invariably result in disaster, because the insurgents simply ambush the patrols, and capture their weapons, ammunition, boots, and other valuable equipment. As he half-jokingly put it: "sending these men out on patrol is a better supply [for the rebels] than the Nicaraguans."[113]

The first large-scale military opposition encountered by the National Plan came, not unexpectedly, at the end of the May–September rainy season. During this perennial period, the fighting always slows down somewhat, if for no other reason than it is nearly impossible to move around in the slop caused by the torrential tropical downpours. Moreover, facing a full-fledged counterinsurgency campaign, the FMLN had to reevaluate its own strategy. But in late August, as the rains died down, the insurgents came alive.

On August 24, the military reported the heaviest fighting in San Vicente since the beginning of the June offensive,[114] a fact confirmed by the FDR leader Rubén Zamora two days later. Describing the shift in FMLN strategy, Zamora noted that Operation Well-Being was predicated on forcing the guerrillas out of the area and winning the support of the people. Claiming that "counting both military and civilian expenses [the cost of the operation] is over $30 million, and neither the Government of El Salvador nor the United States can afford it," he added that "our forces have not retreated back to the north, which the army had hoped for." He went on to explain that "most of them are still in San Vicente or have crossed the Lempa River into Usulután. They are now beginning to resume fighting with classic guerrilla tactics, using ambushes and night raids to hit the enemy."[115] Furthermore, while announcing that the insurgents had inflicted 441 casualties on the Salvadoran armed forces during the month of August alone,[116] a figure supported by the intensified level of combat reported by the international press during this period,[117] Zamora stressed that the FMLN was also concentrating upon fortifying and expanding their zones of control in other parts of the nation.

A concrete example of what the FDR leader meant was provided the following month by an Associated Press reporter after a visit to an insurgent camp in the mountains of San Miguel province, where what he found "made clear the difficulty government forces would face if they tried to oust the seasoned insurgents from the forests and brush lands of these rocky highlands." Glimpsing one small part of the FMLN's support apparatus, or infrastructure, he found particularly surprising an armory "packed with well-oiled rifles, mortars, and heavy machine guns, almost all American-made," as well as a "videotape recorder and television screen rigged to run on automobile batteries," that the rebels took along "from village to village to show propaganda messages and videotapes of victorious guerrilla raids." In summary, the correspondent concluded that "the guerrilla infrastructure is impressive: it has its own farms, radio system, hospital, armory, propaganda office, even a silk-screening operation for printing colorful rebel T-shirts."[118]

In early November, the veteran war correspondent Robert Rivard, who under the protection of the FMLN traveled extensively throughout disputed areas, reported that "the guerrillas are gaining ground in El Salvador and standing American policy on its head." Moreover, this reporter for *Newsweek* gave more specific insights into the rapidly changing nature of the war when he noted that "I was struck by the freedom with which the guerrillas now move about." For example, in Morazán, he noted that previously "the guerrillas had to trek surreptitiously in small bands through rugged terrain, confining their movements to oxcart paths and mountain trails. Now their control over a growing number of towns—and their confidence that civilians will not betray their movements to the government—allows them to maneuver more audaciously. Using heavy trucks and four-wheel drive jeeps seized in recent hijackings, they transport troops and war materiel with relative ease along the country's secondary system of roads."[119]

Although revealed shortly afterwards, with the beginning in early September of the insurgent's offensive "Independence, Liberty and Democracy for El Salvador," during his press conference Rubén Zamora did not mention an equally important change within the guerrillas' military strategy—the amazing growth, sophistication, and reorganization of the FMLN's conventional warfare capabilities. Technically called "Force Concentration," over the summer the five different rebel factions restructured large numbers of their combatants so as to more efficiently coordinate the deployment of new mobile brigade-size units.[120] In this way, they maximized the qualitatively increased fire power made possible through concentration of large numbers of troops and equipment. At the same time, to expand their ranks the rebels opened administrative and recruitment offices in dozens of towns, setting up extra boot camps to provide basic training for the growing numbers of volunteers flocking to join the armed struggle.[121]

Actually, the newly organized insurgent structure consisted of three separate Force Concentrations comprising several battalions each, operating on the central, southern and northern fronts—but by far the most impressive turned out to be the northern forces' 1,500-member Rafael Arce Zablah Brigade. Complete with artillery, modern communications equipment, and even tunnel construction experts, and using camouflage that adapts to vegetation and light intensity, the rebel brigade proved capable of traversing the countryside virtually unimpeded by the Salvadoran armed forces during daylight or nighttime hours.[122] After the rebels occupied five nearby towns, on September 3, two battalions of the Arce Brigade launched a spectacular attack against the provincial capital of San Miguel, the nation's third largest city and headquarters of one of its most effective fighting units, the 3rd Infantry Brigade.[123] During this conventional warfare assault, which was the FMLN's biggest artillery bombardment of the war up to that point, the insurgents shelled the army, police and National Guard barracks, and occupied the city for twelve hours, destroying coffee mills and warehouses, gasoline stations, and at least three major bridges and, in addition, inflicted heavy casualties on the government defenders.[124]

The formidable FMLN military display at San Miguel not only dealt the armed forces a severe psychological blow that intensified the downward spiral in overall morale, it also demonstrated the guerrillas' superior tactical and intelligence capabilities. Referring to the rebels' military planning and precision throughout the operation, in one of the war's classic understatements, a Western military officer who observed the battle from a ringside seat dryly conceded that "you are not playing against a bunch of cadets." Concerning the insurgents' extraordinary intelligence apparatus that undoubtedly included agents within the Salvadoran armed forces, he admitted that "it boggles the mind." Presumably the initial plan was to assault San Francisco Gotera, the provincial capital of neighboring Morazán, twenty miles to the north. But when at the last moment the San Miguel garrison dispatched reinforcements, the rebels quickly learned of this change in troop deployment and took advantage of the situation by immediately switching targets. As the flabbergasted official blurted out, "boy, have they got an intelligence system. It is significantly better than what the government troops have."[125]

Such dramatic operations as the daring San Miguel attack, although useful for capturing world attention and demoralizing the enemy, turned out to be just the beginning of the FMLN's less spectacular, but more practical, overall strategy to counter the National Campaign Plan. The flexibility of the guerrillas to adjust their conventional warfare capabilities to the new situation proved to be the key for an effective counterstrategy. Indeed, as one candid FMLN commander explained, had the CORDS–style counterinsurgency plan been implemented only a year or so earlier, when the rebels still did not possess such strong conventional forces, it might well have dealt them a mortal blow.[126]

By the summer of 1983, however, both the Salvadoran army and the FMLN were undergoing almost diametrically opposite changes in their combat formations. Certainly the government forces maintained their numerical and technological superiority;

yet the rebels could still choose the time and place of confrontations. But while the Salvadoran army, under pressure from its U.S. patrons, moved toward decentralized small units, the insurgents continued to improve their ability to mass large concentrations of troops and fire power.

In what was to become an increasing role reversal, in late June these new military alignments first clashed at the Chinchontepec volcano in San Vicente. Lured by an FMLN contingent dug in on the northern slope, Salvadoran army hunter companies assaulted the volcano. As the bulk of the government forces fought their way up the mountain, they were outflanked by a coordinated maneuver involving approximately 1,000 guerrillas who had been called in from their home bases in neighboring provinces. Catching the army's rearguard by surprise at the base of the volcano, the rebel forces completely annihilated three full hunter companies, sending the rest of the attacking units into disarray and thereby allowing their comrades entrenched further up the mountain to slip away with only minor casualties.[127]

Throughout the summer the insurgents kept up sporadic harassment of the thinly spread government forces through their customary guerrilla tactics—ambushing truck convoys and trains, and attacking outlying military posts—while continuing their economic sabotage campaign against bridges, power lines, communication centers, and sugar, cotton, and coffee processing plants—all of which were rendered even more vulnerable because of the decreased protection that could be provided for these targets.[128] At the same time, they also worked on perfecting the new strategy of deploying larger fighting units to overwhelm the roving 90-man hunter companies, and especially to attack the newly created Civil Defense units assigned to the strategic hamlets.

A vital part of the National Plan, strategic hamlets function to "protect" the inhabitants so that they can leave their homes or refugee camps to enter the depleted work force in order to cultivate the neglected cotton, sugar, and coffee crops so badly needed to bring in foreign-exchange hard currency. As in Vietnam, the futility of attempting to convert these poorly defended towns—whose security depended upon the paramilitary Civil

Defense units—into the textbook strategic hamlets was quickly revealed in San Vicente, the showcase of the hailed counterinsurgency program. For example, the mayor of San Esteban Catarina, situated only twenty miles from the provincial capital, complained that his town fared much better before the implementation of the National Plan; now the presence of the Civil Defense only encouraged rebel attacks. Ultimately, the government found it necessary to install a large security force in San Esteban Catarina to provide the military force required for minimal security.[129] This was precisely what the FMLN intended, since this would limit the number of troops in the field and force the army to revert gradually to its previous strategy of defending urban centers and other strategic positions.

The town of Tenancingo, Cusculatán, serves as an even more dramatic example of the National Plan's unmaking. The rebels seized the town in late August, but withdrew after a short battle against superior government forces sent in to dislodge them.[130] Several weeks into their fall offensive, on September 25, the insurgents virtually walked through the two new army companies deployed to defend Tenancingo. But several days later, following what Archbishop Rivera y Damas denounced as "indiscriminant bombing" by the Salvadoran air force, the rebels once again withdrew.[131] Again, in early October the rebels overran the even more heavily reinforced town, only to be driven out when air force bombs and rockets unleashed another devastating attack that killed at least fifty civilians.[132] Just as in San Esteban Catarina, a permanent army garrison has now been stationed in Tenancingo.

With the exception of the spectacular September 3 attack on San Miguel, the initial thrust of the FMLN's 1983 fall offensive focused on overrunning villages and hamlets guarded by the inept Civil Defense and launching large-scale assaults against towns in order to force the government to either abandon them or permanently deploy large contingents of troops for their defense. By the end of September, the guerrilla offensive had expanded to engulf all seven of the nation's most strategic provinces.[133] The ongoing economic sabotage campaign and the constant mauling of hunter companies by superior insurgent forces drove the Salvadoran military to abandon its aggressive small-unit patrolling and assume once again their defensive, static positions.[134]

While not the type of military actions that grab headlines in the international media—especially with the devastating CIA–planned contra raids against Nicaragua and the Reagan Administration's high profile adventures in Lebanon and Grenada competing for space—by the end of October, *Newsweek* still found room to point out:

El Salvador's FMLN have coordinated more than 60 attacks in recent weeks. FMLN guerrillas have scored some of their most impressive victories in Usulután province by overrunning the coffee-rich town of Jucuapa, El Triunfo and Lolotique. More important, perhaps, the rebels severed the country's two chief roads, holding one stretch of the Pan American highway for as long as three days. . . .

The FMLN campaign undermined the Salvadoran government's plan to extend pacification by securing an area militarily, then sending in teams to provide essential services and encourage local people to rebuild the economy. . . . But the town of San Agustín in Usulután has become a case study in the government's failure. There has been no security presence in San Agustín since the FMLN burned the military barracks months ago; the clinic and public transport are closed and guerrillas stroll the streets shopping for cigarettes.[135]

By late October, the rebels' offensive had proved so effective that they once again could largely determine the pace and tempo of the fighting. In rapid succession, they occupied Cojutepeque, the major city in the province of Cusculatán,[136] and the next day another large FMLN force defeated the Arce Battalion—the first graduates of the intensified program at the U.S. Regional Military Training Center in Honduras—when they took Ciudad Barrios, the second most important city in the province of San Miguel.[137] Furthermore, in an audacious move that vividly depicted the shifting military situation, they then chased the retreating U.S.-trained elite troops, who were joined by elements from two other Salvadoran army battalions, up the Cacahuatique volcano where the besieged soldiers held out at a military base until further reinforcements and the air force could finally come to their rescue.[138]

By this time, the insurgents had not only completely disrupted the National Campaign Plan, they had so demoralized the Salvadoran army that it virtually ceased to attempt to carry out the aggressive counterinsurgency tactics advocated by their Green Beret advisers and sought the safety of their garrison strongholds.[139] Beginning in early November, the rebels stepped up both their guerrilla and conventional-style warfare actions throughout El Salvador, capturing large quantities of ammunition, small arms, mortars, artillery, and other heavy weapons.[140] By the middle of the month it became clear that the war, at least in the strategic northern and eastern parts of the country, had entered a dramatic new phase. Emerging from the summer lull stronger than ever, the FMLN began engaging government forces in ever more frequent and larger confrontations in an all-out effort to secure zones of military, political, and economic control over entire sectors of Morazán, Usulután, San Miguel, and La Unión provinces.[141] Meanwhile, in San Vicente, where the grandiose "full spectrum" counterinsurgency Operation Well-Being first began five months earlier, things were hardly much better: The battered barracks-bound army regressed to their standard operating procedures of sallying forth in the traditional massive sweeping operations and bombings which had proved so ineffectual since the beginning of the war.[142]

As usual, recriminations and plans for escalation followed on the heels of setbacks. One ranking U.S. official openly worried that in the long run the FMLN stood a good chance of winning a definitive victory if the current trends continued. Another repeated the same old complaints that the failures stemmed from a poorly defined chain of command, an ingrained laziness, a "no-can-do" mentality, and the persistence of many Salvadoran commanders in taking weekends off to enjoy the comforts of the nation's capital, San Salvador.[143]

To no one's great surprise, Washington's intention to escalate U.S. involvement also came to light at this time. Not only were plans revealed to build a gigantic new military training base in El Salvador capable of processing up to a thousand soldiers a month,[144] upon his return from a whirlwind dash through Central America, Under Secretary of Defense Fred Iklé announced that military aid to the Salvadoran armed forces would soon be substantially increased.[145]

Overwhelmed by the insurgents' impressive gains, the humiliated Salvadoran army vented its frustration by reverting to what it does best—mounting "search-and-massacre" missions. Outfitted with the best counterinsurgency equipment provided by Washington, these U.S. trained combat elites evidently forgot their lessons about winning the hearts and minds of the people and once again concentrated their talents upon simply killing them. The actions of the elite 1,000-man Atlacátl Battalion, whose officers and enlisted men have received the best U.S. counterinsurgency instruction, provide a shocking example. After weeks of adamantly denying as absurd Communist propaganda the rebel charges that on November 4 his men massacred hundreds of civilians in Chalatenango and Cuscalatán provinces, Atlacátl Battalion commander, Colonel Domingo Monterroso, was forced to admit the truth of the matter. Evading government efforts to seal off the area, a group of six enterprising foreign correspondents defied the travel ban and finally managed to make the dangerous trip to two of the killing sites, where some courageous survivors showed them the mass graves and gave them a partial list of 118 victims.[146] Confronted with this evidence, Colonel Monterroso cynically passed off the atrocities by casually explaining that his troops had merely "confused the civilian population with the guerrillas that operate in that zone."[147]

In any event, even this embarrassing exposé failed to diminish enthusiasm among the pride of the U.S.–trained elite counterinsurgency soldiers to carry out their duty. On November 20 these fearless fighters returned to San Nicolás, Cuscalatán, and slaughtered another twenty or so women and children.[148] Perhaps not to leave any loose ends to spoil a job well done, and to leave no doubt as to the purpose behind these Nazi-style reprisals, one further human being was tortured and murdered: During the December 4, 1983, Sunday mass, Archbishop Rivera y Damas, accusing the armed forces of perpetrating the crime, de-

clared that "I cannot avoid denouncing, because it is such a typical case of abuse of authority, the murder of Santiago Vitelio
Alas, the boatman that was hired by the six journalists." [149]

While Washington's allies carried on with their merciless war
against subversion, the FMLN stepped up its own capaign. During the middle of November, elements of the Rafael Arce Zablah
Brigade surrounded several hunter company encampments near
Sociedad, Morazán, and then stayed on for the next week or so
to engage in furious combat the government reinforcements sent
to retake the strategically vital area. Moving on after causing
heavy casualties, capturing large amounts of arms, and taking 50
prisoners,[150] the rebels stopped long enough to assault the neighboring town of Anamoros, only eight miles from Sociedad.
There they quickly overran the military garrison, killing 12 soldiers and making off with enormous quantities of war materiel—
along with all 135 remaining government troops, the largest single
surrender of the war.[151]

Here another prominent dynamic of the Salvadoran civil war
stands in relief. In the six-week period from mid-October to the
beginning of December, according to official Salvadoran military
sources, 800 soldiers died in combat while another 400 fell cap-
tive.[152] From the government's point of view these prisoners of
war, like all others, might as well be dead since they no longer
serve any useful purpose. This is not because the FMLN exe-
cutes their prisoners—unlike the Salvadoran army, which
does—but rather due to the enlightened policy by which the rebels treat them. With extremely few exceptions, the insurgents
hold their captives for only a short time, usually less than a
week, during which time they give them a crash course in revolutionary ideology. Trying to convince the soldiers that they are
fighting on the wrong side, the FMLN insists that its cause is the
only way to eliminate the age-old system of oppression and
change the structure of society for the betterment of the common
people—that is to say, since the vast majority of enlisted men
come from the poor, to improve their own lives and those of
their families. After this brief period of indoctrination, the prisoners have the choice of joining the rebels, simply slipping back
into society or perhaps out of the country, or being released to

the International Red Cross, which returns them to the military.

Through experience, the armed forces have found that as a group, freed prisoners of war are no longer trustworthy soldiers; for if they surrendered once they might very well do it again, perhaps even taking other troops with them the next time—and besides, how can one be sure that they have not been turned by the rebels and are not actually spies serving the insurgents' intelligence networks? Since any type of punishment—or, worse, yet, interrogations to determine an individual's loyalty—is not quite appropriate, especially as it would severely damage what little *esprit de corps* that exists in the armed forces, the only practical choices are to assign them to noncombat duty or simply discharge the entire lot.

Yet this too presents problems, because the word gets around. Realizing the relatively benevolent treatment that awaits them— as vividly demonstrated by the mass surrender at Anamoros— after putting up a token resistance against the ever more powerful insurgent forces, increasingly the Salvadoran soldiers choose to surrender rather than fight to the death in a war that they neither fully understand nor believe in. The dimensions of the phenomena are depicted by the insurgents' claim that in the three-year period from January 1981 to December 1983, they had taken 1,825 prisoners of war,[153] 400 of which, according to the Salvadoran army, were captured in the preceding six weeks alone.[154]

So the FMLN's humane, and pragmatic, policy of dealing with prisoners of war reaps them a fine harvest: They win goodwill among the people—especially the families of the captives that they release; disrupt the fighting spirit of the Salvadoran armed forces, thereby suffering fewer combat casualties and making it easier to capture larger amounts of war materiel; as well as of course adding to their ranks a considerable number of trained soldiers from the former prisoners who end up staying with them. Sometimes small things tell a lot. By early 1983, there had occurred a significant change in the national vocabulary: Even in public, most people in El Salvador had stopped calling the insurgents "subversives," referring to them instead as *los muchachos*—"the boys."

By any standards, the rebels' military and political advances are impressive. For example, of the 80 medium-size towns in the eastern part of the nation, the insurgents exercise undisputed control over 25, while 30 are still in dispute and the remaining 25 are controlled by the government.[155] With coordinated FMLN offensives on all three fronts,[156] during a late November press conference Secretary of Defense Caspar Weinberger conceded that the military situation "is not good," while at the same time Peter Romero of the State Department's El Salvador desk elaborated by estimating that their analysis showed that the Salvadoran armed forces were incapable of defeating the insurgents for at least the next six years.[157] Moreover, within their "zones of influence," according to a diplomatic source in El Salvador, the guerrillas display a remarkable political maturity: Rather than destroying the cotton and coffee crops, FMLN policy is to intervene on behalf of the farmworkers by "negotiating" labor contracts with the landowners for higher wages and an eight-hour work day.[158]

December 1983 was one of those months when every week saw new records set. It started on the 7th when for the first time the FMLN simultaneously occupied five major coffee plantations,[159] and then stayed on to disrupt the precious harvest and face off the government troops for more than a week.[160] Next, at the Cacahuatique volcano in Morazán, on the 13th they destroyed a strategic military communications center, scoring their most important purely military victory of the war—a record that was broken before the end of the year. Further demonstrating their vastly improved combat capabilities, during the attack on the heavily defended communications center, supporting rebel forces harassed all military bases within a thirty-mile radius of Cacahuatique to prevent the army from sending in reinforcements.[161] The FMLN operation proved so devastating that the Salvadoran high command called an emergency meeting, during which even their U.S. advisers agreed upon a "new strategy" of regrouping the armed forces to conduct enormous brigade-size search-and-destroy sweeps in an attempt to catch large concentrations of enemy troops.[162] During the last week of the year, the government mounted its largest offensive of the war, fielding some 20,000 soldiers to carry out massive coordinated operations throughout the country.[163]

With the army busily beating the bush, the insurgents did it again—this time in the province of Chalatenango, where on the 30th they captured the modern U.S.–designed El Paraíso military base, marking "the first time in the four-year-old civil war that the insurgents had overrun a major army installation."[164] The defeat was so severe and humiliating, coming precisely at a time when the rebels were supposed to be scattered in disarray before the huge army onslaught, that the government absolutely forbade reporters from traveling to El Paraíso and—in another first—slapped strict censorship on the international press.[165] Even so, according to United Press International reports the FMLN completely destroyed all eight buildings in the compound, killing hundreds of defenders (whose bodies were buried by the army in mass graves scooped out by bulldozers), and taking hundreds more prisoner who, as usual, a week later were released to the International Red Cross. Moreover, the operation again displayed the insurgents' remarkable tactical skill: At the same time that they sent their main force against the El Paraíso army fort, they launched twenty-five diversionary raids against all nearby military bases, including the army headquarters for the region in the capital city of Chalatenango.[166] To wrap up the weekend activities, and start off the new year, on Sunday, January 1, 1984, the FMLN finally destroyed the largest and most heavily defended bridge in El Salvador. By blowing up the Cusculatán suspension bridge on the Pan American Highway that used to span the Lempa River, they finally severed the last remaining commercial road transversing the nation.[167]

No room remains for any reasonable doubt concerning the gravity of the situation faced by the Salvadoran government. The only question is what to do about it. On a scale of 1 to 10, while the Salvadoran armed forces have been pushed back to square two, a conservative estimate places the insurgents well past the halfway mark. Given that since 1980 Washington's generous assistance program, along with providing prodigious amounts of arms and training, has already tripled the size of the Salvadoran army, even if the Administration does force through

Congress major new military allocations, the best that can be hoped for from this escalation would be to fend off an insurgent victory for another short period. By the end of 1983, some expert observers, such as former U.S. Ambassador to El Salvador, Robert E. White, already viewed the situation as hopeless. In November he wrote that "we may have pushed the Salvadoran military as far as it is able or willing to go—and, indeed, it may be time to cut our losses and accept the revolutionaries' repeated offers to negotiate."[168] By December he had become even more pessimistic: "There is no way that the military can win in El Salvador—it does not matter how much assistance we give their army."[169]

Unfortunately, the powers that be in Washington and San Salvador have no inclination to accept the necessity of entering into serious negotiations with the FMLN–FDR insurgents to end the civil war. Still trying to shape up the Salvadoran army into an effective counterinsurgency fighting machine, on November 25, Defense Minister Vides Casanova and his Pentagon benefactors restructured the entire army high command, reassigning or dismissing twenty two officers and placing the conduct of the war in the hands of the military's most "aggressive" leaders. A few examples serve to make the point: Colonel Adolfo Blandón, the ranking officer known to favor the Green Berets' counterinsurgency tactics, became chief of staff; Colonel Jaime Flores Lima, considered the "most aggressive" field commander, replaced him as head of San Salvador's critical 1st Infantry Brigade; and Colonel Domingo Monterrosa, perhaps in part because of his proven fearlessness in slaughtering civilians as the commander of the elite Atlacátl Battalion, took Colonel Flores's former command of the 3rd Infantry Brigade in San Miguel province.[170]

Recognizing the obvious, however, Washington is planning well beyond the outside chance that pumping fresh injections of aid into the restructured Salvadoran high command will be enough to turn the tide of battle. For it seems all but inevitable, as the FMLN continues to inflict military and political defeats upon the Salvadoran government, that outside help will be required for their defense. Colonel Larry Tracy, the Defense Department's Inter-American Affairs officer, gave a hint of the likely scenario at the November press conference mentioned above; he pointedly noted that the Guatemalan and Honduran armed forces possess the necessary capability to launch coordinated operations with the Salvadorans against the insurgents.[171] These and other developments give strong indications that the next stage toward regionalizing Salvadoran civil strife will take the form of direct military intervention of foreign troops from the Central American Defense Council (CONDECA)—the military alliance among Guatemala, Honduras, and El Salvador resurrected in early October 1983 at the behest of the Reagan Administration.

It is nothing less than reckless wishful thinking to hope that hiring CONDECA soldiers will stop Washington's slide into the Central American quagmire. The inexperienced Hondurans will be of little help, especially because they have their hands full playing nursemaid to the CIA-backed contras and maintaining their armed forces in a constant state of alert against the eventuality of an armed conflict with the powerful Nicaraguan army. The Guatemalans face a somewhat different problem. To the degree that they commit any sizable portion of their army to El Salvador, they give the Guatemalan insurgents an unprecedented tactical opportunity, leaving themselves vulnerable to stepped-up rebel activity at home.

The biggest flaw in this plan to further regionalize the Salvadoran civil war, however, lies in El Salvador's fervent nationalism. The introduction of foreign troops, especially from the traditionally rival nations of Honduras or Guatemala, unquestionably would provoke ardent opposition throughout the entire society, strengthening the FMLN movement in countless tangible and intangible ways—from greater sympathy for the rebels to passive resistance to the invaders, from a swelling of the insurgents' popular base to unprecedented numbers of recruits for their infrastructure and combat ranks. So while the first phase of foreign military escalation may very well begin with CONDECA forces from Honduras and Guatemala, it is even more probable that such a move will not only miserably fail to crush the guerrillas but will end up being little more than a stepping stone upon which U.S. Marine boots will march across to sink into the morass of Central American revolution.

SEVEN

HONDURAS

Stemming back to the brief period during the last century when all of the region was linked in a loose confederation, the United Provinces of Central America (1823–1838), there has been a tradition of Central Americans fighting in each other's revolutions. In fact, with the still vaguely defined and relatively open borders that permit the virtually unimpeded passage of people and supplies across national boundaries, the Sandinistas drew upon the tradition to wage their war against the regime of Anastasio Somoza from bases in Costa Rica and Honduras. By 1978, when their extraordinary successes clearly had numbered the dictator's days, the United States began looking around for another best friend.

While the Carter Administration did not bemoan Somoza's fall, the event did present new security considerations. The Sandinista victory, U.S. analysts concluded, demonstrated the ultimate inability of an exclusively national armed force—regardless of the degree of its experience and the level of its military technology—to defeat a popularly supported insurgent movement. Not surprisingly, U.S. military strategists set out to develop a new regional military strategy; to do so they needed another reliable ally to fill the leadership vacuum left by the deposing of the Nicaraguan dictatorship.

Actually, Washington did not really have much choice in the matter. Congressional prohibitions on military assistance to El Salvador and Guatemala (because of their disgraceful human rights violations) and the growing opposition movements in both nations made them politically awkward possibilities. Therefore, almost by default, Honduras, boasting excellent geopolitical qualifications, emerged as the prime candidate: With borders on the three "problematic" nations of Nicaragua, El Salvador, and Guatemala, since 1963 it had offered the region's most stable sociopolitical atmosphere with its almost constant military rule.* But even Honduras's availability and reliability did not quite fulfill Washington's requirements for a new regional linchpin with which it could continue exercising its historical hegemony over Central America.

Consequently, the Carter Administration initiated a number of measures to preempt social discontent, clean up the image of its government, and strengthen its military. Because of Honduras's relative tranquility (although worker and peasant unrest pointed to future problems), in the opinion of U.S. diplomats and Administration officials the nation still stood a good chance of avoiding the leftist insurrections that had erupted in all of its neighbors. Therefore they encouraged the implementation of mild reforms, primarily in the agrarian sector and in the holding of national elections to return Honduras to civilian government.

The other thrust of Carter's policy required that Honduras no longer ignore the regional crisis, but rather, take an active part in it. Washington sent a clear message to the Honduran leaders: Achieve political legitimacy through elections, placate rural unrest through simple agrarian reforms, and increase military strength in order to play the appropriate regional role, and we shall pay the bill.

Indeed, then U.S. Assistant Secretary of State for Inter-American Affairs, Viron Vaky, unequivocally expressed these two themes during a major policy address in September 1979. After commenting on how impressed the Carter Administration was

---

*In 1963, Colonel Oswaldo López Arellano seized power in a military coup, and two years later had himself "elected" president in blatantly fraudulent elections. His repressive reign, briefly interrupted by the 18-month presidency of Ramón Ernesto Cruz (1971–1972), came to an end immediately after the 1975 suicide of the United Brands banana company chairman, Eli M. Black, over the bribery scandal involving high Honduran officials. His successor, Colonel Juan Melgar Castro, lasted until 1978 when General Policarpio Páz García ousted him to take his turn at the helm.

with the democratic process since General Policarpio Páz García had come to power through a military coup in August 1978,[1] he went on to emphasize that Honduras must play a key role in preventing "regional conflicts and the potential infiltration of supplies and guerrillas to other places and struggles."[2]

Consistent with this overall plan, the Carter Administration proceeded to convert Honduras into its new regional bastion of strength. While in fiscal year 1978 only Panama, due to the canal treaties, surpassed Honduras in U.S. military and economic aid, in fiscal year 1979, Honduras became the largest Central American recipient.* Of greater significance, during the three-year period from 1978 to 1980, as can be seen in Table 4, Washington granted Honduras by far the largest amount of economic and military aid in the region.[3]

The first steps in building up the Honduran armed forces taken by the Carter Administration were relatively low-key in comparison with what was to follow after President Reagan occupied the White House. The long stretch of military governments had treated their own institutions generously. The Honduran air force, long considered the best in Central America, needed little attention; neither did the well-stocked army present any urgent requirements for vast new quantities of war materiel. The greatest deficiency of the Honduran armed forces at this time consisted in the poor quality of its personnel, and it was in this area that Washington directed its efforts. Between 1971 and 1980, a total of 2,259 Honduran officers and enlisted men received training by U.S. Army instructors, more than double the number trained during the whole 1951–1970 period;[4] and, moreover, between 1976 and 1980 nearly one hundred Honduran officers attended the "Command and General Staff" courses at the U.S. Army School of the Americas in the Panama Canal Zone— three times more than any other Latin American nation.[5]

In addition, U.S. military assistance also involved assigning Green Beret advisers to conduct "in country" training for the

---

*The U.S. fiscal year begins on October 1 of the preceding year. Thus, for example, the figures for FY 1978 actually represent aid given from October 1, 1977, to September 30, 1978, and for FY 1979 the corresponding dates are from October 1, 1978, to September 30, 1979.

TABLE 4. U.S. ECONOMIC AND MILITARY AID TO CENTRAL AMERICA,
1978–1980
(Millions of Dollars)

Country	Economic Aid			Military Aid			Three-Year Total
	1978	1979	1980	1978	1979	1980	
Honduras	17.1	29.1	52.6	3.2	2.3	23.6*	127.9
El Salvador	10.9	11.4	59.0	—	—	17.8	99.1
Panama	23.1	21.2	2.1	.5	1.4	29.8	78.1
Nicaragua	14.0	18.5	37.1	.4	—	1.1	71.1
Guatemala	10.6	24.7	13.3	—	—	.4	49.0
Costa Rica	9.0	17.9	15.1	—	—	.2	42.2
							467.4

*This figure includes the minimum value of one million dollars for each of the ten UH-1H helicopters "leased" to the Honduran armed forces at no charge.

Source: U.S. Department of State, Congressional Presentation, Security Assistance Programs; fiscal years 1981–1983, Washington, D.C.

armed forces. The purpose of this training presumably was to enhance the Honduran army's capability for interdicting the supply lines that were thought to run from Nicaragua to the FMLN insurgents in El Salvador. As explained to Congress by a top Defense Department official, "Honduras plays a crucial role in the movement of men and supplies to the Salvadoran insurgents. The Hondurans believe, and our intelligence sources agree, that their territory is being used by the insurgents as a conduit for men and arms into El Salvador with Cuban support."[6] To this end, U.S. Special Forces personnel conducted basic courses in tactical small-unit operations and border patrolling, in what the U.S. Defense Department calls "border security operations."[7] But the Green Berets not only trained, they actually organized such units, as was the case with the six Special Forces advisers who, from June to September 1980, formed a Border Patrol Unit.[8] Moreover, to increase the military's mobility and strike capacity, at the same time Washington leased at no charge to the Hondurans, ten Huey UH-1H helicopters valued at well over one million dollars each.[9]

While in 1980 yet another 37 advisers accompanied the ten Huey helicopters,[10] the 27 military advisers sent to Honduras early the following year included more Special Forces counterinsurgency experts. Even though U.S. law expressly forbids such personnel from actively participating in military operations, confirmed reports placed at least some of the Green Berets in the company of Honduran troops on patrol along the Salvadoran border, dressed in full camouflage fatigues and carrying M-16 assault rifles.[11]

The buildup of Honduras as the U.S. military citadel in Central America, although conducted quietly, did not escape attention. The March 1980 visit to Washington of President Policarpio Páz García—when the Carter Administration took the opportunity to publicly demonstrate its support for the military dictator by announcing new loans and grants to Honduras— touched off strong protest. One of the most caustic articles— "Why Another Somoza?" by Jack Anderson, drawing upon classified information—proved prophetic:

> The President seems determined to add still another sorry chapter to the chronicle of Yankee imperialism in Central America. The administration apparently has chosen Honduras to be our new 'Nicaragua'—a dependable satellite bought and paid for by American military and economic largesse.
>
> In secret meetings with the Pentagon's emissary . . . the Honduran military junta was told specifically that it is expected to assume the regional role played for years by Nicaragua's Anastasio Somoza—to become the bulwark of anticommunism against the pressure of popular revolt.[12]

TAKING CONTROL

In the following few years, Honduras's history proceeded precisely according to its U.S. benefactor's schedule. The national elections held in late 1981 won the presidency for Dr. Roberto Suazo Córdova, an unassuming country physician, and the traditionally popular and antimilitary Liberal Party. But on January 25, 1982, the day of his inauguration, U.S. Ambassador John D. Negroponte, made it plain to the new president just who was really in charge. Established as the Reagan Administration's proconsul, several days later Ambassador Negroponte appointed his favorite army officer, Colonel Gustavo Alvarez Martínez, as the nation's highest military officer—the chief of the Honduran armed forces. The significance of this unorthodox promotion can only be appreciated from the perspective of the political power structure so common throughout Latin America, especially in military-dominated Honduras, where the top armed forces officer is in reality the de facto ruler of the nation.

Alvarez's meteoric rise to Honduras's most powerful position, considering his background and coinciding precisely with the U.S.-backed expanded role of the military, leaves little to the imagination as to how and why he got the job. Advocating a political philosophy somewhere to the right of generals Erwin Rommel, Hitler's "Desert Fox," and Ariel Sharon, Israel's former defense minister who was sacked because of his responsibility in the 1982 massacre of Lebanese civilians—both of whom he openly admires—Alvarez, speaking fluent English, must have appeared to the Reagan Administration as the almost perfect person to take under its wing.

Alvarez's military education included study of police operations in Washington, D.C., under the Office of Public Safety program (which, because of the brutal techniques that it taught, was dismantled by Congress in the 1970s), as well as advanced infantry and counterinsurgency training at Fort Benning, Georgia, and the School of the Americas in the Panama Canal Zone. He also studied at the Peruvian Superior War College, a unique military institution known throughout the hemisphere for its in-depth courses on political ideology. Moreover, Alvarez attended Argentina's National Military Academy where he embraced the neo-fascist National Security State doctrine which, like its Nazi predecessor, is founded upon the concepts of geopolitics and war without quarter, admitting no distinction between combatants and civilians, against domestic and international communist subversion.[13]

Not only his training, but also his career, may have endeared him to the right-wing ideologues in Washington. Putting into practice the lessons he had learned, as commander of the San Pedro Sula military region the Colonel built up a reputation as a strike breaker for the U.S.-owned banana companies. In 1980, as U.S. interest and influence grew in Honduras, he advanced from this relatively obscure post to be the head of the powerful Public Safety Force (FUSEP), which is in effect the Honduran secret police, with special responsibility for political and trade union repression. There he distinguished himself as a fearless peasant-beater by crushing left-wing campesino and trade union organizations, and courageously took on the task of driving radical students from the National University. He further showed what he was made of during his tenure as chief of FUSEP by introducing a policy of systematically "disappearing" those foes of the fatherland whom he calls "politically incorrect people"—a common practice in the Southern Cone dictatorships where he probably picked up the habit from his Argentine mentors.

But his real break came in January 1982, when President Suazo Córdova promoted the then Colonel Alvarez to head of the armed forces. Since his appointment so drastically violated the Honduran army rules of promotion—which stipulate that to occupy the nation's highest military post, the candidate must already possess the rank of general, and that to become a general all officers must first complete at least five years as a colonel, another requirement that Alvarez had not fulfilled—it soon became evident that the decisive factor in Alvarez's "good luck" was Washington's support. The Pentagon saw in this ambitious officer precisely the type of person they needed: a ruthless executor of their geopolitical plans for the region. Needless to say, however, Alvarez's controversial rise to power did not sit well with the top echelon of the Honduran officer corps.

Following the time-honored Latin American tradition of dealing with contenders for high-level positions that are too powerful to purge or simply eliminate, the U.S.-backed Honduran strongman sent his two chief rivals into "diplomatic exile." Colonel Leonidas Torres Arias, the new head of FUSEP and previous chief of military intelligence, found himself shipped off to Argentina as military attaché; and Colonel Hubert Bodden Cacacers, commander of the 1st Infantry Battalion, the country's most important military force, was dispatched to the Honduran Embassy in distant Taiwan.

Two other developments provide further indications of the direction in which General Alvarez has steered the nation. By reorganizing the army's command structure through consolidating all of its various units into only three brigades, he has institutionalized a centralization that strengthens the army's counterinsurgency capacity, increases its overall combat effectiveness, and minimalizes the potential of a military coup against him.[14]

The other change, which undoubtedly carries far greater consequences for Honduras's future, came on November 10, 1982, when the high command presented a number of constitutional reforms to the national congress. The most important of these, which was hastily passed by the legislative body, elevated the head of the Honduran armed forces to the position of commander-in-chief, until then an authority that always rested with the president of the republic. In turn, the president became the nation's supreme commander, a title and position that remains ambiguous and one that nobody has been able to define satisfactorily. What does come through loud and clear, however, is that these changes confer unprecedented powers upon General Alvarez, who also holds the post of minister of defense.[15]

As Washington has learned through its counterinsurgency programs in Southeast Asia, Chile, and El Salvador, proxies are not always puppets. Indeed, the headstrong General Alvarez proved to be not the best of team players, a highly regarded quality in the Reagan Administration, and had to be reined in by his masters. Evidently carried away by Honduras's evermore important role as the new regional guardian of Western civilization, and his pivotal position within the overall scheme, in August 1982, the minister of defense made the almost fatal mistake of initiating independent action. Placing the Honduran armed forces on full mobilization, he steadfastly rebuffed U.S. efforts to dissuade him from continuing with his plans, that most observers believed amounted to nothing less than mounting a "pre-emptive strike" against Nicaragua.[16]

Although alarmed by the disruption of their game plan—which called for Honduras not to be identified as the aggressor in a war with the Sandinistas, or worse yet, prematurely drawing the United States into direct military intervention in Central America—it appears that Washington was already prepared for such a contingency. Unexpectedly abandoning his diplomatic exile in Argentina, Alvarez's antagonist and former head of the Honduran secret police, Colonel Leonidas Torres Arias, suddenly showed up in Mexico City. With remarkable dispatch Torres Arias managed to publish an incredibly well-documented full-page spread in the prestigious newspaper *Excélsior*.[17] In this impeccably written missive, the Colonel detailed abuses and improprieties committed by Alvarez, and denounced the minister of defense as an unprincipled megalomaniac whose illusions of military grandeur were leading the nation to disaster.

Because of the timing, the exceptionally high cost of the publication, the fact that the article contained many details that Torres Arias could not possibly have had access to even in his capacity as the chief of FUSEP, and that the Colonel now is living in the United States, few insiders doubt that the U.S. intelligence community engineered the scandal by providing him with finances and information. In any event, the insubordinate Alvarez, finding himself fighting not the Sandinistas but the bombast of criticism generated by the article (that somehow quickly found wide distribution in Honduras), was finally forced to cancel his war preparations against Nicaragua. The significance of what had happened was understood by everyone—in a devastatingly effective maneuver, the United States had put down the upstart general, leaving no room for doubt about who was captain of the team; or, as Alvarez resentfully but correctly put it, "The U.S. wants vassals, not allies."[18]

Indeed, the United States, faced with increasing insurgent strength in El Salvador, was refining its game plan. Several weeks after the October 1982 FMLN offensive began, the U.S. Undersecretary of Defense, Fred Iklé, met with the Honduran and Salvadoran ministers of defense, generals Alvarez and García, respectively.[19] Less than a week later, then Commander of the U.S. Army Southern Command, General Wallace H. Nutting, accompanied by the head of one of the U.S. Rapid Deployment Divisions, held another conference with the same men.[20] Considering the fact that immediately following these high-level conferences, Honduran troops began brazenly to enter Salvadoran territory to participate in massive coordinated military operations,[21] it is reasonable to assume that the agenda of the meetings was to escalate the regionalization of Washington's counterinsurgency strategy.

Although neither nation will officially admit that Honduran forces entered El Salvador, in separate statements, both defense ministers confirmed the collaboration between their armed forces. Flanked by the president of the Interamerican Defense Board College, General John McEnry, and the director of the Interamerican Defense College, Rear Admiral Saypre Swartztrauber, General García announced that "just as there are soldiers of other nations that fight in El Salvador on the side of the guerrillas, soldiers from other nations could perfectly well come to combat these sectors that are sowing chaos in a war that they have imposed upon us from abroad." [22]

General Alvarez, once again securely back on the U.S. team's line-up, was even more specific when he revealed the formation of "an alliance of the Salvadoran, Guatemalan, and Honduran armies to fight subversion," and that "we are already working in a coordinated fashion, exchanging intelligence information and supporting each other's operations, but we need to increase our level of coordination, perhaps to operate jointly." [23]

Echoing the rhetoric of the Reagan Administration's hard line, which dogmatically insists upon defining the Central American insurrections in terms of the East–West conflict, the General took the occasion to accuse the Sandinista government of being the beach head of the "Communist conspiracy." Reflecting the seriousness with which he views his role as the military leader of the emerging regional "holy alliance," Alvarez evidently felt obliged to emphasize that "in Central America a war to the death has been unleashed. . . . The democracies of Honduras, Guatemala, and El Salvador [sic] are faced with an uprising of international Communism." Finally, in a dire warning of the high stakes, the fanatical local strong man faithfully concluded in an almost liturgical tone when he dramatically said that "only when El Salvador has fallen, and Honduras and Guatemala follow, only when all of Central America is Communist, when it is already too late, we will realize how important this war to the death is." [24]

Another step in the late 1982 U.S. escalation toward regionalization came the following month. Since one of the purported purposes for CIA sponsorship of the contras is to interdict supplies to the Salvadoran insurgents from Nicaragua, perhaps it is not entirely coincidental that in December the Honduras-based contras launched the first in their series of continuing major offensives. Credibility is added to the idea of linkage between systematic Honduran involvement in the Salvadoran civil war and the contras' commando raids, when the relationship is made between the increase of these two activities and the corresponding success of the FMLN insurgents in the 1982–1983 campaign.

Contrary to the widely held assumption that Honduran military collaboration with their Salvadoran counterparts began under the tutelege of the Reagan Administration (although it did become formalized during 1982), its first expression and foundations are found much earlier, while President Carter still occupied the White House. The tragic first major instance of the ongoing collaboration between the two armed forces occurred just nine days after the top-ranking Salvadoran and Honduran brass held their first summit conference since the brief 1969 war fought between their two nations. In a macabre expression of the new détente on May 14, 1980, Honduran troops prevented more than one thousand Salvadoran refugees, fleeing from pursuing soldiers who were indiscriminately slaughtering all those whom they came upon, from crossing the Sumpúl River to safety into Honduras. Trapped between the Hondurans who shot those who attempted to come ashore and the Salvadorans at their backs, these unarmed peasants floundered in the river for hours, some finally swimming back to the Salvadoran side. But as they reached the shore, their own countrymen slaughtered as many as possible while others were being murdered by machine-gun fire directed from the U.S.–provided Huey helicopter gunships hovering over the river.[25] According to Catholic Church sources, along with a host of international human rights organizations that have investigated the Río Sumpúl massacre and come up with virtually the same conclusions, approximately 600 noncombatant men, women, and children perished in this orgy of death.[26]

In order to facilitate future joint operations, a formal end of the 1969 war between Honduras and El Salvador, a move supported by the Carter Administration, proved expedient. Following the October 30, 1980, signing of the peace treaty, both the Honduran and Salvadoran military could legally enter the Bolsones Territorial, the two-mile demilitarized zone running along either side of the border that had been patrolled by the Organization of American States forces since the cessation of hostilities. The elimination of the formal restrictions forbidding either nation's armed forces from operating in the Bolsones (since it was generally assumed that these neutral zones provided sanctuary for guerrilla bases) opened up greater possibilities for coordinated counterinsurgency actions. The Hondurans could now openly attack suspected insurgent camps on their side, and the Salvadorans were freed to pursue the rebels into the formerly neutral territory in the hope of catching them in hammer-and-anvil operations.[27]

Until the spring of 1982, the Honduran armed forces by and large limited their operations to their own national territory—primarily sweeping maneuvers in an attempt to disrupt the FMLN's rearguard areas. As described in detail in chapter 6, the standard pattern in which the Salvadoran and Honduran armies collaborated after signing the peace treaty in late 1980 was the hammer-and-anvil tactic, in which the Salvadoran hammer of troops attempts to drive retreating insurgents into the Honduran anvil of soldiers waiting on their side of the border.[28] Although embarrassingly ineffectual against seasoned guerrillas, this clever military maneuver works just fine for massacring panicked and unarmed peasant families, as brilliantly demonstrated at the Río Sumpúl engagement.

In July 1982, the Hondurans began expanding their joint actions by entering Salvadoran territory to carry out coordinated operations. Early in the month, a force estimated at 3,000 Honduran troops marched five miles into northern Morazán in a futile attempt to attack the guerrillas from the north while the Salvadoran armed forces pushed up from the south.[29] In a typical circumlocution to explain the reasons for the Honduran incursion, without admitting that it actually occurred, General Alvarez put aside the old wartime animosities and declared: "We are in a war in which our physical borders are not in danger, but rather democracy, our tranquility, way of life and religious faith are endangered, and we ought to join together to defend ourselves."[30] Similar noble pronouncements, reflecting the National Security State's doctrine of "war without borders," followed the November 1982 and January 1983 Honduras military interventions. The martial courtship continues to develop: The couple announced plans in August 1983 to move in together with the proposed stationing of Salvadoran forces inside Honduras to facilitate flanking maneuvers and attacks on the insurgents' base areas.[31]

In comparison with the relatively few combat casualties inflicted upon the insurgents by Honduran–Salvadoran military collaboration, the true victims are the tens of thousands of Salvadoran refugees who seek a haven in Honduras from the atrocities of their own country's military and paramilitary forces. It has become a sad fact of the civil war that these displaced people—the majority are women, children, and old people—cannot find safety anywhere. The major reason for their plight is the assumption widely held by Salvadoran, Honduran, and U.S. officials that many of the refugees continue to function as the insurgents' popular base, providing to the rebels food, medicines, and other supplies received from international relief organizations. In any case, the refugees are certainly considered to be FMLN–FDR sympathizers, which is more than sufficient cause to mount regular incursions of Salvadoran soldiers into Honduran territory in attempts to terrorize them into abandoning any support for the guerrillas. During these raids not only do Salvadoran troops and their ORDEN accomplices rampage through the refugee camps, brutally interrogating and torturing "potential subversives," they routinely carry out extrajudicial executions of any suspected member of the insurgents' infrastructure.[32]

So that Honduras could reliably continue collaborating with the Salvadoran armed forces, provide a sanctuary for the CIA-backed contras, and fulfill other U.S. aspirations, Washington undertook a long-term commitment to stabilize the nation through unprecedented amounts of military and economic assistance. In order to assure social tranquility, the sociopolitical underpinnings for maintaining Honduras's façade of democracy, the Reagan Administration made sure that enough developmental aid arrived to shore up the economy.

On top of suffering the same economic disaster that befell the rest of the Third World—low commodity prices together with the high cost of imported oil and exorbitantly high interest rates for international financing—Honduras was already the region's poorest country, with a yearly per capita income of just 520 dollars[33] and unemployment conservatively estimated at 22 percent of the economically active population.[34] Moreover, its gross domestic product (GDP) fell into a steady downward spiral: While in 1979 it increased by an impressive 6.7 percent, the following year it dropped to a discouraging 1.6 percent growth rate; and in 1981 the GDP plummeted to minus .4 percent,[35] only to continue its fall in 1982 to a disastrous minus 1.2 percent.[36] By 1983, the combination of Honduras's nosediving GDP with its high 2.8 percent birth rate[37] ended up leaving 60 percent of its people living in extreme poverty.[38]

Rather disingenuously claiming to be simply "adjusting" for its "strategy of economic development," the Honduran government in 1982 imposed a harsh austerity budget. Yet even with these radical measures, the Honduran national budget requires that at least 30 percent of its funds come from international financial sources to keep it afloat.[39]

Regardless of the severe reduction in the people's standard of living caused by the economic crisis, Honduras's acute problems would have assumed far graver proportions without U.S. economic assistance. Reflecting President Reagan's emphasis on the security aspects of Central American policy, while continuing with the generous pattern established by the Carter Administration, the President did reduce somewhat the levels of economic aid to Honduras: for fiscal year 1980 President Carter granted 52.6 million dollars, while in FY 1981, economic assistance was reduced to the still magnanimous sum of 38.5 million dollars; for FY 1982, the figure rose to 43.9 million dollars, growing to 45.6 million dollars in FY 1983; and for FY 1984 the Administration has requested a further increase to 46.2 million dollars.

The scope of Washington's generosity to its client state is better depicted in Table 5.[40]

TABLE 5.   1983 FOREIGN ECONOMIC CREDITS FOR HONDURAS*
(Millions of Dollars)

International Monetary Fund	$ 84.3
Inter-American Development Bank	54.0
World Bank	53.0
U.S. economic assistance†	45.6
Canadian International Development Agency	10.0
Caribbean Basin Initiative	37.0
Total	$283.9

* With the exception noted below, all statistics come from *Inforpress Centroamericana,* No. 511, September 23, 1982.

† This figure is taken from the U.S. Department of State, Congressional Presentation, Security Assistance Programs, Fiscal Year 1984, Washington, D.C.

Certainly not all of these monies came unilaterally from the United States, but even those funds from multilateral institutions are largely determined by Washington's enormous influence in these organizations. The Inter-American Development Bank's (IDB) lending record for the past few years serves to exemplify the effectiveness of U.S. pressure. While in 1979 the IDB awarded Somoza's Nicaragua, in the midst of its war against the insurgents, 36.5 percent of its total loans to Central America, once the Sandinistas won, it radically reversed its lending pattern, steadily reducing the amounts of its loans to Nicaragua, so that by 1982 they amounted to only 9.7 percent of its awards in the region.[41] Table 5 does not include funding from other sources, such as private banks, the European Economic Community or other governments and multilateral financial institutions. Therefore, it is safe to assume that Honduras's foreign borrowing in 1983 exceeded the 283.9 million dollars detailed in the table.

The long-term effects of Honduras's ballooning foreign debt turns out to hold another plus for the United States, beyond the fact of stabilizing its floundering economy. By so substantially increasing its already staggering foreign debt of more than 2 billion dollars,[42] since Honduras already must commit more than 18 percent of its 1983 budget just to service its existing debt,[43] this dramatically increased borrowing further deepens the country's dependency upon foreign sources of capital and its necessity to submit to the geopolitical pretentions of U.S. policy in Central America.

The interface between U.S. policy and its Honduran execution finds its clearest expression in the triangle of mutual support among U.S. Ambassador Negroponte, President Suazo Córdova, and Defense Minister Alvarez. As diplomatic and government sources outline their relationship, the functions that these three colleagues perform complement each other in an extraordinarily convenient manner.[44] Of course, the Ambassador commands enormous resources that allow him to steer the nation in the direction set by Reagan Administration policy, a policy of maintaining an unequal relationship between the armed forces and the civilian government.[45]

From the Reagan Administration's point of view, the set-up is just about perfect. Ultimately, of even more importance to its designs on Honduras than buoying up the economy and the façade of democracy is insuring that the military remains the nation's key institution, a priority amply demonstrated in the largesse of its security assistance: The 14.2 million dollars accorded in 1981 paled beside the 78 million dollars pumped in during FY 1982; as does the 68.9 million dollars for FY 1983 compared to the Reagan Administration's requested 134 million dollars for FY 1984.[46]

Ever since taking office, Suazo Córdova, a novice in foreign affairs and defense matters, deferred to Negroponte and Alvarez. Since his 1983 heart attack,[47] President Córdova has relinquished even more of the pitifully limited power that he possessed, electing to spend more of his time in the country at his ranch near the Salvadoran border.[48] Still, as elected head of state, Suazo Córdova continues to confer national and international legitimacy upon the United States' militaristic policies in Central America. For his part, Alvarez gets to play out his fantasies by swimming around as a big fish in a little pond; he duly carries out Washington's macho game plan, keeping tight control over the armed forces, thereby insuring discipline and minimizing the possibility of a military coup.

FORTRESS AMERICA

Regardless of the Reagan Administration's incredible insistence upon categorizing joint United States–Honduran military ma-

neuvers as "routine," a review of the facts clearly shows its absurdity. Traditionally, U.S. practice military activities in the region have taken the form of occasional multilateral exercises
conducted with Central American armed forces until the late
1970s under the auspices of CONDECA, as well as more frequent bilateral maneuvers with individual nations, such as the
24 Honduran "Hawks View" exercises held since 1965.[49] But
beginning in 1982—with CONDECA as dead as Somoza, Guatemala ruled out because of congressional human rights restrictions, and El Salvador engaged in a real war—the Pentagon radically changed the nature of its relationship with Honduran
armed forces.

Rather than playing war games together, the special "Combined Movement" maneuvers initiated an escalating trend of
broadening the purpose and frequency of joint operations. Since
these two-week exercises, held during late July and early August
1982, joint U.S.–Honduran maneuvers have increasingly taken
on the character of advanced training for the Honduran armed
forces. They have provided the opportunity to unilaterally cir-
cumvent congressional oversight by upgrading existing facilities
and building new installations, leaving behind enormous quantities of ordnance, and covertly supplying the CIA–created contra
army based out of Honduras.

Alarmed by the extremely poor performance of the Salvadoran
military in its war against the FMLN, in preparation for Combined Movement a U.S. Army planning team visited Honduras
to check out the situation. Perhaps inadvertently hinting at
Washington's shift in policy, a Pentagon spokesman explained
that the evaluation had to be conducted "while no one is shooting at us."[50] According to the same official source, the immediate objective of the exercise was to "test people and equipment
movement, and the communication procedures needed to move
them."[51] Its long-term purpose can hardly be called a normal
function of maneuvers: the establishment of a permanent military base at Durzuna, situated some 25 miles north of the Nicaraguan border in the province of Gracias a Díos. The largest
military installation in eastern Honduras, the new Durzuna
airport facilities are designed to accommodate the full U.S.

arsenal of fighters and even the gigantic C-5 Galaxy transport, the largest aircraft in the North American fleet. The full significance of its existence also lies in its strategic location—only six miles from Mocorón, the site of an existing army garrison and adjacent camp for several thousand Nicaraguan Miskito contras.[52] (It was this same contra faction that in January 1983 carried out underwater sabotage raids against port facilities in Nicaragua's Puerto Cabezas just across the border.)

The operational aspects of Combined Movement centered upon an elaborate airlift of more than 1,000 Honduran troops and their equipment by a U.S. Air Force flotilla to the Nicaraguan border in a simulated combat operation.[53] Denounced as "provocative" by the Sandinistas because of its proximity to the contra raids beginning at this time, the Combined Movement exercises certainly were more than routine on a number of counts.[54] They provided cover for the delivery of supplies to the FDN contras, as well as for the enormous quantities of military equipment left behind when the U.S. forces departed.

Marking another development in the Reagan Administration's Central American policy, the exercises introduced a new mechanism for evading congressional control over foreign military assistance levels. Normally, to expend funds to build bases or provide munitions to a foreign government, the Administration by law first must obtain the consent of Congress, an increasingly difficult process because of the strong opposition to granting greater amounts of military aid to Central American nations. By financing the building of Durzuna and leaving behind military equipment from Defense Department funds designated for military maneuvers, which are administered from special accounts directly by the Joint Chiefs of Staff, the Pentagon bypassed all congressional oversight. Consequently, Congress did not have any say in the granting of this military aid. In this way the Administration violated the spirit of the law if not its letter. Since this money and equipment does not appear in any category of U.S. security assistance to Honduras, it serves to hide the true amount and proportion of military aid that the public knows about.

The next step in the escalating war-games game came with

Ahuras Tara—which means "Big Pine" in the Miskito Indian language—originally scheduled to commence on December 5, 1982. The unprecedented scale of U.S. Army, Navy, and Air Force's involvement caused moderate civilians and a dissident group of military men to voice their concern that the joint operation far exceeded the boundaries of legitimate military exercises. Perhaps knowing the true nature of the Combined Movement exercises, the officers charged that U.S. intelligence personnel were using Big Pine to once again intimidate and destabilize Nicaragua; especially since just the announcement of the maneuvers had provoked another round of strong Sandinista protests that heightened the already tense relations and risk of war with their neighbor. In one more demonstration of where the real power lies, despite Honduras's objections, in an October 1982 interview, a senior Pentagon official arrogantly insisted that "we are not going to stop the exercise just because we have got a bunch of screaming Sandinistas over there."[55] However, the exposure of the CIA's illegal organization of the Honduras-based contra army at this time, and President Reagan's inclusion of stops in Costa Rica and Honduras during his Latin American trip (December 4 and 5, 1982) forced Big Pine's postponement. But not for long.

On February 1, 1983, the one-week Big Pine maneuvers, whose undisguised purpose according to Honduran authorities was to provide training for their armed forces at a cost of 5.2 million dollars, got under way. Again the action centered in Mocorón in the coastal province of Gracias a Diós just a few miles from the Nicaraguan border. Dwarfing Combined Movement, Big Pine involved 4,000 Honduran troops along with 1,600 U.S. soldiers utilizing several troop ships complete with landing craft, as well as sophisticated reconnaissance and observation aircraft, at least four different types of military helicopters, and ten Hercules C-130 transports; all this while a destroyer, the USS William V. Pratt, provocatively cruised the Caribbean coast.[56]

The execution of Big Pine seemed to confirm that the Reagan Administration finally had adopted the recommendations of the so-called Santa Fe document, *A New Interamerican Policy for the 80's.* Prepared in 1980 for President-elect Reagan by the reac-

tionary Santa Fe Committee of Latin American specialists—
some are currently serving as advisers in the Administration—
its ultra-right thesis contends that the United States must pursue
an aggressive Latin American policy of providing military leadership, backed up by unprecedented security training programs
and supplies of war materiel to combat domestic and international threats from Soviet–Cuban subversion. In other words,
once defining the hemisphere's problems in terms of the East–
West conflict, the only rational course for Washington is to re-
lentlessly crush the Communist menace through a militaristic
foreign policy.

The announcement on July 18, 1983, of Big Pine II dispelled
any remaining doubts concerning the thrust of Reagan's Central
American policy. The decision to conduct these extraordinary
"maneuvers" seems to have been made on July 12, following a
series of high-level meetings which stressed the necessity to
counteract Cuban assistance to Nicaragua.[57] In turn, this priority
appears to flow from the disastrous performance of the Administration's two principal military adventures in the Isthmus: the
embarrassingly ineffectual attempts of the contra armies to challenge the Sandinista government and the devastating beatings
inflicted upon the Salvadoran armed forces by the FMLN insurgents. Given the internal logic of the rightist East–West analysis
held by the Reagan Administration, Big Pine II makes perfect
sense. Without Cuban aid, which in their minds really means
backing from the Soviet Union, the Nicaraguans would be rendered more vulnerable to the contra attacks and less able to assist the Salvadoran insurgents. Moreover, such an enormous display of U.S. might would discourage any Sandinista thoughts of
sending their powerful army to strike the contras' rearguard
bases in Honduras or Costa Rica. Such action quite likely would
prematurely spark full-fledged war in which neither ally stood a
chance, thereby jeopardizing Washington's long-term regional
plans.

If Combined Movement paled beside Big Pine—the biggest
U.S. joint exercise in Central American history to that date—
then the duration and magnitude of U.S. sea, air, and land forces
involved in Big Pine II make its namesake look like a nickle-

and-dime operation. In fact, as its principal characteristics show, in comparison with its predecessor, Big Pine II was in a league by itself; instead of one measly destroyer cruising the coast, it involved two full naval battle groups, one in the Caribbean and another in the Pacific. Rather than 1,600 U.S. troops, it brought in up to 5,600 soldiers. Instead of lasting only one week, its duration was initially scheduled to run for six months. Billed from the beginning as an unabashed display of raw power to intimidate the Sandinistas, top Administration officials pointedly announced with extraordinary arrogance, even by superpower standards, that if Cuba did not halt its arms shipments to Nicaragua, President Reagan "had not ruled out establishing a military quarantine around Nicaragua."[58] This demand had absolutely no juridical basis in international law, since sovereign nations possess uncontested legal prerogatives to enter into whatever security relationship they mutually decide upon. Indeed, several days later, senior Reagan officials confirmed that the President viewed the exercises in part "to test and refine plans for imposing a military quarantine around Nicaragua."[59] Another Administration official was even more explicit when he boasted that "We want to persuade the bad guys in Nicaragua and Cuba that we are positioned to block, invade, or interdict if they cross a particular threshold."[60]

Moreover, the same high-ranking officials revealed that the classified Big Pine II plans approved by the President detailed the mechanisms to lay the foundation for an expanded U.S. military presence in Central America.[61] Bombarded by a concerned nation, four days later Reagan called a nationally televised press conference to allay fears that he was anything more than a determined, but peace-loving democrat. Explaining that the purpose of the military exercises was only to provide the necessary "shield for democracy and development" in Central America, he insisted that "we are not seeking a larger presence in the region." But when pressed by reporters to assure the world that he would not escalate U.S. military involvement by sending more troops to the Isthmus, Reagan found it convenient to duck the question with the old standby that "Presidents never say never."[62] Unfortunately, as events subsequently showed, the President had good reason to be less than candid that night.

In late July, a U.S. Navy battle group, centered around the aircraft carrier *Ranger* with its seven escort ships, took up positions along the Pacific coast of Nicaragua. At the same time, Pentagon officials made public other details of Big Pine II, which they claimed would last until January 1984: In August and September two other battle naval task forces would arrive, one on Nicaragua's Caribbean coast led by the aircraft carrier *Coral Sea,* and the other in the Pacific headed by the battleship *New Jersey* to relieve the *Ranger* flotilla.[63] All told, the battle groups stationed off both Nicaraguan coasts comprised about 20 ships, carrying 16,000 military personnel and 140 of the most sophisticated fighter bombers possessed by the United States.[64] Within a week after the arrival of the first Pacific coast task force, Washington flexed its muscles. In what universally was interpreted as a brazen act to intimidate the Sandinistas, a U.S. destroyer harassed a Soviet freighter by demanding to be told its cargo and destination, then shadowing it for the next forty miles until it turned into Nicaraguan territorial waters to enter Corinto, the nation's largest port.[65]

Big Pine II's unexpected display of gunboat diplomacy immediately resulted in several new developments. The details of the operation, which leaked to the international diplomatic community a week or so before the Administration had made any official announcement, so concerned the Sandinistas that they decided to radically change tactics. In order to plainly demonstrate to the world that Washington, not Managua, was the aggressor, the Nicaraguan government on July 19 offered to negotiate the Reagan Administration's public demands: entering regional peace talks, stopping all supply shipments to the Salvadoran insurgents, and ceasing to import any offensive weapons.[66] Even President Fidel Castro, in conjunction with the Nicaraguans, offered to work out a deal with President Reagan to pull out all foreign military advisers from Central America.[67] Although the Administration duly expressed cautious interest in these proposals, it did not make a forceful attempt to pursue them.[68] This is precisely what the Sandinistas expected, since they believe that the United States harbors no real interest in finding a peaceful solution to the region's civil strife, but its true goals are the overthrow of their government and the total defeat of the Salvadoran FMLN insurgents.

Another upshot of the Administration's dramatic escalation of U.S. military intervention turned out to be a sharpening of differences with Latin American nations working to bring about a negotiated settlement to the fighting.[69] Perhaps the growing distance between the United States and these countries was most poignantly dramatized during mid-August in Mexico when President Miguel de la Madrid cautioned President Reagan against aggravating the Isthmus's problems through U.S. "shows of force."[70] Certainly de la Madrid did not completely share the Administration's confidence that its display of military power had pressured the Sandinistas into softening their position. Since the Nicaraguan stratagem was being openly discussed throughout Central American diplomatic circles at this time, surely the Mexican president knew that this was only the opening finesse, and that the Sandinistas were far from being cowed.

According to a very senior Sandinista official, their plans ran as follows: While they would do everything possible to avoid war, if forced into hostilities with Honduras they felt confident that their battle-seasoned army would easily defeat the corrupt and inefficient Honduran armed forces. Hedging their bet, in August, Nicaragua announced plans to institute national conscription to bolster its already formidable fighting forces.[71] Their scenario assumed that the outbreak of war would likely result in some form of stepped-up U.S. military intervention to save its client state, perhaps at first through air cover for the Hondurans, more aggressive contra attacks directly supported through U.S. logistics, and even the bombing of Nicaraguan troop formations and military installations. In that eventuality, in order to alleviate the pressure on themselves, the Sandinistas intended to "activate their contacts with the insurgent forces in El Salvador, Guatemala and Honduras." By "activate," the official clarified, they meant providing the rebels with unprecedented amounts of weaponry—"enough so that they could give a rifle to every peasant who wanted one—and more." Moreover, he claimed that the Sandinistas would further "raise the level of the war" by distributing enormous amounts of explosives, mortars, recoilless rifles, bazookas, and artillery, along with "more than sufficient ammunition." As a final step, they would introduce weapons as yet unknown in the fighting, such as shoulder-held surface-to-air rockets, which are deadly against helicopters and other light aircraft. Estimating that within ten days to two weeks these measures would regionalize the civil strife to involve all six Central American nations and their 23 million people, he predicted that full-scale direct U.S. military intervention with combat ground troops would shortly follow, a contingency that the Sandinistas have been preparing for since the election of Ronald Reagan.[72]

In retrospect, one further observation might be made concerning the immediate reaction to Big Pine II: The Administration pulled off its largest escalation of U.S. military intervention in Central America at minimal political cost to itself. Certainly this move contributed to the largely symbolic vote on July 28 in the House of Representatives, by the unexpectedly large margin of 223 to 203, to cut off funding for CIA clandestine support of the contras.[73] While in practical terms the passage of the Boland Amendment in the House did not affect covert CIA funding for the contras—because the Republican-dominated Senate refused to support the legislation—it did represent a major revolt against the Administration in Congress. The initial shock of Big Pine II heightened by the reckless challenge of the Soviet cargo ship raised fears of a Gulf of Tonkin–type incident that could lead to a direct confrontation with Moscow, as in the 1962 Cuban missile crisis. The dynamics of this situation helped the Administration.

As the potential Soviet freighter crisis passed and the naval battle groups caused no further interference with shipping bound for Nicaragua, the initial enormous outcry[74] soon died down to a resentful grumble from a relieved nation.[75] By the time the Big Pine II's land operations began in early August 1983, according to the new commander of the U.S. Army Southern Command in Panama, General Paul F. Gorman, their duration had been moved from January to February 1984,[76] and a month later the date was once again advanced to "at least through" April 1984,[77] thereby extending the originally announced six-month operation to a minimum of eight months. Nobody seemed to notice.

Another facet of these "routine" maneuvers that have hardly raised an eyebrow is the incredible expense and the unusual emphasis on strengthening Honduran armed forces facilities. On top of the more than 165 million dollars for operational expenses, the local material and labor required for Big Pine II amounted to at least another 30 million dollars;[78] not an exorbitant sum considering its vast building program, which includes extending three or more airfields,[79] establishing a new military hospital,[80] installing a second radar base in the Gulf of Fonseca,[81] expanding port facilities,[82] building roads and communications centers,[83] and transforming the Honduran Air Force School into a sophisticated command center for the Joint Task Force.[84] Although all of these construction projects fit into a larger plan, the renovation of the Trujillo airport takes on special importance because it is located only a few miles from the Regional Military Training Center where, since mid-June, 120 Green Berets have been running thousands of Salvadoran troops through intensified counterinsurgency courses. All these permanent improvements to the Honduran armed forces' infrastructure will be left behind with whatever else the Pentagon decides to donate. Since their cost comes out of the U.S. Joint Chiefs of Staff's budget for maneuvers, Congress exercises no influence over this multimillion dollar military assistance.

As ambitious as the physical aspects of Big Pine II appear, the actual military operations are even more impressive. Calling for both conventional and unconventional warfare training, Big Pine II's more than 5,600 U.S. soldiers included contingents from the Army Special Forces, the navy's SEALS and the air force's Special Operations Wing.[85] As one of its stated purposes was to train the Honduran armed forces in special techniques to stop the Salvadoran insurgents' supplies of weapons from Nicaragua,[86] one detachment of 70 Green Berets offered extensive instruction to two Honduran army battalions in counterinsurgency tactics in the southern border province of Choluteca, the suspected main supply route.[87] Since U.S. officials in El Salvador and Washington had conceded that such supplies had dwindled to a trickle[88] since the spring of 1983, many observers question precisely for what these elite battalions really will be used. The most widely held guess contends that they will be employed in increased joint operations with the Salvadoran armed forces against the FMLN insurgents, to join the contras in the event of war with the Sandinistas, and be deployed against the growing force of Honduran insurgents that several months before began guerrilla operations.

The same is true for the three other battalions whipped into shape by 1,800 U.S. Marines, who after holding at least one amphibious assault landing on the Caribbean coast—a maneuver difficult to justify as defensive in nature—pushed on to the nearby mountains to instruct their charges in unconventional warfare tactics. It appears that a glimpse of the nation's future was given by General Gorman's explanation that this training is designed "to combat guerrillas"[89]—especially since Honduras faces only low-level insurgent activity, a stage that the official U.S. Army Special Forces counterinsurgency scheme still calls for predominately police, not military, countermeasures. Even so, the combination of insurgency and the so-called exercises quickly blurred the lines between war games and real war, when in September, U.S. forces participated in a military operation by helicoptering Honduran troops to the Río Patuca area as part of the Honduran armed forces counterinsurgency campaign against the guerrillas.[90]

The Honduran and U.S. air forces air control exercises to plan tactical air strikes,[91] which used fighter bombers from the U.S. aircraft carrier,[92] as well as Big Pine II's extensive artillery training, present similar doubts about their ultimate purpose. Assuming that the Honduran armed forces, even under the distinguished leadership of General Alvarez, do not plan on unleashing air and land bombardment upon their own people, the question naturally arises as to where these skills are intended to be employed. The emphasis upon heavy artillery training raises yet another imponderable: since the Honduran army did not possess this equipment, the field artillery pieces and the enormously expensive ammunition to fire them was provided by the U.S. forces.[93] Given their penchant for forgetting to take along war materiel when they finally leave, the prediction is that the Honduran army may very well be the beneficiary of new artillery batteries that it could not possibly have afforded to purchase from its limited budget.

The idea that Big Pine II's objective merely amounted to building up the Honduran armed forces is actually only half the picture. As senior Reagan officials bluntly explained, the military operations were "designed to lay the ground work for the expanded American presence" in Central America.[94] To begin with, in the words of the commander of the Joint Task Force, Colonel Arnold Schlossberg, Big Pine II was "a marvelous opportunity for the practice and employment of American forces from the United States to another country."[95] But the Administration's plans are far more ambitious than the Colonel let on.

In late July 1983, a senior national security official boasted that "We have developed a program for a significant and long-lasting increase in the U.S. military presence in Central America," which included the building of new electronic surveillance posts and radar sites throughout the region,[96] in addition to the sophisticated radar station staffed by sixty technicians just south of Tegucigalpa that had been in operation since mid-June.[97] Washington's plans, moreover, call for the pre-positioning of large stockpiles of military supplies and equipment,[98] the modernization of a half dozen more airfields,[99] and perhaps most telling of all, the construction of a 150-million-dollar air and naval base on the Honduran Caribbean coast.[100] Within this context, Big Pine II's extensive construction program makes more sense. The roads, water supplies, port facilities, communication centers, hospital, and airports are not meant only to support these "routine maneuvers," but to lay the foundation for Fortress America.

POLARIZATION

The most tragic repercussion so far of Washington's overbearing policy toward Honduras is the rapid polarization of the body politic, forcing moderates to abandon their centrist positions and join the extremes on the right and left. Among the critics' fears is that their nation will be dragged into a regional war through the government's support of the contras, its military collaboration with the Salvadoran armed forces, and the transformation of Honduras into the forward base of illicit U.S. activities in Central America; all of which violate a number of international treaties to which both Honduras and the United States are signatories.

The Havana Convention on Civil Strife states that all contracting states bind themselves "to use all means at their disposal to prevent the inhabitants of their territory, nationals or aliens, from participating in, gathering elements, crossing the boundary or sailing from their territory for the purpose of starting or promoting civil strife."[101] The Charter of the Organization of American States stipulates that "no State or group of States has the right to intervene, directly or indirectly, for any reason whatever, in the internal or external affairs of any other State. The foregoing principle prohibits not only armed forces but also any other form of interference or attempted threat against the personality of the State or against its political, economic and cultural elements."[102] The Charter of the United Nations prohibits all members from using "the threat or use of force against the territorial integrity or political independence of any state, or in any manner inconsistent with the Purposes of the United Nations."[103] The Inter-American Treaty of Reciprocal Assistance states that the "High Contracting Parties formally condemn war and undertake in their international relations not to resort to the threat or the use of force in any manner inconsistent with the provisions of the Charter of the United Nations or of this Treaty."[104]

Since these treaties carry the force of law, there is little wonder that neither Honduras nor the United States has admitted to their role in assisting the contras or joint Honduran–Salvadoran military operations. Although the World Court lacks the power to enforce the provisions of these treaties, given the documented facts of multiple and continuing violations, what worries a growing number of Hondurans is that, should war break out with Nicaragua, the Sandinistas would not only emerge victorious, but in the court of international opinion they most likely would stand vindicated as well.

One measure of the growing polarization can be seen in the

208

THE MORASS

factionalization of the governing Liberal Party. For instance, in late 1982 a former Liberal Party presidential candidate, Modesto Rodas, Jr., publicly accused the United States of "pushing us into a war with Nicaragua." Echoing the concerns of many opposition leaders, Rodas went on to specify that "there are irresponsible elements in the armed forces that, by protecting Nicaraguan counterrevolutionary camps and by supporting the army of El Salvador in the fight against the guerrillas, have tried to do away with the Honduran doctrine of the internationalization of peace."[105] The peace doctrine to which the outspoken politician made reference was an early attempt to maintain Honduras's neutrality in the regional strife. First presented to the Organization of American States in March 1982, it called for the general disarmament of the Isthmus, although some analysts feel that it was also directed at the rapid militarization of Honduras itself.[106] Rodas's denunciation proved prophetic. It was precisely at this time that Honduras abandoned any further attempts at pursuing a peaceful foreign policy, taking a more belligerent stance in regional politics.[107] By mid-1983, one of the two factions within the Liberal Party—the Popular Liberal Alliance—openly denounced "the existence of Nicaraguan opposition camps," claiming that they endanger "the security of Honduras."[108]

Of even more immediate concern, although intricately tied to the government's militarism and the threat of war, are the effects on the nation of the U.S.–supported counterinsurgency policy. Most of the reform aspects, even though largely funded by Washington, have met with approval, as might be expected. During his January 1983 address to Congress on the occasion of his first year as president, Suazo Córdova emphasized these programs, especially the 11-million-dollar U.S. Agency for International Development–funded agrarian reform that has provided land titles to 4,000 peasant families. Furthermore, the president listed other achievements, including the building of 1,063 new schoolrooms and AID's 7-million-dollar housing project, along with advancements in health facilities and improvements in the nation's infrastructure.[109] Another project subsequently initiated with the assistance of a U.S. legal commission is the badly needed reform of the judicial system.[110] In his January speech, however, the president failed to mention the clamor over the improvements on the 100-mile road stretching from Tegucigalpa to the southern border province of Gracias a Díos. In past years, this controversial 7.5-million-dollar AID-financed operation has been the target of severe criticism because one obvious use to which it could be put is more easily supplying the contras. Even several conscientious AID officials strongly oppose its construction, since, in their opinion, it constitutes less a valid economic development project than, in their words, "a road for tanks."[111]

By far the most important factor polarizing Honduras is General Alvarez's energetic application of the repression component of counterinsurgency doctrine. Supported by his omnipotent Washington benefactors, Alvarez's increasingly autocratic ways alienated even some of the government's top officials. For example, after arranging for an arms-selling visit in December 1982 by Israel's former minister of defense, Ariel Sharon, Alvarez did not bother to inform the cabinet of the deal until just a few days before Sharon arrived,[112] far too late for them to have any say in the matter.

A more revealing example of the General's true position in the Honduran power structure can be seen in the arrangements to establish the U.S. Regional Military Training Center in Puerto Castilla. During a May 1983 trip to Washington, Alvarez signed the agreement establishing the base, without consulting the Honduran congress—which, under the Constitution, must approve the entrance of all foreign troops into Honduras.[113] Forced to take action by the clamor of opposition leaders, he worked out a unique face-saving solution.[114] Instead of asking the Honduran congress to ratify his unilateral decision, which would in effect confirm the legislature's authority over him as required by the constitution, Minister of Defense Alvarez openly ridiculed the democratic principle of subordinating the military to civilian authority by forcing the congress to vote that the 2,400 Salvadoran troops undergoing training at the base were in the country under the status of students rather than soldiers.[115]

Under the fanatical leadership of Alvarez, who attributes the country's problems to Communist agitation, Honduras is experiencing a drastic rise in repression and human rights violations.[116]

In support of the armed forces' crackdown, in April 1982 the Honduran congress rubber-stamped a harsh "anti-terrorist" law which prescribes severe penalties for those who commit "crimes against the security of the state."[117] Declaring a "preventive war" against subversion,[118] the army has taken to setting up frequent roadblocks and raking entire neighborhoods, allegedly in search of weapons and subversive literature. Furthermore, a nation-wide "civil defense" network was organized—the Committees of Civil Defense—patterned along the lines of the Salvadoran paramilitary organization, ORDEN.[119] Since mid-1982, a further development no longer made it necessary for Honduras to take a back seat to El Salvador and Guatemala in another area important to the military: At that time, its first death squad appeared, the Honduran Anti-Communist Movement, appropriately known by its Spanish acronym MACHO.[120]

Since Alvarez's ascendance to power, Honduras has also joined its brutal neighbors in practicing extrajudicial executions and disappearances. According to Ramón Custodio, the president of the Honduran Commission for the Defense of Human Rights, by early 1983 this fate had befallen at least eighty-one people. The local head of the Jesuits, Father José María Tejeira, places the figure at 100 victims.[121] Indeed, for the first time in the nation's history, clandestine cemeteries started sprouting up in the outskirts of Tegucigalpa and in the countryside.[122] While of dubious honor, in early 1983, for first time, Honduras made the United Nations' exclusive list, which includes only thirty-eight other members, of nations that "arbitrarily execute people."[123]

The armed insurgent movement, despite Alvarez's questionable claims that more than 2,000 Honduran terrorists and guerrillas received training in Nicaragua,[124] certainly is not strong enough to present any serious threat to the government. The rising level of repression, however, is helping to change that situation. In April 1983, several small guerrilla groups announced the formation of a new coalition, the National Unity Directorate of the Revolutionary Movement of Honduras.[125] Their ranks seem to be growing.

The major factor helping the insurgents, as a liberal Honduran politician complained, is that Alvarez "cannot distinguish the difference between legitimate dissent and subversion."[126] Along with the Catholic Church, students, and teachers, organized labor has been especially hard hit. Labor unions throughout the country denounce the murders and disappearances as an officially sponsored pattern to eliminate their leadership, particularly since so many unions of peasants and workers have expressed strong opposition to the conversion of their nation into Fortress America.[127] Demanding that the government put an end to its repressive policies, on May Day of 1983 more than 150,000 demonstrators took to the streets in Tegucigalpa and San Pedro Sula, the country's second largest city.[128]

By this time, however, little hope remained for reversing the polarization of the nation, a trend that already had driven many authentically democratic dissidents leftward to continue their organizing work underground or out of the country. Writing in the *New York Times,* Barbara Crossette vividly summed up the situation: "And so the tragic dance begins, with a restless left and a suspicious right locked in a tentative but potentially lethal two-step of fear and counterfear. When the music stops—or somebody blows up the band—each side may have fulfilled the other's worst prophecies."[129]

COSTA RICA

Even though coffee and bananas make up its major exports, in many impressive ways Costa Rica broke the traditional stereotype of the "banana republic." Since the enactment of the 1948 constitution that ended a particularly bloody civil war and abolished the army, this so-called Switzerland of Central America has prided itself as a model of democracy and social stability. Adopting a pacifist foreign policy of neutrality, during the past decades Costa Rica has not only stayed clear of any serious international problems, but by welcoming the exiles from the upheavals of its volatile neighbors, also has become the asylum capital of the turbulent region.

Guided by the humane policies of the Social Democrats, who first came to power immediately following the civil war, its record of social justice has been equally extraordinary. Placing a high value on education, Costa Ricans also developed a wide-ranging social security system, which it generously extends even to the newcomers who seek haven there. Including unemployment, welfare, and retirement benefits, it also provides the best health-care system of any Latin American country, as can be seen in the nation's low infant mortality and long life expectancy.*

*Although the official government statistics claim that 95 percent of the population is literate, a more realistic estimate of functional literacy would be closer to a still respectable 80 percent. Moreover, according to the *Encyclopedia of Developing Nations* (1982 edition), there are only 38 infant deaths per 1,000 live births, while life expectancy at birth is an astounding 70.3 years.

The reasons behind Costa Rica's admirable stability and social justice are not some mysterious trait of its people or extraordinary wealth. On the contrary, with no rich mineral deposits or native labor force to exploit, the misnamed Costa Rica—which means Rich Coast in Spanish—also presented other obstacles for the development of a traditional Latin American export economy. Since the country lacked an efficient infrastructure, the high cost of getting agricultural products to market made it unprofitable to establish plantations by importing slaves from Africa, as occurred in Brazil, with its rich coastal region and political importance to the Portuguese empire. Therefore, the system of large landholdings did not take root in Costa Rica, as reflected by the fact that today 75 percent of its farms are operated by their owners.[1] Consequently, neither did a landed elite class emerge to take control of society and its institutions. Without an oligarchy to align themselves with, the nation's military never became as powerful as in other Latin American countries, thus making it possible to abolish the army after the 1948 civil war. So Costa Rica, freed from an ambitious officer corps eager to jump into bed with a selfish oligarchy, escaped the classic Third World pitfalls, and was able to develop its uniquely humane society.

These qualities, together with liberal tax laws and the incredible natural beauty of its mountains and tropical beaches, have attracted an unusually large number of retirees from around the world, especially the United States. In fact, Costa Ricans have traditionally held an affinity for their neighbors to the north. As former president Daniel Oduber pointed out in a recent interview: "Costa Rica is basically a pro-Yankee country, perhaps the only one truly so in all of Latin America."[2]

Because of Costa Rica's pro–United States sentiments and its established credentials as an authentic democracy, in the past Washington has called upon it to lend legitimacy to its side of the East–West conflict. The most obvious example is the 1961 Declaration of San José (the nation's capital), that condemned Fidel Castro's growing ties with the Soviet Union and virtually isolated Cuba from the other members of the Organization of American States. But, while Costa Ricans may harbor deep sympathy for the United States, their own nationalism takes first place.

This helps to explain in part why San José cooperated in the late 1970s with the Sandinista-led coalition during their struggle against Anastasio Somoza Debayle. The special resentment toward the neighboring Nicaraguan dictatorship dates back to the early 1950s when Anastasio Somoza García, the father of the dictator that the Sandinistas finally defeated, backed an unsuccessful coup to overthrow their new democratic government. So when the tables turned decades later, and with the tacit approval of the Carter Administration, Costa Rica got its chance to repay the Somoza dynasty in kind. Breaking its policy of strict neutrality, San José not only let the rebels quietly use the northern province of Guanacaste as their principal base of military operations, it also permitted them to receive arms shipments from Venezuela, Cuba, and other countries. It even went so far, during the last stages of the war, as to allow the insurgents to openly use their territory as the supply route and launching pad for the final military offensives in 1979.[3]

The courtship between San José and Managua, however, did not initiate a lifetime of close relations, for the fast-moving events sweeping Central America shortly put an end to their affair. Within just a few years, the Managua government's drift to the left and San José's swing to the right, combined with the nation's devastating economic crisis and pressure from Washington, resulted in a 180-degree shift in relations with the Sandinistas.

BROUGHT INTO THE FOLD

Within Washington's regional scheme, the role designed for Costa Rica is to confer political legitimacy upon its counterrevolutionary crusade and provide a sanctuary for Edén Pastora's contra forces. Confronted by San José's reticence to join the flock, the Reagan Administration brought it into the fold by squeezing its vulnerable economic pressure point.

The magnitude of Costa Rica's economic crisis had already become apparent during the last years of President Roberto Carazo's government (1978–1982), when the world recession threw the nation into a now-familiar dilemma. The international market price of coffee, its chief export crop and foreign exchange earner, plummeted to an all-time low at the same time that oil import bills and interest rates on foreign loans rose sharply. Consequently, in the absence of investment financing, Costa Rica's gross domestic product fell from its already measly 1980 growth rate of 1.7 percent to a minus 3.6 percent the following year, only to continue its plunge to a disastrous minus 6 percent in 1982.[4] One result was that the 1979 foreign debt of 800 million dollars skyrocketed to about 3 billion dollars by the time Carazo left office in early 1982; and this on top of the private sector's foreign debt of another 1.2 billion dollars. For a small agricultural country of just 2.3 million inhabitants, the weight that this staggering burden represents can be seen in the facts that, after Israel, Costa Rica is saddled with the highest per capita foreign debt in the world,[5] with a 1981 GDP of only 3.3 billion as a base from which to pay it off.[6]

After twice appealing to the International Monetary Fund (IMF) for emergency loans and twice refusing to implement the harsh "austerity measures" that the powerful lending institution demanded as a condition for granting these funds, in September 1981 President Carazo declared a moratorium on the interest payments of Costa Rica's foreign debt.[7] The vehemence with which the international financial community reacted surprised most observers, to say nothing about the Costa Ricans who suddenly found themselves placed on the Third World debtor countries black list. One of the consequences of its inability to borrow abroad was the almost immediate devaluation of its currency, for the first time in 32 years. In terms of 1980 parity, the colón—which had remained stable between six and nine colónes to the dollar for the past decades—virtually collapsed. By the end of the year, it had devalued a full 400 percent,[8] touching off a run that devalued the colón by 700 percent by mid-1983.[9]

Confronted with the additional problem of a 1982 inflation rate of over 90 percent,[10] upon taking office in May 1982 the new president, Luís Alberto Monge, agreed to the IMF's severe conditions. The capitulation to international finance capital, at least in the short term, paid off. Once again Costa Rica began receiving hundreds of millions more in new loans.[11] In fact, the IMF issued a further 100-million-dollar contingency credit in the first days of 1983, at the same time that a consortium of 170-odd private banks announced that they were granting another 230 million dollars in other loans.[12]

Contingent upon Costa Rica's keeping its agreements with the IMF to cut back on government spending and subsidies on food, transportation, and other basics, the Reagan Administration earmarked lesser but still substantial amounts of assistance. On top of the 70 million dollars from the Caribbean Basin Initiative funds,[13] together with other assistance that Washington promised this vital ally, the total amount of bilateral U.S. aid for fiscal year 1982 was scheduled to exceed 123 million dollars, reaching an estimated 292 million dollars in FY 1983, and climbing further to a proposed 396 million dollars by FY 1984. (See Tables 6, 7, and 8, pages 234–238.)

In order to get the loans to pay off its 1982 foreign debt interest installments of 280 million dollars,[14] the government agreed to, and in large part succeeded in, imposing upon the country the cutbacks dictated by the IMF and Washington. Costa Rica's economic trauma serves to demonstrate another familiar pattern of the dependency of Third World nations upon the developed countries of the North Atlantic complex and Japan. Invariably, international economic assistance ends up not satisfying basic human requirements or raising the standard of living in these countries. Instead of permitting the debtor nations to declare a moratorium on repayments during these cyclical periods of uncontrollable crisis, the international financial system insists upon maintaining its own good health over the human needs of the already impoverished. In fact, the deeper in debt these nations fall, the better the private banks like it. Backed up by the awesome power of the multilateral lending institutions, the financiers have a greater opportunity to make even bigger guaranteed loans at the exorbitant interest rates that they dictate, and ultimately to reap millions more in profits. Of course there are limits. The international bankers' great fear is the formation of a debtor nations' cartel that en masse would announce a moratorium on repayments or, worse yet, default on their loans by declaring themselves bankrupt—a sound business procedure practiced throughout the developed countries.

But as yet, any such type of unified action still remains in the talking stage, and Costa Rica, like the rest of the Third World, remained vulnerable to the pressures applied by Washington and its allies in the international financial community. This was even more true when, in early 1982, President Monge capitulated to IMF demands, which many Costa Ricans saw as part of an overall betrayal of the Social Democratic values of the National Liberation Party, that historically advocated government spending for social programs, pro-labor legislation, participation of the state in the economy, protection of human and civil rights, and respect for ideological pluralism. Veering to the right, the new president broke his party's liberal tradition by enacting a stringent program of sharply cutting back on government subsidies for food and basic consumer goods, lending increasing support for the private sector of the economy while pursuing antilabor policies, and, most significantly, adopting strong law-and-order measures.[15] This surprising hard line touched off an uproar among the people that took the form of unprecedented numbers of mass demonstrations, the creation of popular organizations, and an increasing number of labor strikes, which the government responded to with unexpectedly severe repression.[16] Although still restrained by Latin American standards, the growing social unrest is interpreted by many concerned Costa Ricans as the beginning of a polarization process that could end up tearing the country apart.

Costa Rica had to pay yet another price for Washington's assistance in arranging the 1982 financial bailout. As something of a quid pro quo for this critical economic support, San José ideologically endorsed the Reagan Administration's East–West interpretation of the region's problems. Similar to its part in the isolation of Cuba in the early 1960s, Costa Rica played both host to and chief critic of Nicaragua's Marxist totalitarianism during the formation of two new U.S.–initiated regional organizations: the Central American Democratic Community, and the Forum for Peace and Democracy, commonly called the San José Forum.

The establishment in January 1982 of the Central American Democratic Community (CDC) turned out to be, despite its deceptive name, an attempt to launch a new regional military alliance, along the lines of the defunct CONDECA. In fact, because of its overbearing military objectives, the CDC became so discredited that Washington decided it was necessary to sponsor the formation of yet another organization. Through the October 1982 creation of the San José Forum, the Reagan Administration attempted to bring together the "democratic regimes" of the Caribbean basin in an effort to diplomatically and politically isolate Nicaragua. But it turned out to be little more than a paper organization because Mexico and Venezuela—the region's largest and most influential countries—refused to attend in an act of solidarity with the Sandinistas. Consequently, the participants consisted only of Costa Rica, El Salvador, Honduras, Panama, Belize, Colombia, Jamaica, the Dominican Republic—and of course, the United States.

The United States showed an extremely unusual interest in such a small nation, evidently holding high hopes for the role that Costa Rica would play in its regional policy. In the last six months of 1982, the presidents of these two countries held three highly publicized face-to-face meetings: in July and November, President Monge visited the White House; while in December, President Reagan decided to make San José the first stop on his Central American tour. One other detail adds further weight to the developing special relationship between the two nations. Monge helped break the ice of the region's glacial attitude toward the United States by being the first Latin American head of state to come to Washington during the post–Malvinas/Falkland Islands period of resentment caused by Reagan's support of England against Argentina during the war.

Linking the Sandinistas' ideology to the sudden rise of popular discontent and "terrorist" activity in Costa Rica, the new Monge government further played into the Reagan Administration's plans by casting the blame for its problems on revolutionary Nicaragua. The highlight of the anti-Sandinista campaign came in September 1982 when, aping the tactics of their benefactor, the government published an 87-page "white paper." Along with accusing Managua of exporting revolution to Costa Rica, the document presents in chronological order a long list of Nicaraguan border violations. While it does appear true that Sandinista troops have often crossed into Costa Rica in pursuit of contras, in general, Monge's white paper is hardly more credible than its many U.S. predecessors. Consistent with the government's new policies, the president welcomed back to Costa Rica Edén Pastora, who had been banned from returning to the country because of his contra activities, an act that violated the nation's traditional pacifist stance.[17]

Perhaps the most radical change instituted by the Monge government came in the buildup of the security forces, which have increasingly taken on the characteristics of regular armed forces. With a standing army constitutionally banned, Costa Rica's security requirements have been met by the 7,000 members of the Judicial Police, the Rural Guards, and, most important, the Civil Guards. Since December 1982, however, they have been supported by a new paramilitary force created under Monge's "New Security Policy."[18] The official explanation claims that the 10,000-man Organization for National Emergencies (OPEN), which consists exclusively of those of "proven democratic creed," is only a reserve militia. However, former Security Minister Juan Echéverria charges that OPEN is in reality a "paramilitary ideological organization."[19] Be that as it may, OPEN, which is trained and armed by the Ministry of Security, constitutes a new blemish on the countryside of pacifist Costa Rica.[20]

If OPEN altered the view of the landscape, then the enormous increases in U.S. security assistance have changed the picture entirely. In fiscal years 1980 and 1981, total security assistance to Costa Rica amounted to 202,000 dollars and 92,000 dollars respectively, almost all of which was accounted for by the routine purchase of small arms and ammunition for the Guards. By Costa Rican standards, the agreements that Reagan and Monge arrived at are nothing less than startling: For FY 1982, Washington provided 22.2 million dollars in security aid; while in FY 1983, the figure leapfrogged to an astounding 127.8 million dollars; and for FY 1984, the initially projected sum, which almost always gets raised, is 72.2 million dollars. (See Table 6, pages 234–236.)

Just as the first military assistance in 1980 to El Salvador was justified by labeling it "non-lethal" military materiel, Costa Rica's initial installments consist of such items as uniforms, communications equipment, river patrol boats, and helicopters.[21] But, again comparing the Salvadoran experience, such "non-lethal" war materiel is essential to counterinsurgency operations. The suspicion that there might be more behind the Reagan Administration's generosity than meets the eye is heightened by the content of the U.S. military training programs. During 1982, 4,000 members of the regular security forces received counterinsurgency training at U.S. facilities in Panama.[22] The 10,000 OPEN militiamen have also been trained in counterinsurgency tactics by in-country U.S. military advisers.[23] Furthermore, in late 1982, four more teams of Green Berets arrived in Costa Rica to conduct additional courses.[24]

Too much visible U.S. military involvement, however, could end up causing problems for both governments: The Reagan Administration already has enough trouble getting military aid appropriations through Congress, and the Monge government has come under growing criticism from some of Costa Rica's oldest democratic friends in Europe and Latin America because of Washington's embrace.[25] So they worked it out in the regular way. As of November 1982, the second month of the fiscal year 1983 enormous security aid package, five other countries had contracted to provide Costa Rica with military weapons, uniforms, vehicles, and training, as well as antiriot equipment and advisers.[26] The only hitch arose when it came, in the depths of the worst economic crisis in its history, to Costa Rica's paying the tens of millions of dollars for these military goods and services. However, since the lion's share of U.S. security assistance comes in the form of loans and grants that can be used to pay for military equipment and training, the problem was solved.

IN OVER ITS HEAD

For the sake of accuracy, it should be emphasized that Costa Rica is not another Honduras. While the Honduran Commander-in-Chief General Alvarez might, without fear of character assassination, be labeled an ambitious neo-fascist fanatic, President Monge is more of a naïve democratic opportunist. With Costa Rica's economy buffeted by world recession and breaking up under the costs of its welfare state, Monge thought he could ride out the storm by joining with the Reagan Administration's armada. But as the torment increased, he seemed to have second thoughts about committing his ship of state to the flotilla.

In 1982, Costa Rica's role consisted primarily of lending its good name to legitimize the U.S. antirevolutionary crusade in Central America. But by mid-1983, the situation had changed dramatically. By then, Pastora's ARDE contras numbered in the thousands, carrying out increasingly provocative attacks against Nicaragua—which included dropping bombs from light aircraft on Managua and the Pacific coast port of Corinto[27]—and Washington no longer bothered to hide its intention of overthrowing the Sandinistas. As the Honduras-based contras stepped up their incursions into Nicaragua, Costa Rica found itself serving as the military southern flank in the escalating war against the Managua government.

Certainly the feuding over the past two years within the exile community in San José, amounting to little more than a couple of kidnappings and a few assassination attempts, had proved embarrassing.[28] But with Pastora's April 1983 declaration of war against the Sandinistas, the situation began to get out of hand. Although everybody knew about the contra radio station and offices in San José, tensions with Nicaragua rose as Pastora's rebels openly bragged about their arms depots, fleets of trucks, boats, airplanes, and small factory for manufacturing military uniforms, which they maintained in Costa Rica. But of even greater concern, along the nation's northern border from whence the contras operate, violence began spreading among Costa Ricans themselves. In a number of villages, fighting between Costa Rican supporters and opponents of the contras resulted in closing schools, burning shops, and a half dozen political killings.[29] Clearly, all this was much more than San José had bargained for.

Evidently realizing that he was in over his head, Monge ordered a crackdown on rebel activities. Although previously making occasional gestures to control the contras, such as throwing a couple of Somocista troublemakers out of the country in May 1983, the government now made a forceful effort to maintain its neutrality.[30] In late August, authorities expelled as mercenaries seventeen Cuban-Americans who arrived to join Pastora's commandos, and in early September the minister of security, Angel Solano Calderón, arrested several dozen contras and seized their weapons and vehicles. Furthermore, on September 17, the Civil Guard captured a raiding party of eleven Sandinistas who had crossed into Costa Rica.[31]

However, Costa Rica had already been drawn too deeply into the dynamics of the Reagan Administration's plan for it to easily maintain its traditional neutrality. Needless to say, Washington was less than impressed with San José's evenhanded measures in sternly dealing with mercenaries and foreign soldiers in its territory: The disgruntled U.S. ambassador, Curtin Winsor, complained that Minister Solano was being "overzealous in interpreting President Monge's policy of neutrality."[32] Since in the understated language of diplomacy such a rebuke amounts to nothing less than a furious protest in normal life, it should come as no great surprise that Washington's emissary did not speak from a position of impotence. Although cloaked in a "conspiracy of silence" that limited public exposure, events soon began to give strong indications of the bitter division raging within the San José government over how to deal with the situation.

Never an ideological question, due to the ardent anti-Sandinista stance held by all parties, the infighting divided along pragmatic lines.[33] The "interventionist" factions—based in the ministries of the Interior and Exterior, as well as (of course) the U.S. Embassy—advocated that the overthrow of the Managua government could be accomplished in a "surgical" fashion, with the fighting contained exclusively in Nicaragua. On the other hand, the "neutralists"—led by President Monge and the Ministry of Public Security—feared that if Costa Rica became too closely identified with the contras, their country could not escape becoming a battleground in the inevitable regionalized conflagration.

The interventionists made the first move on September 28 when ARDE commandos devastated the Peñas Blancas Nicaraguan border station. Adamantly rejecting Managua's strong protest that the Costa Ricans had abandoned their own border post, thus giving the contras carte blanche to operate from their territory—and thereby incurring a serious violation of that nation's "strictly enforced" neutrality—San José countered with the charge that it was actually the Sandinistas who had attacked one of their frontier checkpoints.[34] By mid-October, however, unnamed high Costa Rican officials, evidently realizing that the contras did in fact commit the aggression, warned the ARDE leadership that the entire group would be expelled if proof was found of "armed military action against Nicaragua."[35] More than a month passed before Minister of Public Security Solano, confronted with overwhelming evidence, finally admitted the truth of the Nicaraguan allegations.[36] Even so, the government failed to carry out its threat to throw the rebels out of the country.

The neutralists did toughen their stance, resulting in the resignation of the Minister of the Exterior, Fernando Volio; and on November 17, 1983, President Monge gave a widely publicized address during which he reaffirmed Costa Rica's "perpetual neutrality."[37] This noble, if dubious, declaration, unfortunately, did not represent the end of the factionalism; just two days later, from their Costa Rican bases, ARDE launched its largest military offensive of the war with "Operation Blazing Tooth" that sent approximately 1,000 contras deep into Nicaraguan territory.[38] Playing his advantage to the hilt, at this same time Ambassador Winsor took the opportunity to declare that an invasion of Nicaragua "is not impossible," and went on to elaborate that "to achieve our objective, we must use persuasion as well as pressure. If this does not work, it is possible that we will have to do something more."[39]

Strong indications suggest that the Sandinistas were not the only objects of persuasion and pressure. The new Minister of the Exterior appointed by President Monge—none other than the nation's second vice-president, Fernando Arauz—made headlines several weeks later when on December 3 he surprised everyone by declaring his support of the hard line position toward Nicaragua.[40]

The following day, two further developments added to the suspicion that powerful behind-the-scene forces were in motion. Because of unexpectedly strong opposition—in the form of mass demonstrations, strikes by organized labor, and even congressional legislation—Monge's government technically had failed to impose all of the "austerity measures" demanded by the International Monetary Fund.[41] Consequently, it had been threatening to withhold the next installment of its loan. But on December 4, 1983, the IMF unexpectedly granted the financially strapped nation a "special dispensation," releasing the 20 million dollars and thereby giving Costa Rica another few months to meet the harsh requirements.[42] The other, perhaps related, development came on the same day, just after President Monge concluded a week-long visit to the United States. Dropping a not so subtle hint, Monge made his most pessimistic public appraisal of the region's future when he gloomily predicted that "the Vietnamization of Central America is not something impossible, on the contrary [it is] very probable. Up to a few days ago I still held great hope that the danger of war was diminishing. But now . . . I am afraid that I have been too optimistic."[43]

Since the Reagan Administration and the IMF dole out their assistance in periodic payments contingent upon the Costa Rican government fulfilling their conditions, the international economic ax hovers precariously over its neck. How these forces will ultimately play themselves out still remains to be seen, but for the time being President Monge and his neutralists are positioned somewhere between the fire and the bottom of the frying pan.

NINE

REFORMS VERSUS REPRESSION

The damning pronouncements leveled by liberal decisionmakers against the Reagan Administration's Central American policy have contributed as much confusion in the public's mind as the complex events themselves. Often it appears that these critics actually oppose counterinsurgency, but upon close examination it turns out this is not the case. More accurately, they object only to the manner in which Washington is applying counterinsurgency doctrine. This "loyal opposition" type of criticism amounts to no more than an intramural squabble among the U.S. governing elites as how best to implement what since the early 1960s has been a state policy.

Both liberals and conservatives view insurgency in the Third World primarily in the East–West terms of the capitalist–communist struggle, lumping together wars of national liberation under the rubric of opportunities for the Kremlin to replace U.S. friends with pro-Moscow puppets. While liberals are somewhat more sophisticated regarding the local causes of social unrest and the vital difference between socialism and communism, the bottom line is that neither faction is prepared to accept the establishment of another nationalistic socialist state in the hemisphere. In terms of policy, this translates into neither group permitting the people of these nations to determine their own destiny: If social change cannot be controlled, then it must be stopped; the way to stop it is counterinsurgency.

The center of the conflict between the liberals and the conservatives is not whether or not Washington should do everything in its power to defeat the Central American insurgents, rather, the dispute centers upon the technicalities of implementing counterinsurgency doctrine. More specifically, the basic disagreement lies in the emphasis that should be given to reform or repression within the overall scheme. While neither camp relies exclusively upon one or the other of these two major components of counterinsurgency doctrine, in general terms, liberals place priority upon reforms, attempting to employ repression more as a shield to hold off an insurgent military victory until the reforms have time to take effect and undermine the rebels' popular base. The conservatives, while paying lip service to the importance of reforms and even implementing them to some degree, tend to charge ahead with massive repression to plaster "the Communists and their dupes."

Charles Maechling, Jr., the staff director of the National Security Council's Special Group (Counterinsurgency) during the Kennedy and Johnson administrations (1961–1966), recently provided a fine example of this difference in emphasis upon reform or repression. Shortly after President Reagan's inauguration, he reasserted the liberal position on counterinsurgency in his article "Counterinsurgency, Yes—But with Controls," in which he counseled: "Properly applied, the counterinsurgency doctrine was, and is, a unitary one—aimed at helping nations that aspire to democracy to build effective and disciplined military and police forces within a framework of social justice and economic improvement. Far from being a blank check to worthless oligarchies, much less to dictator-lackeys posing as 'friends,' the counterinsurgency doctrine is predicated upon political and economic reform."[1]

Maechling's noble-sounding explanation of counterinsurgency doctrine, while helping to justify U.S. intervention in the affairs of the Third World nations, unfortunately has no basis in historical fact or current-day practices. Counterinsurgency simply has no record of ever working in this majestic fashion. A more current actor, Robert E. White, inadvertently clarified further the distinctions between the liberal and the conservative approaches to counterinsurgency in a revealing article of his own, which will be discussed further on.

First, though, it should be remembered that White was President Carter's outspoken ambassador to El Salvador from February 1980 until he was fired a year later, almost immediately after the Reagan Administration assumed office. Secretary of State Alexander Haig, derisively labeling the liberal diplomat a "social reformer," recalled him from his post in San Salvador and drove him out of the Foreign Service altogether. It is safe to say that Robert White ranked among the most experienced, respected, and progressive of all the U.S. envoys. In fact, his strongly reformist policies so inflamed the Salvadoran oligarchy that for the first time the right wing found cause to hold demonstrations in front of the U.S. Embassy. Once, they even surrounded the ambassador's residence for three days, making him a virtual prisoner in his own home, where he took to sleeping with a shotgun under the bed. Finally, losing patience, he broke through the armed demonstrators in a caravan of armored cars, further protected by battle-ready U.S. Marine guards, and returned to his duties at the Embassy compound. After he was canned by the Reagan Administration, the Salvadoran extreme right literally fired their guns in celebration, and the former ambassador opened up with a verbal barrage of his own, emerging as the most articulate high-level critic of Washington's Central American policy.

Despite obligatory public rhetoric, every nation's foreign policy, not just that of the United States or the Soviet Union, is based upon what the nation's leaders perceive to be the country's material well-being—primarily economic considerations and security interests—and not upon higher ethical principles, such as a people's right to self-determination or the nonintervention of a more powerful nation into the internal affairs of a weaker one. In keeping with these realities of the diplomatic game, White persistently denounces the Reagan Administration's pursuit of a military solution to the civil strife in Central America, but he does so not on moral grounds, but upon the premise that such a policy is impractical and even counterproductive.

For example, in his 1982 *New York Times Magazine* cover story, he opposes "raking operations" by the security forces in El Salvador not because they invariably leave a wake of innocent dead in their trail, but because "each time the Salvadoran military invades a poor neighborhood in San Salvador with United

States–furnished weapons, hundreds of recruits and sympathizers are incorporated into the revolutionary movement."[2] As for actually defeating the insurgents, he pragmatically points out that "military assistance plus covert action will not do it. Vietnam-style use of American combat troops would seem to be ruled out by national consensus." Addressing the Reagan Administration's interventionist policy, he does not argue for nonintervention, rather he disagrees on the basis that Washington's approach is "a textbook case of boldness, ignorance, and ideological certitude combining to weaken the region's defenses against Communist penetration." In an even more recent article, White restated this same concept in a more literary fashion when he counseled that "As we examine our actions in Central America, we should recall Florence Nightingale's words: 'The first responsibility of a hospital is not to spread disease.'"[3]

Judging from certain statements that he constantly expounds, including the following ones from his 1982 article, one would think that former Ambassador White gained a firm understanding of many Third World dynamics. He accurately identifies that "it is not Russia, Cuba or Nicaragua, that make the revolutions of Central America—it is injustice, brutality and hunger." And in an apparently even more enlightened vein: "It is racist nonsense to assert that the people of Central America are not capable of democracy. . . . What they are not capable of is achieving democracy if the United States gives its support to military domination of their society." One could think that these insightful concepts came from the mouth of a Latin American revolutionary, rather than a skillful infighter trying to save the United States from, in his opinion, following a misguided foreign policy.

The illusion that White grasps the matrix of social change in the Third World is shattered by the central theme of this article, where he contends that "President Reagan is right to concern himself with denying Communism a new foothold in the Western Hemisphere. He is wrong only in his methods." Put in other words, reform, not repression, should be the principal weapon of Washington's East–West confrontation in Central America. To support this thesis, and his policies as ambassador to El Salvador, he extols the progress made under his reform-oriented policy.

By the end of 1980, he claims, his liberal program of implementing reforms, particularly the agrarian reform conducted under the direction of Roy Prosterman (whom the Ambassador considers a "genius"[4]) already showed results. Again pragmatism rather than human values dominates his justification of reforms, in which category he even places the human rights component of the Carter Administration's foreign policy. It was "precisely because of our emphasis on human rights and the reconciliation of the Salvadoran family," he writes, "that popular support for the Government had increased over the previous year and the revolutionary threat had thereby diminished."[5] Understandably, if not in total candor, White neglects to mention the millions of dollars in "non-lethal" military assistance provided during this same period and the many millions more in weaponry sent during the final days of President Carter's tenure in office.

As if to dispel any remaining doubt that U.S. liberal policymakers might somehow have escaped superpower arrogance, White paternalistically pontificates that "those who argue that the people of Latin America should be allowed to have their revolutions without any involvement on our part misunderstand both the nature of power and the struggle between democracy and Communism. If we do not do what we can to achieve our objectives in Latin America, others will fill the vacuum and the outcome will be bad for the United States and bad for the people of the area." Of course this is no more true than the old self-serving cliché that "what is good for General Motors is good for America." Making the false assumption that what is good for the United States is also good for the people of Latin America, he moves on to even greater heights of haughtiness, by claiming that the United States has the right to intervene in order to impose its version of what is "good for the people of Latin America," and to wrap it all up, the only real question that remains, as the liberal diplomat concludes, "is not whether to involve ourselves in the affairs of our Central American neighbors, but the form and substance of that involvement." Translated from the diplomatic-ese into everyday language, the point of contention is not whether the United States should intervene, but the best way for it to carry out its interventionist policy.

Conservatives also suffer from more than their share of superpower arrogance. In a speech delivered several months after the Reagan Administration took power, then Assistant Secretary of State for Security Assistance, James L. Buckley, felt obliged to take head-on the often-reiterated accusation that the United States is an "imperial power." Citing the neo-conservative ideologue Irving Kristol, Buckley asserted that "Americans have never sought the responsibilities of world leadership," and then went on to give what might be described as a modern-day version of the "white man's burden":

There are a great many people who appear to think that a great power is only the magnification of a small power, and the principles governing the actions of the latter are simply transferrable, perhaps with some modification, to the former. In fact, there is a qualitative difference between the two conditions, and the difference can be summed up as follows: A great power is 'imperial' because what it does *not* do is just as significant, and just as consequential, as what it does. Which is to say, a great power does not have the range of freedom of action derived from the freedom of inaction that a small power possesses. It is entangled in a web of responsibilities from which there is no hope of escape, and its policy makers are doomed to a strenuous and unquiet life.[6]

Although phrased in stronger terms, Buckley's conservative concept of U.S. foreign policy ends up being basically the same as White's liberal explanation of "the nature of power and the struggle between democracy and Communism." Both "extremes" of Washington's political spectrum not only agree that the United States has the right to impose its will. They further insist that it is actually obliged to do so.

There do exist, however, some esoteric differences, as Buckley went to lengths to clarify in the same speech. "I know that conservatives are often accused of being simplistic: and as a self-confessed, card-carrying member of that fraternity, I might as well confess that I harbor the simplistic notion that on the world's stage today it is possible to divide the principal actors between the good guys and the bad guys: and we might as well understand that the bad guys are serious and playing for keeps." The Under Secretary ended his address in almost spiritual terms, when with a straight face, he announced: "We *are* the last best hope on Earth: and we have no responsible choice but to act accordingly."[7]

As detailed in the following chapter, the Reagan Administration's pursuit of a military solution to the turmoil in Central America reflects the manner by which it has chosen to carry the heavy burdens that it evidently feels history has unkindly thrust upon it. In a 1982 policy address, then Assistant Secretary of State for Inter-American Affairs, Thomas O. Enders, rather ingeniously put forth Washington's position when he explained that "we could not and will not stand idly by and watch, in El Salvador or elsewhere, internationally recognized governments—undertaking reforms we support—having to throw untrained recruits short of ammunition into battle against Cuban-trained guerrillas supplied and coordinated from abroad."[8]

Other than reforms receiving more attention than repression in the application of counterinsurgency doctrine in Central America, had Jimmy Carter defeated Ronald Reagan in 1980, it is doubtful that U.S. policy would be very much different today. As long as Washington continues to formulate its foreign policy with the arrogance of an uncompromising superpower, it matters very little whether a Republican or a Democrat sits in the White House.

TEN

IT DEPENDS ON THE WAY YOU COUNT

Reiterating a claim often made by his Administration officials, President Reagan, in his April 1983 address to the joint session of Congress, bragged that: "Seventy-seven cents out of every dollar we will spend in the area this year goes for food, fertilizers, and other essentials for economic growth and development."[1] To arrive at this relatively benign statistic the President took full advantage of the complex structure of the multiple foreign-aid programs that permits calculating what goes where on the way you count.

Evidently the 77 percent figure came out of the most advantageous manner of playing with the data. After subtracting the three obvious categories of military aid from the total U.S. aid package officially designated for Central America, he simply counted the remainder as developmental or economic assistance.* Although convenient for minimizing the amounts of mili-

---

*The three programs that clearly fall under the category of military aid are: (1) the Military Assistance Program (MAP), which provides direct grants to foreign countries for military equipment, facilities, technical assistance, repair, and rehabilitation of equipment, and supply operations and administrative support; (2) the International Military and Training program (IMET), which provides grants for the training of foreign military personnel; and (3) the Foreign Military Sales program (FMS), which provides financing in the form of credits and loan repayment guarantees to foreign governments for the purchase of defense articles, services, and training. Since all components of the United States Foreign Assistance Program are in constant flux because of reprogramming, supplemental funding requests, and presidential discretionary "draw down" monies, the exact figures that were employed to arrive at the 77 percent statistic are extremely difficult, if not impossible, to determine.

tary aid while maximizing the sums of so-called economic assistance to the region, this simplistic fashion of tallying up the count is extremely misleading to the press and the public.[2]

At least three other categories of the Foreign Assistance Act should be considered as military or security aid (see Tables 6 and 8). Two of these regulate the commercial exports of everything legally classified as "defense items and services,"[3] while the deceptively named Economic Support Fund (ESF) is even officially classified by the government as security assistance.[4] While the ESF provides cash in the form of grants and concessionary loans to foreign countries for such purposes as the purchase of necessary imports and to help meet their balance-of-payments deficits, the reason that it falls under the Security Assistance Program becomes obvious. ESF funds are provided upon the security considerations of the recipient nation and are used, for example, to purchase military equipment or to pay for military training programs.

The way it works is that Washington gives millions of dollars to its Central American friends, publicly calling it economic support; then these "friends" turn around and buy war materiel or hire military instructors, such as the case of Honduras's purchase of weapons from Israel, or Costa Rica's contracting with third-party nations to sell them military goods and services. It is the old story of the difference between facts and truth. It is factual that the ESF program provides cash and not military aid; therefore, it technically can be labeled economic aid. The other fact not mentioned, which is that this money is used for military and security purposes, makes the truth of the situation an entirely different story.

So, when calculated in the more honest way of only counting as economic aid the categories that the government itself classifies as economic assistance,* President Reagan's 77 percent for fiscal year 1983 turns out to be more than a little off the mark. Of all goods, services, and loans provided by the United States

---

*Economic Assistance Program consists of three categories for Central America: the Peace Corps; P.L. 480 (Food for Peace); and Developmental Assistance (the Agency for International Development), which accounts for nearly all of U.S. economic assistance to the region.

TABLE 6. U.S. SECURITY AID PROGRAMS TO CENTRAL AMERICA, 1950–1984 (Thousands of Dollars)

	1950–1979	1980	1981	1982	Estimated 1983	Proposed 1984*
Military Assistance Program (MAP)						
Costa Rica	930	—	—	2,000	2,500[a]	2,000
El Salvador	4,322	8	25,000[b]	63,500[b]	33,500[c]	55,000
Guatemala	16,250	—	—	—	—	—
Honduras	5,615	11	—	11,000	27,500[d]	40,000
Nicaragua	7,633	—	—	—	—	—
Panama	4,492	2	—	—	—	—
Total	39,242	21	25,000	76,500	63,500	97,000
International Military Education and Training Program (IMET)						
Costa Rica	901	—	35	58	125	150
El Salvador	5,843	247	492	2,002	1,300	1,300
Guatemala	7,495	—	—	—	200	250
Honduras	8,469	441	535	1,275	800	1,000
Nicaragua	11,601	—	—	—	—	—
Panama	4,772	289	378	401	450	500
Total	39,081	977	1,440	3,736	2,875	3,200
Foreign Military Sales Financing Program (FMS)						
Costa Rica	5,000	—	—	—	—	—
El Salvador	3,373	5,700	10,000	16,500	46,800[c]	30,000
Guatemala	10,718	—	—	—	—	10,000[e]
Honduras	12,500	3,530	8,400	19,000	10,000	—
Nicaragua	8,000	—	—	—	—	—
Panama	3,500	—	—	5,000	5,000	5,000
Total	43,091	9,230	18,400	40,500	61,800	35,000

Foreign Military and Construction Sales Agreements Program (FMSA)

Costa Rica	1,480	—	—	—	—	125,000
El Salvador	3,375	2,517	13,917	19,000	60,000	10,000
Guatemala	31,988	11	5	—	2,000	50,000
Honduras	9,659	5,045	4,332	9,388	15,000	—
Nicaragua	5,302	1	100	—	—	5,000
Panama	5,125	277	410	478	5,000	—
Total	56,929	7,851	18,764	28,866	82,000	190,000

Commercial Exports Licensed Under Arms Export Control Act—Export (AECA)

Costa Rica	968	202	57	150	150	75
El Salvador	2,013	207	17	300	200	200
Guatemala	4,674	417	7	750	100	100
Honduras	3,986	666	923	500	500	3,000
Nicaragua	4,243	—	750	50	—	—
Panama	9,384	29,241	752	1,000	1,000	1,500
Total	25,268	30,733	2,506	2,750	1,950	4,875

*The figures for fiscal year 1984 are the originally requested figures. In the majority of cases they have later been increased.

a Includes $1.5 million in reprogrammed funds.

b Includes funds allocated under Section 502(a), executive draw down authorization monies that do not require the approval of Congress.

c Includes $55.3 million in reprogrammed and supplemental funds.

d Includes $17 million in reprogrammed and supplemental funds.

e Congress rejected this funding request, and therefore it is not included in the total figures.

f Includes $58,875 of the supplemental aid to Central America funds left over from fiscal year 1980.

g These figures do not include Economic Support Funds.

Sources: U.S. Department of Defense Security Assistance Agency, Foreign Military Sales, Foreign Military Construction Sales and Military Assistance Facts, Washington, D.C., September 1981; U.S. Department of State, Congressional Presentation, Security Assistance Programs: fiscal years 1981–1984, Washington, D.C.; Cynthia Arnson, "Background Information on Honduras and El Salvador and U.S. Military Assistance to Central America," Update #8, Institute for Policy Studies, Washington, D.C., March 1983; The New York Times, August 10, 1983.

Continued

TABLE 6. U.S. SECURITY AID PROGRAMS TO CENTRAL AMERICA, 1950–1984 (Thousands of Dollars) (*Continued*)

	1950–1979	1980	1981	1982	Estimated 1983	Proposed 1984*
Economic Support Fund (ESF)						
Costa Rica	—	—	—	20,000	125,000	70,000
El Salvador	—	9,100	44,900	115,000	140,000	120,000
Guatemala	—	—	—	—	26,350	40,000
Honduras	—	—	—	36,800	15,000	40,000
Nicaragua	—	1,125	66,375[f]	—	—	—
Panama	—	—	—	—	—	—
Total	—	10,225	111,275	171,800	306,350	270,000
Subtotal U.S. Security Aid						
Costa Rica	9,279[g]	202	92	22,208	127,775	72,225
El Salvador	18,926[g]	17,779	94,326	216,302	281,800	331,500
Guatemala	71,125[g]	428	12	750	28,650	50,350
Honduras	40,229[g]	9,693	14,190	77,963	68,800	134,000
Nicaragua	36,779[g]	1,126	67,225	50	—	—
Panama	27,273[g]	29,809	1,540	6,879	11,450	12,000
Subtotal	203,611[g]	59,037	177,385	324,152	518,475	600,075

Total U.S. Security Aid, 1950–1984

Costa Rica	231,781
El Salvador	960,633
Guatemala	151,315
Honduras	344,875
Nicaragua	105,180
Panama	88,951
Grand total	1,882,735

TABLE 7. U.S. ECONOMIC AID TO CENTRAL AMERICA, 1980–1984*
(Thousands of Dollars)

	Economic Assistance Program (EAP)					
	1980	1981	1982	Estimated 1983	Proposed 1984†	Total
Costa Rica	15,098	15,035	31,639	40,615	36,198	138,585
El Salvador	49,942	59,069	71,084	87,100‡	75,478	342,673
Guatemala	13,291	18,735	15,188	19,673	26,556	93,443
Honduras	52,627	38,548	43,879	45,561	46,182	226,797
Nicaragua	35,975	14,814	—	—	—	50,789
Panama	2,104	10,489	13,044	11,316	11,932	48,885
Total	169,037	156,690	174,834	204,265	196,346	901,172

*These figures include Developmental Assistance (Agency for International Development), Peace Corps, and P. L. 480 (Food for Peace).

†The figures for fiscal year 1984 are the originally projected figures. Following the pattern of previous years in the vast majority of cases it can be expected that they will be increased.

‡These figures include supplemental and reprogrammed funds in addition to the initial fiscal year 1983 requests.

Source: *U.S. Department of State, Congressional Presentation, Security Assistance Programs, fiscal years 1981–1984,* Washington, D.C.

TABLE 8. TOTAL U.S. SECURITY AND ECONOMIC AID TO CENTRAL AMERICA, 1980–1984
(Thousands of Dollars)

	1980	1981	1982	1983	1984*	Total
MAP	21	25,003	76,500	63,500	97,000	262,024
IMET	977	1,440	3,736	2,875	3,200	12,228
FMS	9,230	18,400	40,500	61,800	35,000	164,930
FMSA	7,851	18,764	28,866	82,000	190,000	327,481
AECA	30,733	2,506	2,750	1,950	4,875	42,814
ESF	10,225	111,275	171,800	306,350	270,000	869,650
Security total	59,037	177,388	324,152	518,475	600,075	1,679,127
EAP	169,037	156,690	174,834	204,265	196,346	901,172
Economic total	169,037	156,690	174,834	204,265	196,346	901,172
Total	228,074	334,078	498,986	722,740	796,421	2,580,299

*The figures for fiscal year 1984 are the originally projected figures. Following the pattern of previous years, in the vast majority of cases it can be expected that they will be increased.

Source: U.S. Department of State Congressional Presentation, Security Assistance Programs: fiscal years 1981, 1982, 1983, 1984, Washington, D.C.

Foreign Assistance Program for Central America that year, only 28.3 percent comprised economic aid, while the remaining 71.7 percent should properly be identified as security aid.*

An insight into the liberals' charges against the Reagan Administration's militaristic policy toward Central America is found in the spending trends revealed by the government's own statistics on foreign aid to the region. For fiscal year 1980 the Carter Administration spent a total of 228 million dollars, with economic aid accounting for 74.1 percent while security assistance amounted to the other 25.9 percent. In FY 1981, when the new Administration could partially determine the level and proportioning of Washington's program, the total rose to 334.1 million dollars and economic assistance dropped to less than half (46.9 percent) while security aid climbed proportionately (53.1 percent). In FY 1982, the first year that the Reagan Administration formulated the foreign assistance requests for Central America, the total jumped to almost half a billion dollars (499 million dollars), and the economic component continued its downward trend to 35 percent, while 65 percent was accounted for by the security component. Reflecting the U.S.–financed military build-up throughout the Isthmus, by FY 1983 the total leaped to 722.8 million dollars, with the portion of economic aid falling to 28.3 percent, while security assistance continued to climb to 71.7 percent. For FY 1984 the trend continues: higher total expenditures of 796.4 million dollars with proportionately smaller economic-aid allocations dipping to less than a quarter (24.6 percent), and a larger percentage of security assistance—more than three quarters (75.4 percent). It should be mentioned, moreover, that the figures for FY 1984 are only projected sums and likely will increase in favor of the security assistance part, as they have done consistently for the past four years. A glance at these statistics places in relief the priorities of the two administrations: In FY 1980 the Carter Administration allocated only about one fourth of total assistance for security purposes and three fourths in economic aid; by FY 1984, the Reagan Administration, while more than tripling the total amount, had reversed its distribution,

*The following statistics have been calculated on the data contained in Tables 6–8.

channeling three fourths into security assistance and only one fourth for economic aid (see Fig. 2).

In reality, the percentages are even more heavily weighted on the side of security because the above calculations do not take into account the extra hundreds of millions of dollars in military aid being slipped in through the Joint Chiefs of Staff's "maneuvers" accounts, or the tens of millions spent on CIA operations. Actually, it would not be unfair to add to the security assistance figures the money "we will spend in the area" for the two naval battle groups (which according to a member of the Senate Intelligence Committee, who asked to remain unidentified, costs much more than a million dollars a day each), as well as the Defense Intelligence Agency's spy plane over-flights of Central America from Howard Air Force Base in Panama and even the cost of the National Security Agency's satellite surveillance, which has produced invaluable intelligence data.

These billions of dollars in security assistance that Washington has pumped into Central America, moreover, still only partially reflect the financing of the Reagan Administration's counterrevolutionary and counterinsurgency policy. To begin with, some of the U.S. security assistance comes in the form of loans, which, although granted at concessionary terms, must be repaid. Of course, this raises the region's foreign debt. So, in step the private bank consortiums and the multilateral lending institutions—primarily the International Monetary Fund, the World Bank, and the Inter-American Development Bank—bail out Washington's friends. But not all of this international financing goes for balance-of-payments support; an even larger share of it gets used up in the indirect costs of carrying out the militarization of the region, largely in the expenses of national infrastructure building programs, such as communication facilities, roads, bridges, airfields, and port installations—all of which are essential for efficiently moving about troops and military supplies.

During the Vietnam era, the strengthening of the client state's infrastructure was explicitly considered part of the overall counterinsurgency doctrine. Today, like so many other key words and phrases, "infrastructure" is out of vogue because of its association with Washington's intervention in Southeast Asia. Even so,

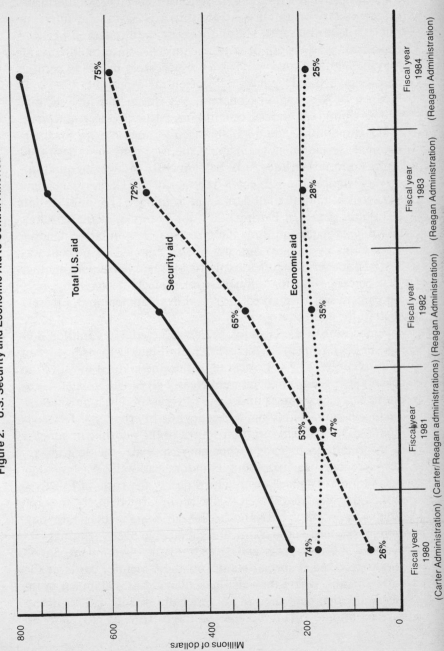

Figure 2. U.S. Security and Economic Aid to Central America

its critical function as the foundation of effective counterinsurgency military operations and for direct U.S. military intervention remains the same. As one Reagan Administration official explained, the purpose of national infrastructure building is so that the United States will "have the necessary means to become heavily involved if we have to" in Central America.[5]

Much of Washington's bilateral aid, from both the security and economic categories, goes into infrastructure programs, such as the Honduran "tank road" financed through Agency for International Development grants, and the replacement of destroyed bridges and power lines in El Salvador. By influencing multilateral assistance, the Reagan Administration is able to channel hundreds of million of dollars more to finance U.S. intervention in Central America. During 1983, for example, of the 964 million dollars requested from the three major multilateral lending institutions by the governments of the region, 20.7 percent was destined for servicing their exploding foreign debts, and another 30.4 percent went for infrastructure projects. Conversely, only 8.8 percent was earmarked for social development and a mere 7 percent for education.[6]

By focusing on El Salvador, which received 416.4 million dollars, or 43.2 percent of these 1983 multilateral loans,[7] an even more accurate view is presented of the fine-grained mesh of the counterinsurgency financial web. Nearly all of U.S. bilateral economic assistance comes under the category of developmental assistance, administered by the Agency for International Development (AID), which in turn funds most of the reform components of the counterinsurgency campaign—especially the agrarian reform program, as it does in Honduras as well. Washington's "economic assistance" even helped defray the costs of El Salvador's widely heralded March 1982 elections. Incidentally, the U.S. took extraordinary measures to insure a high voter turn out, thereby supporting the claim that the people overwhelmingly repudiated the insurgents and supported the government. Salvadorans received a special stamp on their identity cards at the voting booths, where they also had their thumbs stamped in invisible ink that only showed up under ultrared light. This procedure intimidated many because failing to vote, as proven by an unstamped identity card or thumb, was sufficient evidence of subversion and punished accordingly. Given the circumstances, it is safe to say that these "free elections" were tainted both figuratively and literally by the invisible ink—which was so generously paid for and supplied by the CIA.

Through the various AID projects, the Reagan Administration's so-called economic aid not only directly contributes to the counterinsurgency effort, it is also employed to prop up the wartorn Salvadoran economy. Because of the insurgents' economic sabotage campaign, Washington's economic assistance helps supply the government with extra funds to cover the extraordinary indirect costs of the war, including widespread damage to the nation's infrastructure and productive plant, as well as lost production and the lack of capital because many of the wealthy have transferred their funds abroad for safekeeping. Indeed, the Reagan Administration openly, if quietly, concedes the military importance of keeping the Salvadoran economy afloat. In its fiscal year 1983 presentation to Congress for foreign assistance to El Salvador, the Administration justified its requests for economic aid in unequivocal terms: "To support the Salvadoran economy is an essential element of the United States policy, not only as an economic objective, but as a military objective as well."[8]

In fact, military, security, and economic assistance given to a country in a counterinsurgency and/or counterrevolutionary context really boils down to the same thing. Since within this framework, regardless of its official title, all aid functionally serves the purpose of supporting the war effort, these distinctions end up being a false issue.

This very point was blandly made during a January 1983 interview with a high-level U.S. diplomat in San Salvador, who asked to remain unidentified. When asked if he would agree that "all aid, be it economic or military, is counterinsurgency aid in a civil war situation," he candidly replied: "Economic resources are almost by definition fudgeable. We would not have to give them a nickel's military aid if we gave them enough economic aid. Because the Israelis, South Africans, Argentines, and Brazilians would keep them in all the arms that they need to run the war. One of the great sillinesses in the U.S. is talking about big distinctions in economic and military aid. . . . You know, money buys guns."[9]

A more accurate appraisal of the means by which economic assistance serves as counterinsurgency aid is not as mechanical as the fact that "money buys guns." A top-ranking U.S. military adviser, who also requested to remain anonymous, was closer to the truth when he answered the same question: "Well, if you mean that . . . whatever kind of aid comes into Salvador is ultimately to keep Salvador from losing the war, what is wrong with that?"[10]

ELEVEN

RATIONALIZING WASHINGTON'S POLICY

Similar to President Kennedy's obsession with insurgencies and revolutions twenty years ago, President Reagan's ideological commitments lead him to devote a disproportionate amount of foreign policy effort and resources to attempting to deal with the crisis in Central America. In large part, this preoccupation stems from the Administration's perception of the region's geopolitical significance, which, of course, is gauged through the prism of the East–West conflict. For example, had Nicaragua's nationalistic, nonaligned and socialist revolution taken place in another geographical location that placed it in a different political context, instead of attempting to overthrow the Sandinistas, Washington likely would be offering them its support, as it does with Yugoslavia. Likewise, if El Salvador's civil war broke out in Afghanistan, no doubt the Administration would be doing all that it could to promote insurgency, with the rebels receiving arms and training instead of the government. However, since the revolutionary movements are sweeping not the Soviet Union's backyard, but the United States' traditional Central American sphere of influence, the story is completely different. By defining these historic changes within the Cold War priorities of global competition with the Soviets, Washington subordinates their intrinsic content to a point of almost total irrelevance, as if these nations amounted to nothing more than chips in the superpower game with no legitimate rights or interests of their own.

Once this arrogant perspective is accepted, an internal logic takes over to rationalize protecting U.S. hegemony at whatever cost to its unfortunate protectorates. During a November 1982 speech before the General Assembly of the Organization of American States, Secretary of State George P. Shultz went a long way in explaining the double standard of this operational principle. Attempting to repair the damage to Washington's primacy in the Inter-American system caused by its support of England during the Malvinas/Falkland Islands conflict, Shultz declared that when the United States is confronted with crisis in the hemisphere, it will react with "good intentions, urging negotiations, offering good offices." The Secretary quickly clarified, however, that such political solutions for dealing with crises do not apply to Central America because "most states in this area are challenged by insurgency." Continuing by expounding upon the necessity to defer "democracy, human rights, [and] socioeconomic equity" there, he went on to justify the Administration's military rather than political solution to the social turmoil in the region with the standard superpower logic that "U.S. security assistance programs for El Salvador and for our other threatened friends . . . stem from the basic consideration that peace requires strength."[1]

As utilized in superpower propaganda, such concepts as "peace" conveniently become extremely relative and open to a wide range of distorted interpretations. Imagine, for instance, a situation in which Washington sends security assistance to the puppet Afghan government to help the Soviets crush the insurgents and bring an end to the fighting. Although apparently ridiculous, in absolute terms it is hardly more bizarre than selling arms to China, a major point of discussion during Secretary of Defense Caspar Weinberger's September 1983 visit with that nation's Communist leadership. From the Administration's point of view, of course, "peace" is only acceptable within the context of "what is good for America." Or to paraphrase a U.S. general in Vietnam after a Viet Cong–held town had been leveled: "We had to destroy it in order to save it." So the last link in the self-serving chain of internal logic ends up in the contradictory position that if peace cannot be imposed in terms favorable to the

United States, then even intensified warfare becomes the only rational course of action.

But times have changed since the days when Washington could, without inhibitions, impose its will through direct military intervention. The more critical international attitude and the post-Vietnam domestic anti-interventionist consensus in the body politic require that the Reagan Administration seek more indirect means of exercising power. Consequently, U.S. intervention in Central America now employs the Vietnamization strategy of mobilizing regional client states to do the dirty work. Given the long record of direct military intervention and the current course of events, sending in the Marines is a very real eventuality—especially in light of the predilection shown by Reagan's invasion of Grenada and the development of new "rapid reaction" military strategies, facilities, and units developed over the past few years to implement them.

For the immediate future, however, it seems that the United States has opted for a long-range commitment to prop up its regional troupe of proxies through ever-increasing infusions of security and "economic" assistance, in their common objective of eliminating insurgent movement and strangling Nicaragua's revolution. In a fall 1982 policy speech before the Inter-American Press Association, then Assistant Secretary of State for Inter-American Affairs, Thomas O. Enders, clearly enunciated the reasons and scope of this strategy: "In the past, the United States has generally neglected Central America only to send in troops when things got out of hand. U.S. troops are no solution now. What can help is a dependable U.S. commitment. The United States will help its friends in the area defend themselves from violent minorities within—and hostile neighbors from without—and as long as it is necessary."[2]

After evaluating the effects of the devastating 1982–1983 Salvadoran insurgent offensive, by the spring of 1983 the "pragmatic" Enders tried to get into step with the increasing influence of the Reaganite ideologues. In congressional testimony supporting President Reagan's requests for emergency grants to El Salvador, he raised the specter of falling dominoes.

Major national interests of the U.S. are at stake. In El Salvador, if we allow a government that is reforming itself . . . to be knocked off by guerrillas who don't have the people with them, then no government in the Isthmus will be safe. Nicaragua's Cuban and Soviet-supported 'revolution without frontiers' would spread. It would head south across Costa Rica, which has no Army toward the [Panama] Canal. It would head north putting enormous pressure on Honduras and reviving the guerrilla war in Guatemala and move toward the Mexican border. So the struggle would go on, but on battlefields where the stakes would be much higher.[3]

But the ideologues in the Administration were more than a full stride ahead. Already in the fall of 1982, President Reagan's newly appointed ambassador to Colombia, Lewis A. Tambs, conceptualized an even more alarmist scenario that portended the next escalation in U.S. intervention in Central America.

The former Arizona State University professor and member of the Santa Fe Committee warned of a Soviet plan, utilizing Cuba and Nicaragua as its hemispheric bases, to encircle the United States. One of the more serious consequences of this perceived Communist aggression, as President Reagan began emphasizing six months later, was to endanger the nation's mineral ore and oil sea lines of communication. Yet of even greater concern than these strategic considerations was the frightful possibility, should the Communist plan successfully proceed, of an uncontrollable "human wave" of millions of Latin refugees that would flood the United States and threaten the "American way of life." In a most vivid version of the updated domino theory, Tambs depicted a grim scenario:

As insurgency inches northward from Nicaragua, to El Salvador to Guatemala and into Mexico, thousands of refugees will not only flee by sea. They will also work their way overland toward the open, unguarded and probably unguardable southern frontier of the United States. For there exists the possibility that the turmoil in Meso-America may induce a ripple effect which might inundate the U.S. with a human wave which could destabilize and capsize the Republic . . . if only 10 percent of the Isthmus's 24 million people along with an equal percentage of Mexico's 70 million inhabitants stampede, and only half of these insurgency-driven innocents recoil across the international line, America may be swamped under a tidal wave of terror-stricken refugees. Consequently, it is time to shake off the somnolence of the Vietnam syndrome and stem the tide at its source in Central America and in El Salvador.[4]

Having shattered the Vietnam syndrome in his own mind, the reactionary ideologue evidently felt qualified to counsel that the formula for "victory in El Salvador depends on winning three battles—in the field, in the media, and in Washington within the Administration."[5] In 1983, in a swing to an even more uncompromising rightist position by the Reagan Administration, new offensives were launched on all three fronts.

Beginning in March, President Reagan came out of the closet and personally began pitching for increased assistance to El Salvador, while at the same time Washington let the inept Minister of Defense García be forced aside and replaced with the brutally efficient General Vides Casanova. To further tighten up field operations, the conducting of the war was at last placed in the hands of the U.S. Special Forces, who devised the first full-spectrum counterinsurgency National Plan in an all-out effort to defeat the insurgents and pacify the nation. Providing essential support to El Salvador's intensified counterinsurgency campaign, moreover, the Administration set out to train at least half of the army in special warfare methods at the newly created Regional Military Training Center in Puerto Castilla, Honduras.

The power struggle within the Administration culminated in the May 1983 purge of the pragmatists in the State Department, shifting the formulation of Central American policy to a group of ideologues headed by then Director of the National Security Council, William P. Clark.[6] The Assistant Secretary of State for Inter-American Affairs, Thomas O. Enders, who served as the architect of Washington's policy since taking office with Secretary of State Alexander Haig (and who, like his former boss is a protégé of Henry A. Kissinger, the father of the pragmatist diplomatic school), headed the ideologue's hit list. Drawing upon his extensive Vietnam and Cambodian experience during his 28 months running the show, Enders came to believe that a purely military solution was simply out of the question. Following in the footsteps of his mentor Kissinger's Vietnam strategy of "bomb and talk," beginning in February 1983 he began to push

strongly for a "dual track" policy of stepped-up military activity
and assistance, combined with negotiations. Clearly, this "con-
ciliatory" course was anathema to the ideologues, who as soon as
they acquired the strength dumped him along with the U.S. Ambassador to El Salvador, Deane R. Hinton. Their replacements—Langhorne A. Motley, the former ambassador to Brazil,
and Thomas R. Pickering, the former ambassador to Nigeria,
without previous Central American experience—present no
challenge to the preeminence of the new decisionmakers. Indeed,
the entire State Department, according to a high officer there,
was "suddenly out of the information loop on a lot of stuff";[7] in
every day language that means the power shift had dealt them
out of the picture.

Anticipating opposition to this undisguisable swing to a far-
right policy, the President made several gestures to defuse the
critics' attacks. Acting on the Democratic congressional proposal
to appoint a special ambassador for Central America, who would
play a mediating role among the contesting parties much like
Washington's Middle East envoy, in April Reagan named former
Senator Richard B. Stone to be Ambassador at Large to the region. At first, there was some doubt about Stone's Senate confir-
mation because during 1981–1982, after leaving the Senate, he
served as a registered foreign agent lobbying in the nation's capital for the Guatemalan dictator General Romeo Lucas García.
But the outcome never was seriously in doubt; as one Senate
aide put it, "Sure, he's going to be confirmed, because he's a
former colleague. Senators are going to hold their nose and vote
for him, but they have reservations about both his competence
and his views."[8] To no one's astonishment, despite his frequent
trips to Central America and several meetings with the insurgents and Sandinistas, Ambassador Stone has racked up an un-
blemished record of producing not a single positive step toward
a peaceful solution to the area's problems.

Again responding to congressional pressure and in a further
move to legitimize its policy, in July 1983 the Administration
agreed to form a National Bipartisan Commission on Central
America. Although the stated purpose of the Commission is to
"lay the foundations for a long-term unified national approach"

to the region's problems,[9] many observers feel that President Reagan displayed the greatest of cynicism by appointing Dr. Henry Kissinger to head it. Nor does its mandate—the President proclaimed it was to "help us warn the American people that, for the first time in memory, we face real dangers on our borders, that we must protect the safety and security of our people"—help inspire confidence in its objectivity.[10] For the people of Central America the former Secretary of State's best-known achievements (opening relations with China, establishing détente with the Soviet Union, and the progress made in the Middle East) are all overshadowed by his devising and concealing secret invasions and bombings in Laos and Cambodia.

Undoubtedly the issue of greatest sensitivity throughout the hemisphere lies in Kissinger's unabashed disdain for Latin America, which he once described as "a dagger pointed at the heart of Antarctica," and especially his pivotal role in the 1973 military coup by General Augusto Pinochet that overthrew the democratically elected socialist government of President Salvador Allende in Chile, which he arrogantly justified in the now infamous remark that "I don't see why a country should be allowed to go Communist through the irresponsibility of its own people."[11] Tom Wicker captured the predominate Latin American opinion of appointing the "Great Destabilizer of Chile" to head the commission when he railed that "a less appropriate person to act as arbiter of policy anywhere in Latin America could not be found this side of General Pinochet. Dr. Kissinger's well-known world view, moreover, does not allow the possibility that an insurgency in El Salvador might not have been conceived in Moscow and planned in Havana; and even if it did, his oft-proclaimed geopolitical concepts won't tolerate even an *elected* Marxist government in this hemisphere, let alone one achieved by revolution."[12]

During the spring of 1983, in an attempt to dramatize their concerns to the public, media, and Congress, Administration officials increasingly began echoing Lewis Tambs's "human wave" fear-mongering propaganda. In a May 17 study, the Refugee Affairs Office of the State Department contributed statistics to the Calamity Jane mutterings by predicting that 2.33 million people could end up sweeping across the border. Clearly the media remained unimpressed, for as a *New York Times* editorial retorted: "Not 2 million, not 2½ million, but 2.33 million. Such precision means sophistication, and credibility, right? The figure, it turns out, is what you get if you make the dubious assumption that 10 percent of the region's population will take flight."[13]

In early June, a U.S. general entered the argument from a different angle, insisting that to protect the homeland from this disaster it would be necessary to recall troops from Europe in order to seal off the Mexican–United States border.[14] Why fully trained soldiers and not National Guard units, for instance, would be needed to carry out the high-risk mission of manning a defense line against the hypothetical mobs of bedraggled refugee families evidently escaped the attention of this clear-headed Pentagon planner.

Actually the general seemed to have been following up on a closely related point made in early March by his Commander in Chief, when the President revealed to the country the sinister plot of Soviet military theorists who "want to tie down our forces on our own southern border and so limit our capacity to act in more distant places, such as Europe, the Persian Gulf, the Indian Ocean, the Sea of Japan."[15] In his June speech before a Mississippi catfish dinner rally, Reagan climbed to new heights of demagoguery when he insisted that the United States absolutely could not permit "the Soviet–Cuban–Nicaraguan axis to take over Central America" because "the result could be a tidal wave of refugees—and this time they'll be 'feet people' and not 'boat people'—swarming into our country seeking a safe haven from Communist repression to our South."[16]

About a month later, as the polls continued to show that the message was not getting through, the President began his nationwide televised speech in a more statesmanlike fashion by quoting from a 13-year-old admirer's letter: "'Don't you wish sometimes you could just stamp your feet and shout at the press or Senators to be quiet, sit down and listen to what you're saying?'" While somberly looking the camera straight in the lens, he continued by answering the question with, "Well, yes, Gretchen, I sometimes do feel that way, and particularly over the past week." Likely his irritation stemmed from the leaks detailing the plans for the Big Pine II military maneuvers, which contributed to the House of Representatives' largely symbolic vote two days later to cut off covert aid to the contras. Taking a swipe at the media, when pressed by a reporter to respond to the widespread public disapproval of the massive military exercises, Reagan suggested that "maybe the people are disturbed because of the confused pattern that's been presented to them and the constant drumbeat with regard to the fact of suspicion that somehow there is an ulterior purpose in this." [17]

Several weeks later, during his August address to the Veterans of Foreign Wars convention in New Orleans, President Reagan followed up the "constant drumbeat" slap with a roundhouse punch at the media. Decrying the "discouraging hype and hoopla" that was giving "a distorted view of what's actually taking place" in Central America, he concluded with his customary fairness: "I don't blame the media alone because in many cases they are just reporting the disinformation they hear coming from people who put politics ahead of our national interests." [18] Regardless of the President's attempt to spread the culpability around, judging from the press's strong reaction, the Fourth Estate was not appeased, intimidated, or amused.

CONCLUSION

By Washington's insistence upon defining Central America's convulsions within the context of the East–West competition for world power, and without a radical change in U.S. policy, the forces already set into motion leave little hope but that the final outcome will spell disaster for everyone involved. While denouncing outside influence and assistance to the Salvadoran insurgents as a Communist conspiracy to foment "revolution without frontiers," whereas in reality it is just as marginal as that provided by the United States to the Afghan rebels, the Reagan Administration has created an immensely greater military network. The structure of Washington's "counterrevolution without borders" is found in its creation of the contra armies and in several regional military alliances, specifically the Central American Democratic Community (CDC) and the reconstituted Central American Defense Council (CONDECA).

Actually the seamy martial saga begins more than a year before President Reagan even took office. The 1979 Sandinista victory in Nicaragua threatened Washington's historical hegemony in the area by disrupting the pro-U.S. ideological consensus. Along with sounding the death knell for CONDECA, it also precipitated the further deterioration of the already fragile Central American Economic Community. The establishment of socialist Nicaragua and the fear that it would fan the flames of revolution in El Salvador and Guatemala prompted new efforts to form fresh counterrevolutionary covenants against the Sandinistas and apply counterinsurgency doctrine against other revolutionary movements in the Isthmus.

Only one month after Somoza's fall, in August 1979, the Carter Administration made the first attempt to pull together an official regional military pact among the Northern Triangle states of Guatemala, El Salvador, and Honduras "to prevent the coming of Communism in Nicaragua and coordinate efforts so that democratic values will predominate in that country."[1] However, due to the internal situations of these three nations, rivalries among them, and the Administration's own policies, the timing and the circumstances proved unfavorable. With El Salvador caught up in the political chaos following the October 1979 coup, the Lucas García regime in Guatemala was busily consolidating its power by killing off the political center; and Honduras's military dictatorship was maintaining a low profile in the hope of forestalling pressures leading to elections. These countries' dominant orientation was still their own internal problems. Moreover, the international climate also posed stumbling blocks, such as the residual animosity left by the 1969 war between Honduras and El Salvador, as personified by the Organization of American States patrolled demilitarized zone that still separated them at that time. Furthermore, the Carter Administration's strikingly different policy toward these nations hardly promoted unity. While courting Honduras by pouring in enormous amounts of security and economic assistance, in El Salvador it attempted to manipulate and control the initial stages of the counterinsurgency campaign of reform and repression, causing violent reactions from the extreme right and left. In addition, during this period Washington had turned its back on the Guatemalan dictatorship by cutting off military aid because of its disgraceful record of human rights violations.

But the new Reagan Administration's unwavering counterrevolutionary policies and developments within the region overcame these difficulties. The substitution of President Carter's foreign policy of "promoting human rights" with President Reagan's fight against "international terrorism" led directly to the formation of the first regional military pact. The consolidation of Nicaragua's socialist revolution and the dramatic growth of the insurgent movements in El Salvador and Guatemala laid the groundwork for the region's reactionary regimes to view internal problems from a wider perspective, while at the same time serving to lessen the tensions among them. Ten months after assuming office, in November 1981, the new Administration scored its first tentative success at the XIV Conference of the American Armies,* when all of the Central American armed forces reached a vaguely worded general agreement to coordinate their efforts to fight insurgency and oppose Nicaragua.[2]

Washington's big breakthrough in militarizing the Isthmus, however, came several months later in San José, Costa Rica, with the creation in January 1982 of the Central American Democratic Community (CDC). Openly sponsored by the United States, the founding members—Costa Rica, Honduras, and El Salvador—subsequently attempted to include Guatemala. But the effort failed because even by the wildest stretch of the Reagan Administration's elastic imagination, Guatemalan-style dictatorship just could not be sold as democracy.[3] Although the charter of the CDC includes political† and economic resolutions,‡ from its inception its principal purpose has been the reactivation of a mutual defense pact, as unequivocally stated in the first and last of the four "premises" establishing its basic principles and objectives: "1st—to make available appropriate military assistance to defend governments against guerrilla military offensives," and "4th—to promote a joint operation against the Cuban government and the revolutionary movements that it foments."[4]

Bringing the powerful Guatemalan armed forces into its counterrevolutionary military block still presented a problem for the Reagan Administration. Undeterred by technicalities—such as that its erratic President Efraín Ríos Montt had lost interest in the venture, and the country in no way could be passed off as a democracy—Washington still did not lose heart. The solution to

*The Conferences of the American Armies are periodic gatherings of the hemisphere's armed forces convened under the auspices of the 1947 Inter-American Treaty of Reciprocal Assistance, commonly referred to as the Río Treaty (because it was signed in Río de Janeiro, Brazil), which was initiated by the United States as a post-war anti-Communist military alliance.

†These are aimed at conferring, through elections, international and domestic legitimacy to the Central American regimes.

‡The purposes of these are to initiate a process of economic reactivation, along the lines of the nearly defunct Central American Economic Community and to ease the flows of U.S. bilateral and transnational capital that is expected to increase because of the Caribbean Basin Initiative.

the dilemma, undoubtedly, will enter the annals of history as one of the more imaginative examples of cutting a Gordian knot. Under extreme circumstances strongly pointing to United States involvement, in August 1983 the idiosyncratic Ríos Montt was overthrown in a military coup. This got rid of one problem, since the new dictator, General Oscar Mejía Víctores, desperately wanted to join the club. But military dictatorships, unadorned with even a minimum of window dressing, still did not quite fit the Central American Democratic Community's image. Side-stepping that entire issue, Yankee ingenuity lived up to its well deserved reputation. Immediately following a weekend conference during early October in Guatemala City with the head of the U.S. Army Southern Command, General Paul F. Gorman, the defense ministers of Guatemala, El Salvador, and Honduras announced the resurrection of the Central American Defense Council (CONDECA). Echoing almost verbatim the Reagan Administration's line, the northern tier states emphasized the danger posed to the region from "Marxist-Leninist aggression,"[5] and insisted upon the "vital need" to reactivate CONDECA in order to "jointly strengthen the isthmus' armies, using force, both to defend democracy and protect development."[6]

Through its militaristic policies, centered upon the illegal creation of the Nicaraguan contra armies and escalating intervention in El Salvador's civil war, the Reagan Administration has transformed Central America into an intricately woven mesh of intertwined, overlapping, and intensifying conflicts.

As the linchpin of the Reagan Administration's Central American policy, Honduras serves as the base for Washington's myriad covert and overt activities, hosting the CIA's contras and the Pentagon's "routine maneuvers" as well as its Regional Military Training Center where U.S. Special Forces train thousands of Salvadoran troops on a continually rotating basis. The recipient of massive aid, its military infrastructure—from hospitals and communication centers to air bases and port installations—is being fortified, and further strengthened by the construction of new U.S. facilities that range from radar sites to air and naval bases. In fact, even the distinction between war games and real Honduran military operations increasingly has become blurred, with U.S. forces providing logistical help such as airlifting Honduran soldiers to areas where they are carrying out counterinsurgency operations.

Moreover, the escalating Salvadoran civil war, which can continue only with ever-increasing amounts of Washington's assistance, counts upon joint military operations with the Honduran armed forces inside El Salvador. The conflict shows signs of spreading beyond its borders with the proposed stationing of Salvadoran forces inside Honduras, and the Salvadoran air force flying missions to resupply the contras fighting deep inside Nicaragua. Furthermore, the new Guatemalan dictatorship entered the picture when in August 1983 it made a deal with El Salvador to train its troops in exchange for weapons and ammunition from their U.S.–supplied stockpiles, a manipulative move that ridicules the congressional prohibition against providing any military aid to Guatemala.

Of course, Honduras has long been the contras' northern home, where they maintain permanent bases, complete with modern hospitals and facilities to service and repair their equipment. The Honduran armed forces, channeling U.S. ordnance to them, also provide logistical and even tactical support for their incursions into Nicaragua. To complete the scenario, Costa Rica serves as the southern flank of the counterrevolutionary assault against the Sandinistas. From there, the contras not only conduct commando raids, but like their northern-based comrades, bomb Nicaraguan cities and ports from light aircraft and specially equipped boats provided by the CIA.

When viewed individually, the pieces of Central America's chaotic mosaic confuse anyone who casually relies upon the media for information. Washington's rhetoric about supporting negotiations to arrive at a peaceful settlement of the region's problems further muddies the waters, so the resulting hodgepodge of conflicting words and actions is nothing less than mind-boggling even for the well-informed and best-intentioned people. The cord that ties together all of the seemingly disparate parts into a coherent whole can be found in the Reagan Administration's uncompromising policy of settling for nothing less than an unconditional military victory.

Gearing up for the perennial budget battle with Congress to increase aid to Central America, one of the Administration's ideologues came close to laying it all out. The Under Secretary of Defense for Policy, Fred C. Iklé, in a widely publicized September 1983 speech cleared by the White House, blasted away at the legislature for "crippling the President's military assistance program" and thereby condemning the United States to "a policy always shy of success." Shedding his tattered sheep's clothing, the Under Secretary bluntly stated that "We do not seek a military defeat for our friends. We do not seek a military stalemate. We seek victory for the forces of democracy." Concluding with a virtual declaration of war, Iklé insisted that "We must prevent consolidation of a Sandinista regime in Nicaragua that would become an arsenal for insurgency," because "if we cannot prevent that, we have to anticipate the partition of Central America. Such a development would then force us to man a new military front line of the East–West conflict, right here on our continent."[7]

A week later another bend in the Administration's warpath was leaked to the press in the form of a series of Pentagon decision memorandums for the fiscal year 1985 budget. On top of the large FY 1984 increases, in these documents the Deputy Secretary of Defense, Paul Thayer, ordered all branches of the armed forces to increase funds for operations in Central America and, along with beefing up their counterinsurgency capabilities, to formulate a plan for "force structure and basing requirements" in the region;[8] for those unfamiliar with military jargon this means planning the details to send in the troops.

In summary, what this all amounts to is that the Reagan Administration's policy absolutely rules out a negotiated or political settlement, despite the President's frequent proclamations favoring them. It recognizes that without committing appreciably greater resources, the United States cannot even hope to defeat the Salvadoran insurgents and therefore is saddled with "a policy always shy of success." It reveals that the Administration's "secret war" against Nicaragua, for the purported purposes of interdicting supplies to the rebels in El Salvador and pressuring Managua to move more quickly in a democratic direction, is nothing but a smoke screen to obscure its real objective of over-throwing the Sandinista government. Moreover, the Administration is prepared, should it fail in this illegal venture, as Under Secretary Iklé threatened, to unilaterally partition the Isthmus by stationing U.S. forces "in these countries, as in Korea or West Germany."[9] To accomplish these goals, it is making plans and channeling funds to build a presidential war chest for direct U.S. military intervention.

An examination of the reasons behind the Reagan Administration's policies may contribute to understanding the mechanisms of the pending disaster in Central America. Some dogmatic Marxists contend that the motivation for U.S. intervention stems from a compulsion to protect its economic interests in the region. But a cost–benefit calculation simply does not support any such mechanical relationship. Compared to the colossal sums being pumped in to prop up the decaying regimes and to "win back" Nicaragua, U.S. investment—primarily in low-yield agro-businesses, a little light manufacturing, and even less service industry—amounts to peanuts. Even adding in the minimal value of present and future markets for U.S. exports, including private bank loans, does not appreciably change the picture. The same is true for primary products imported from Central America: Since the area lacks any strategic minerals, and since there is a chronic world glut of coffee, cotton, sugar, and other agricultural goods, the Isthmus, as far as economics go, is virtually insignificant.

The right-wing strategic argument that somehow the establishment of Communist governments in the continental Western hemisphere would endanger North America's sea lines of communications (SLOCs) is even less credible than a similar rationalization Washington used to justify the disastrous 1961 Bay of Pigs invasion of Cuba. Any harassment of the Caribbean SLOCs could just as well be conducted from the island stronghold of Cuba. In any event, such speculation is absolute absurdity considering the vulnerability of the Soviet's only warm water port of Odessa, which easily could be completely shut down simply by blocking the narrow Bosporus. While the idea of a Red Army, unimpeded by 90 miles of ocean, marching into the United States is laughable, there does remain the hypothetical threat that the Kremlin might deploy strategic nuclear missiles in the region. But logic and common sense dictate against such folly: No advantage in delivery time exists, since Central America lies farther away than Cuba, and new missile technology has rendered obsolete such bases. At the first sign, the United States, like the June 1979 Israeli attack on the Iraqi nuclear plant, would destroy them. Most important, the October 1962 Cuban missile crisis established a quid pro quo by which Washington promised not to overthrow the Havana government in return for Moscow agreeing never to deploy missiles in the Western hemisphere— an agreement that both parties have faithfully abided by.

Actually, economic and strategic considerations constitute the reasons behind Washington's policy, although not in the terms presented above but as viewed through the Reagan Administration's ideological prism that prejudices their interpretation of the world communist–capitalist competition. The President gave a strong indication of this during his April 1983 speech to Congress when he concluded with the dire warning of the stakes in Central America: "If we cannot defend ourselves there, we cannot expect to prevail elsewhere. Our credibility would crumble and the safety of our homeland would be put in jeopardy." The real fear is not the fate of the economically and strategically marginal nations of the region, but the negative effect upon the U.S. position vis-à-vis the Soviet Union, a characteristically rightist world view that judges almost every situation in these ideological terms and then exaggerates their significance beyond all sense of proportion. So, regardless of the fundamentally nationalistic nature of these revolutions, the Reaganites are forcing the people of Central America into a regionalized war based on the Administration's paranoid understanding of the East–West conflict.

Responding to this policy, Roger Hilsman, one of the architects of President Kennedy's counterinsurgency doctrine, now a professor at Columbia University and still no friend of revolution, posed several rhetorical questions during a 1983 symposium on applied history for Central America. Based upon the Vietnam experience, Professor Hilsman, although skirting any moral implications, asked "What is the essential nature of the insurgencies? Are they essentially the creatures of 'world Communism' or are they nationalistic, anti-oligarch, peasant revolts, feeding on social discontent, whose leaders just happen to be Communist party members? . . . does the long history of resentment of 'economic imperialism' by the 'Colossus of the North' and its alliance with Latin American oligarchs mean that, as in Vietnam, American troops would end up recruiting more Communists than they could kill?"[10]

The Reagan Administration is its own worst enemy. The relentless drive to impose a military solution offers not the best, but the worst, possibility of achieving peace or democracy, because its very nature carries destructive repercussions for each of the affected nations and the region as a whole. It might be well to remember that both Ho Chi Minh and Fidel Castro repeatedly sought Washington's help long before they were driven into the Russian bear's embrace. Through its pretentions of reestablishing the Pax Americana as its own actions show, Washington recognizes that things will get worse before they get better. However, perhaps because of ideological blind spots, it evidently fails to realize that the military route amounts to the surest way of dooming noble ideals and embroiling the United States in another Vietnam-style quagmire.

By creating a regional counterrevolutionary block, Washington has embarked on another self-defeating course of self-fulfilling prophecies. As a general rule, military alliances require a compatibility of the member states' military, political, and economic structures. Forcing such an alliance—as the Reagan Administration is trying to do—causes the member nations to suffer profound social and political disintegration. Even placing aside the immorality, on purely pragmatic grounds the domestic effects of U.S. counterrevolutionary policies within these nations have been disastrous. They serve to aggravate, sometimes even create, the very conditions that spawn social turmoil and civil war.

The first self-fulfilling prophecy begins with the buildup of a country's security apparatus and its military forces, thereby strengthening the social and political positions of these institutions, and contributing to the parallel phenomenon of polarizing the body politic between the political left and right. Moreover, the process is characterized by two secondary dynamics: The political center becomes debilitated or even eliminated because, out of self-preservation, many members find themselves forced to abandon their moderate positions and move to the left or the right. Furthermore within these polarized coalitions, a tendency develops to assume even more radical leftist and rightist postures. Since the most powerful sectors of their societies feel threatened and seek authoritarian solutions to a nation's growing crisis, governments react to the upsurge of leftist opposition movements by opting for greater repression and adopting yet harder-line policies. The antithesis of stronger leftist coalitions is the movement of many sectors within the traditional right to more extremist positions, attempting to gain control of the armed forces and perpetuating death squads and other terrorist activities.

Within this context of violent polarization, the militarized regimes "defer" human rights, political democracy, and economic development programs in their campaign to destroy those whom they perceive as real or potential subversives. In large part because of the attacks upon these left-of-center coalitions, which consist predominantly of the remnants of the political centrist and moderate-leftist organizations, leadership is often assumed by the most militant opposition individuals or groups since it is they who have best prepared for this eventuality. The final phase comes with the outbreak of civil war between the leftist insurgents and the rightist government and their extreme right cohorts. In Central America the polarization process has already progressed to this point in El Salvador and Guatemala and has taken root in Honduras, and to a lesser degree in Costa Rica. Regardless of the final outcome of these national wars of liberation, the stated objectives of U.S. counterrevolutionary intervention—the defense of peace and democracy—are not achieved. Historically, when Washington forces national insurrections into the East–West paradigm, they invariably result in the establishment either of Communist regimes, if the insurgents emerge victorious, or of the rightist dictatorships, if U.S. supported client states succeed in defeating the rebels.

Conversely, history demonstrates that when a more normal process of social change runs its course—as in Tanzania or Zimbabwe—although the United States may not particularly like the outcome, the results are far more moderate. After all, people do not fight revolutions to please Washington or Moscow, because nobody wants to exchange one set of masters for another. But if faced with no alternative except defeat or joining the Soviet camp—such as Washington forced upon Cuba during the early 1960s—the question becomes academic. In fact, since 1979 when the Sandinistas came to power, President Castro has repeatedly warned the Nicaraguans "not to make the same mistakes we did." The 1980s undoubtedly offer a far wider range of choices than existed during the 1960s when, at the height of the Cold War, Third World nations had little option other than to align themselves with one side or the other in order to survive. Now, true nonalignment is possible, especially in the Western hemisphere, where the Soviets possess the ability neither to project their power nor to support another Cuba.

Nicaragua offers a prime example of the benefits that a nonaligned socialist, rather than Communist, revolution can count upon. While it is true that the Kremlin and its allies provide material and moral support, so do the nations of the Non-Aligned Movement and other countries (like Mexico, Canada, and West Germany), the twenty-odd governments belonging to the Socialist International (including traditional U.S. allies such as France, Spain, Austria, and the Scandinavian countries), and especially the dynamic liberation theology sector of the Catholic Church. With assistance from these varied sources, and minimal interference from the Carter Administration, the Sandinista revolution began as an authentic moderate and pluralistic experiment in social change. But as the Reagan Administration's "secret war" escalated against the young government, the aggression forced a shift in the center of power within the Sandinista coalition to the hard-line factions. If Managua does finally end up dependent upon the Soviets for survival, little doubt exists that Washington's counterrevolutionary policies will have been the decisive factor, and not some diabolical plot hatched in the bowels of the Kremlin.

Of course, Moscow will take whatever advantage it can reap from the situation. However, trying to keep their own economy afloat while facing off the Chinese along the Sino–Soviet border (where the two nations have deployed the largest standing armies in the world), attempting to run an outlandishly expensive arms race with the United States and Western Europe, paying the political and economic costs of their arrogant Afghan intervention, and maintaining control over Eastern Europe, especially troublesome Poland with its powerful Solidarity trade union movement, the Soviets simply are not looking for more problems. That is exactly what would happen if they got caught sticking their nose in Central America; on top of the enormous loss of world prestige, the United States certainly would retaliate by upping the ante in the Middle East and other places of Soviet vulnerability around the world. Considering how profitable it would be for the Soviets to see increased United States intervention in Central America—in terms of a propaganda coup to offset their own interventions, diverting defense funds and other military resources, and undermining President Reagan's popular support—the really surprising thing is how little they have done to suck Washington deeper and quicker into the mess. It is almost as if the two superpowers operate on a tacit sphere of influence accord along the lines of "you keep your support to Central America at a level acceptable to us, and we will keep a cap on our assistance to the Afghan rebels."

The other self-fulfilling prophecy perpetrated by Washington centers upon the so-called domino theory, which during the Southeast Asian war served as one of the principal justifications for U.S. intervention in Vietnam. If the virus of insurgency was not contained in Vietnam, the reasoning went, the neighboring nations would become infected and fall like dominoes, one after the other, to the Communists. After years of massive direct U.S. military intervention, however, it became painfully clear that the Vietnamese insurgents could not be defeated through counterinsurgency operations limited to that nation alone. Consequently, the Pentagon adopted a strategy intended to destroy their rearguard, sanctuaries, and supply lines by escalating its secret war in Laos, and unleashing invasions and saturation bombing upon Cambodia. Achieving absolutely none of their objectives, these measures only served to regionalize the armed conflict and destroy the political and social fabric of Laos and Cambodia, thereby creating the conditions by which the insurgent movements finally mustered enough strength to topple their governments. Certainly in the case of Cambodia, had the United States not paved the road to victory, it is virtually inconceivable that the marginal Khmer Rouge could ever have seized power. Conversely, in the neighboring Southeast nations of Thailand and Malaysia, which were not dragged into the conflict, the rebels remain as isolated as ever. Reflecting the true regional alignments, moreover, the Vietnamese overthrew the new Kampuchean regime following one of history's most brutal reigns of terror.* (Today the Khmer Rouge find themselves once again the insurgents; and in an even more ironic twist, while still receiving assistance from their traditional Chinese backers, they have developed a new and unexpected source of support—the Reagan Administration.)

Despite the profound changes in the alignment of world power that makes a domino theory even less credible than 20 years ago, President Reagan clings to the outdated rationalization. Following the unexpectedly strong 1982–1983 Salvadoran rebel offensive, the President personally began campaigning for increased U.S. aid to the region in a March 1983 speech: He sounded the "revolution without frontiers" alarm and predicted that if the Communist conspiracy succeeds, "El Salvador will join Cuba and Nicaragua as a base for spreading fresh violence to Guatemala, Honduras, even Costa Rica. The killing will increase, and so will the threat to Panama, the canal and ultimately Mexico."[11]

Without doubt, Nicaragua views the Salvadoran and other Central American insurgencies favorably, even going so far as to send some material support, although of such limited quantities that in spite of their best efforts, Washington and and its allies have failed to intercept a single shipment. Not unreasonably, Managua would prefer to enjoy the security of sister socialist states, instead of the hostility of right-wing dictatorships. However, the leap from sympathy and minimal support for neighbor-

---

*After assuming power in Cambodia, the Khmer Rouge changed the name of the country to Kampuchea, and instituted a vicious policy of resettling and liquidating "undesirables." An extremely conservative estimate is that the Khmer Rouge regime of Kampuchea killed one fifth of the population before the Vietnamese drove them from power.

ing revolutionaries to a worldwide Communist conspiracy is total nonsense. In fact, the idea is so absurd that it would not be an exaggeration to postulate that the Reaganite policymakers are simpletons if they truly believe their own demagoguery. Ranking the motivations spurring on the region's revolutionary movements, nationalism emerges as the strongest by far, followed by, in equal measure, socialism and liberation theology–style Christianity. To assume that the relatively few Communists involved, even taking into consideration their high-profile leadership positions, determine the character of the Isthmus's social upheavals not only flies in the face of historical reality, but amounts to a fundamental conceptual error leading the United States down a primrose path of self-delusion.

Barring a sinking of the *Maine* or a Gulf of Tonkin–type incident against U.S. vessels or forces, at this stage there exist two flash points in the Central American tinder box. In El Salvador, should the insurgents succeed in breaking the will of the government forces—as occurred in Cuba, South Vietnam and Nicaragua—Washington might very well feel obliged to send in the Marines in an attempt to salvage the situation. The other danger spot is the outbreak of war between Nicaragua and Honduras, precipitated by the latter nation's open collaboration with the illegal CIA–sponsored contra armies. Should the Nicaraguans unleash their overwhelming military might, all analysts agree that both the contras and the Honduran armed forces stand virtually no chance of stopping them. Again, in order to save its proxy, the Reagan Administration seems to have painted itself into a corner from which it can escape only through direct military intervention. Given the Sandinista contingency plans for themselves and to provide the area's insurgents with unprecedented amounts of war materiel, the likelihood of containing such a conflict is remote; more realistically, it would quickly touch off a regional conflagration.

In either case, the military scenario ends up pretty much the same: a short initial period of heavy fighting with U.S. forces easily defeating the revolutionary governments and taking control of the major urban centers and other strategic positions. For President Reagan, similar to 1979 when Premier Leonid Brezh-

268

THE MORASS

nev sent the troops into Afghanistan, so far so good. But then the prolonged guerrilla war, that for years the revolutionaries have been preparing for, begins and goes on and goes on and goes on.

While the Central American war would start out differently than the Vietnam war, it rapidly would boil down to about the same thing: a U.S. occupation force continually sending out its soldiers on military counterinsurgency operations with not all of them coming back to their headquarters, but returning home in body bags; Central and North Americans killed and maimed for no clearly defined purpose, and with no end in sight to the televised madness of an unnecessary war. With its iron-fisted control, Moscow can minimize the domestic political repercussions from the casualties and immorality of their protracted counterinsurgency campaign; but the furor in the United States, rekindled on the embers of Vietnam, would once again split the nation apart.

The United States' militaristic policy in Central America bears an uncanny resemblance to the Soviets' arrogance, which trapped them in the Afghan morass, and from which for more than four years they have been unable to extract their more than 100,000 troops. Hardly the solution to the region's problems, Washington's approach is a prescription for the beginning of real trouble.

GLOSSARY OF ACRONYMS AND TERMS

AID Agency for International Development. The official U.S. organization responsible for administering Washington's economic foreign assistance programs. AID's functions include its role as an integral element in U.S. counterinsurgency policy throughout the Third World.

ARDE *Alianza Revolucionaria Democrática* (Democratic Revolutionary Alliance). U.S.-supported Costa Rica-based counterrevolutionaries led by former Sandinista hero Edén Pastora, currently attempting to overthrow the Sandinista government of Nicaragua.

CDC *Comunidad Democrática Centroaméricana* (Central American Democratic Community). Formed in January 1982 as a U.S. initiative, the CDC is fundamentally a military alliance among Costa Rica, Honduras, and El Salvador.

CIA Central Intelligence Agency. The principal U.S. espionage institution responsible for conducting overseas intelligence gathering, counterinsurgency operations, and counterrevolutionary clandestine activities.

CONDECA *Consejo de Defensa Centroamericana* (Central American Defense Council). The mutual-defense pact initially formed in 1964 among the dictatorships of Nicaragua, Honduras, El Salvador, and Guatemala. CONDECA virtually ceased to function after the 1979 overthrow of Anastasio Somoza in Nicaragua, but was revived as part of the U.S. militaristic Central American policy in October 1983. Of course, Nicaragua is not now a member, but Panama and Costa Rica occupy a vaguely defined "observer" status.

CONTRAS The counterrevolutionary armies based on Honduras and Costa Rica that were organized by the CIA to "harass" the revolutionary Sandinista government of Nicaragua. (See ARDE, FDN, and MISURASATA)

CONTADORA GROUP The four Latin American nations—Mexico, Venezuela, Colombia, and Panama—who since January 1983 have led the diplomatic effort to find a negotiated settlement to the Central American conflicts.

CORDS Civil Operation and Rural Development Support program. First developed as a "full-spectrum" counterinsurgency program in Vietnam, the CORDS model of applying reform and repression to defeat insurgency was adopted in El Salvador in June 1983.

FDN *Fuerza Democrática Nicaragüense* (Nicaraguan Democratic Force). The CIA–organized and supported counterrevolutionaries based in Honduras, composed predominantly of former members of General Somoza's National Guard. The FDN is the strongest of the contra armies attempting to overthrow the Sandinista government of Nicaragua.

FDR *Frente Democrático Revolucionario* (Democratic Revolutionary Front). The political arm of the Salvadoran insurgent movement comprising a coalition of various dissident political parties and factions, and closely aligned with the FMLN guerrillas.

FISCAL YEAR The U.S. government's fiscal year runs from October 1 through September 31; thus, FY 1982 covers the period from October 1, 1981 through September 31, 1982 and FY 1983 begins on October 1, 1982 and continues through September 31, 1983.

FMLN *Frente Farabundo Martí de Liberación Nacional* (Farabundo Martí National Liberation Front). The military arm of the Salvadoran insurgents, named after the early twentieth-century Salvadoran revolutionary Farabundo Martí, composed of a coalition of five different guerrilla armies and closely allied with the political FDR.

FSLN *Frente Sandinista de Liberación Nacional* (Sandinista National Liberation Front). The insurgent movement, named after the early twentieth-century Nicaraguan revolutionary César Augusto Sandino, that overthrew the dictatorship of General Anastasio Somoza in 1979.

GDP Gross Domestic Product. The total yearly value of a nation's production and services.

GREEN BERETS U.S. Army Special Forces. Although these "nonconventional" soldiers are highly trained in commando and counterinsurgency warfare, their primary function is to instruct "friendly" armed forces in these skills.

INSURGENT INFRASTRUCTURE The administrative apparatus of the insurgents that provides essential support in the form of intelligence networks, supply and communications lines, manufacture of weapons, medical care and even investment of surplus funds.

KHMER ROUGE   The Communist insurgents of Cambodia (Kampuchea), who seized power after U.S. intervention brought that nation into the Southeast Asia war.

MISURASATA   United States supported coalition of anti-Sandinista Miskito, Rama and Suma Indians from eastern Nicaragua that is bitterly divided into two factions. The largest group, led by Steadman Fagoth, has formed a contra army based in Honduras and has close ties with the F.D.N.; the smaller faction led by Brooklyn Rivera has aligned itself with the Costa Rican based A.R.D.E. contras.

OAS   Organization of American States. The official international organization of North, Central, and South American countries chartered in 1948.

ORDEN   *Organización Democrática Nacional* (Democratic National Organization). The rural vigilantes of El Salvador founded in 1961 as the "eyes and ears" of the armed forces, this ultra-right-wing paramilitary organization has eagerly participated in numerous massacres and death squads. Although officially outlawed in 1979, ORDEN members now form the core of the Salvadoran Civil Patrols and continue to function in their traditional roles.

PATHET LAO   The Lao Communist National Liberation Front of Laos, who seized power after U.S. intervention brought that nation into the Southeast Asian wars.

NSC   National Security Council. The presidential advisory body officially responsible for coordinating U.S. foreign and domestic policy.

POPULAR BASE   The logistical foundation of insurgents that provides essential support in the form of food, medicines, money and overall support of a substantial portion of the population without which no true insurrection can succeed.

SANDINISTAS   The Nicaraguan revolutionaries who have governed the nation since 1979, when they ousted the U.S.–backed dictatorship. (See FSLN)

SEALS   The U.S. Navy's Sea, Air and Land teams. Although these "non-conventional" soldiers are highly trained in commando and counterinsurgency warfare, their primary function is to instruct "friendly" armed forces in these skills.

SOMOCISTAS   Counterrevolutionaries identified with the policies of the deceased dictator Anastasio Somoza, currently attempting to overthrow the Sandinista government of Nicaragua.

USIS   The United States Information Service (known within the United States as the United States Information Agency or USIA) is the "public relations" arm of the White House that sponsors a variety of propaganda programs presenting the current administration's views from their offices and facilities located at U.S. embassies throughout the world.

NOTES

Chapter One: The Origins of Modern Day Counterinsurgency

1. Arthur M. Schlesinger, *A Thousand Days*, (Boston: Houghton Mifflin Co., 1975), p. 274.

2. Cf. "Krushchev's Speech of January 6, 1961, a Summary and Interpretive Analysis," Legislative Reference Service, Library of Congress, 87th Congress, 1st Session, Document No. 14, (Washington, D.C.: U.S. Government Printing Office, 1961).

3. Department of Defense, *U.S.–Vietnam Relations*, (Washington, D.C.: U.S. Government Printing Office, 1971), Vol. 11, p. 17.

4. *Public Papers of President John F. Kennedy, 1961*, (Washington, D.C.: U.S. Government Printing Office, 1962), p. 336.

Chapter Two: Reform as Counterinsurgency

1. "U.S.–Latin American Relations," Thomas O. Enders, Assistant Secretary of State, *United States Department of State*, Bureau of Public Affairs, *Current Policy*, Number 407, 21 June 1982.

2. Unless otherwise cited, the primary source of information concerning Prosterman and his involvement in various land reform schemes is found in his article, "The Unmaking of a Land Reform," *The New Republic*, 9 August 1982.

3. "El Salvador Project Paper: Agrarian Reform Organization" (Unclassified), *Agency for International Development*, AID/LAC/P-060, 25 July 1980; also see *The New York Times*, 4 July 1982.

4. Prosterman, op. cit., p. 23.

5. *The Pentagon Papers*, (New York: Bantam, 1971), p. 195.

6. Ibid., p. 197.

7. Ibid., pp. 206–208.

8. *The Pentagon Papers*, Senator Gravel Edition, (Boston: Beacon Press, 1971), Vol. II, p. 251.

9. *The Pentagon Papers,* Bantam, op. cit., p. 214.

10. Ibid., p. 216.

11. *The Pentagon Papers,* Gravel, Vol. II, p. 123.

12. U. Alexis Johnson, *The Foreign Service Journal,* July 1962, p. 23.

13. Tape-recorded interview, San Salvador, 21 January 1983.

14. Prosterman, op. cit., p. 23.

15. *The New York Times,* 6 May 1982.

16. Prosterman, op. cit., p. 24.

17. The Washington *Post,* 21 May 1982; *The New York Times,* 23, 24, 25, 28 May 1982 and 7 June 1982. See also, "Land Reform Suspension: First Dividend Paid on Oligarchs' Campaign Investment," *Council on Hemispheric Affairs,* press release of 27 May 1982; and "Testimony before the Subcommittee on Inter-American Affairs of Foreign Affairs," by Dick Clark, Commission on U.S.–Central American Relations, Washington, D.C., 10 August 1982, pp. 23–29.

18. Prosterman, op. cit, p. 24.

19. *Legislation on Foreign Relations through 1982,* (Washington, D.C.: U.S. Government Printing Office), Vol. I, Sec. 727, p. 251.

20. *The New York Times,* 27 October 1982.

21. *The New York Times,* 28 October 1982.

22. *The New York Times,* 5 November 1982.

23. The Washington *Post,* 30, October 1982.

24. *The New York Times,* 10 November 1982.

25. *The New York Times,* 11 and 22 November 1982.

26. *The New York Times,* 27 October 1982.

27. *The New York Times,* 16 and 21 November 1982.

28. *The New York Times,* 16 March 1983.

29. *The New York Times,* 7 November 1982.

30. Ibid.

31. *Uno más Uno,* 9 November 1982.

32. *Uno más Uno,* 18 December 1982.

33. *Uno más Uno,* 30 December 1982.

34. *Uno más Uno,* 21 December 1982.

35. *The Miami News,* as reproduced in *Uno más Uno,* 22 December 1982.

36. *Uno más Uno,* 30 December 1982.

37. *Uno más Uno,* 3 January 1983.

38. *The New York Times,* 9 January 1983.

39. *The New York Times,* 12 January 1983.

40. Tape-recorded interview, San Salvador, 20 January 1983.

41. *The New York Times,* 16 January 1983.

42. *The New York Times,* 19 April 1983.

43. Memorandum for the Special Assistant to the President for National Security Affairs, Subject: "Summary Report, Military Counterinsurgency Accomplishments since January 1961," Joint Chiefs of Staff, 21 July 1962, p. 8.

44. Douglas S. Blaufarb, *The Counterinsurgency Era; U.S. Doctrine and Performance,* (London: Free Press, Collier Macmillan, 1977) p. 77.

45. Frances FitzGerald, *Fire in the Lake,* (New York: Vintage Books, 1972), pp. 411, 412.

46. *Massive Extra-Judicial Executions in Rural Areas under the Government of General Efraín Ríos Montt,* (London: Amnesty International, July, 1982).

47. See for example the articles in *The New York Times,* 3, 4, 6, 14, and 17 June 1982.

Chapter Three: The Role of the CIA

1. U.S. Congress, House of Representatives, Committee on Government Operations, *U.S. Assistance Programs in Vietnam, Hearings,* 92nd Cong., 1st Session, 1971, p. 182.

2. Allen Goodman, "The Political Implications of Rural Problems in South Vietnam: Creating Public Interests," *Asian Survey,* August 1970, pp. 677–678.

3. *The New York Times,* 5 November 1982.

4. Tape-recorded interview, Salvadoran Army High Command Headquarters, 24 July 1980.

5. *Nazi Conspiracy and Aggression,* VII, pp. 873–874, (Nuremberg Documents, L-90), 12 December 1941, as cited in William L. Shirer, *The Rise and Fall of the Third Reich: A History of Nazi Germany,* 1959, p. 1248.

6. Ibid., pp. 871–872 (N.D., L-90), February 1942, as cited in Shirer, op. cit., p. 1248.

7. Shirer, op. cit., p. 1248.

8. Ibid., p. 1483.

9. "Democratic Revolutionary Front (FDR) Leaders Are Detained and Disappear in El Salvador," WOLA Press Release, 21 October 1982. See also, *The New York Times,* 23 and 25 October 1982.

10. Ibid.

11. *Uno más Uno,* 24 October 1982.

12. Blaufarb, *op. cit.,* 105–106.

13. Ibid, p. 165.

14. Ibid. p. 107.

15. "Casey and His CIA on the Rebound," *The New York Times Magazine,* 16 January 1983.

16. *U.S. News and World Report,* 1 June 1981.

17. *"Casey and His CIA on the Rebound,"* op. cit.

18. Ibid., p. 39.

19. Ibid., p. 49.

20. *The New York Times,* 27 March 1983.

21. The Washington *Post,* 14 February 1982; and *The New York Times,* 15 February 1982.

22. The Washington *Post,* 16 March 1982.

23. The Washington *Post,* 8 May 1983.

24. By early 1983 these covert operations had cost more than 50 million dollars. See *The New York Times,* 20 April 1983 and *The Central American Update,* Vol. IV, No. 5, April 1983, p. 24.

25. Ibid.

26. Ibid.

27. Ibid.

28. *The New York Times,* 23 December 1982.

29. The Washington *Post,* 8 May 1983.

30. *Newsweek,* 8 November 1982.

31. *The New York Times,* 3 November 1982.

32. *Newsweek,* 8 November 1982.

33. See also, *The New York Times,* 7 November 1982.

34. The Washington *Post,* 15 May 1983.

35. *Inforpress Centroamericana,* No. 507, 26 August 1982.

36. *The New York Times,* 15 July 1983.

37. The Washington *Post,* 23 March 1983; *Newsweek,* 14 April 1983; and *U.S. News and World Report,* 20 June 1983.

38. The Washington *Post,* 15 May 1983.

39. *Newsweek,* 18 April 1983.

40. *The New York Times,* 3 April 1983.

41. *Newsweek,* 11 April 1983.

42. The Washington *Post,* 8 May 1983.

43. *The New York Times,* 3 April 1983; see also, *Central American Update,* Vol. IV, No. 5, April 1983, pp. 24 and 26.

44. *The New York Times,* 21 July 1983.

45. See Tables 6 and 7.

46. *The New York Times,* 3 April 1983; *Time,* 4 April 1983; and *Central American Update,* Vol. IV, No. 5, April 1983, p. 27.

47. The Los Angeles *Times,* 20 December 1982.

48. *Newsweek,* 4 April 1983.

49. *Uno más Uno,* 8 December 1982.

50. *Uno más Uno,* 18 December 1982.

51. *Uno más Uno,* 19 December 1982.

52. *Uno más Uno,* 20 December 1982.

53. The Washington *Post,* 8 May 1983.

54. The Washington *Post,* 22, 25, and 28 March 1983; and 3, 4, and 5 April 1983; and *The New York Times,* 28, 29, and 30 March 1983; and 5, 6, 7, and 8 April 1983; *Central American Report,* Vol. X, No. 12, 25 March 1983, p. 89; *Newsweek,* 4 and 11 April 1983; and *Time,* 4 April 1983.

55. Ibid.; see also the other references in the citations in this section.

56. *CBS Nightly News,* 1 April 1983. For a description of a contra training camp in the province of El Paraíso, Honduras, see *The New York Times,* 28 March 1983.

57. The Washington *Post,* 2 and 15 May 1983; *Newsweek,* 30 May 1983.

58. The Washington *Post,* 8 May 1983.

59. The Washington *Post,* 30 May 1983.

60. *The New York Times,* 23 May 1983.

61. *U.S News and World Report,* 9 May 1983.

62. The Washington *Post,* 5 May 1983.

63. The Washington *Post,* 29 April 1983; *The New York Times,* 31 July 1983.

64. The Washington *Post,* 15 June 1983.

65. *The New York Times,* 23 and 29 June 1983.

66. The Washington *Post,* 15 May 1983; *Newsweek,* 30 May 1983.

67. *The New York Times,* 15 July 1983.

68. *The New York Times,* 29 June 1983; and 21 July 1983.

69. *The New York Times,* 19 July 1983.

70. *The New York Times,* 21, 22, 23, 26 and 27 July 1983.

71. *The New York Times,* 27 July 1983.

72. *El Día,* 20 July 1983; *The New York Times,* 22 July 1983.

73. *Uno más Uno,* 23 November 1983.

74. *Time,* 8 August 1983.

75. *The New York Times,* 26 August 1983.

76. "Pressure Mounts on Nicaragua," *El Salvador Information Bulletin,* Vol. 2, No. 11, September 1983.

77. *The New York Times,* 26 August 1983.

78. *Latin American Index,* Vol. XI, No. 14, September 1983; *Envío* No. 27 (Managua, Nicaragua), September 1983.

79. *The New York Times,* 2 October 1983.

80. *U.S. News and World Report,* 29 August 1983.

81. The Washington *Post,* 25 November 1983.

82. *The New York Times,* 9 September 1983.

83. *Newsweek,* 19 September 1983.

84. *The New York Times,* 6 October 1983.

85. *CBS Nightly News,* 6 October 1983.

86. *The New York Times,* 11 September 1983.

87. *The New York Times,* 20 September 1983.

88. *The New York Times,* 11 September 1983; *Uno más Uno,* 12 and 13 September 1983.

89. *Inforpress Centroamericana,* No. 559, 15 September 1983.

90. *The New York Times,* 20 September 1983; Associated Press, 20 September 1983.

91. Associated Press, 27 September 1983; *The New York Times,* 27 September 1983.

92. United Press International, 1 October 1983.

93. *The New York Times,* 11 October 1983.

94. See the almost daily articles in the Mexican press, as well as the dispatches of Associated Press, 5 October 1983; and United Press International, 7 and 20 October 1983.

95. Associated Press, 11 October 1983.

96. *The New York Times,* 16 October 1983.

97. Associated Press, 5 October 1983.

98. *The New York Times,* 13 October 1983.

99. *The New York Times,* 15 October 1983.

100. *The New York Times,* 17 October 1983.

101. *The New York Times,* 15 October 1983.

102. *The New York Times,* 23 October 1983.

103. *The New York Times,* 24 and 25 October 1983.

104. *Uno más Uno,* 29 October 1983.

105. *Uno más Uno,* 30 October 1983.

106. *Uno más Uno,* 7 November 1983.

107. *Uno más Uno,* 8 November 1983.

108. *Uno más Uno,* 12 November 1983; *The News,* 13 November 1983.

109. The second House vote denying contra funding came on 30 October 1983; *The New York Times,* 31 October 1983.

110. *El Día,* 18 November 1983.

111. *El Día* and *Uno más Uno,* 19 November 1983.

112. *Uno más Uno,* 19 November 1983.

113. Ibid.

114. *El Día,* 21 November 1983.

115. *The New York Times,* 28 December 1983.

116. *The New York Times,* 15 August 1983.

117. *El Día,* 18 November 1983.

118. *The News,* 21 November 1983; *Uno más Uno,* 21 November 1983.

119. "A View from Managua," Tom Wicker, *The New York Times,* 3 October 1983.

Chapter Four: The Development of Counterinsurgency Military Strategy

1. T. N. Greene (ed.), *The Guerrilla and How to Fight Him,* (New York: Praeger Press, 1962), pp. 22–36.

2. Ibid., pp. 25–26.

3. Ibid, p. 29.

4. Gunter Lewy, *America in Vietnam,* (Oxford, England: Oxford University Press, 1978), p. 63.

5. In South Vietnam alone, 3.5 million tons of bombs were dropped by the U.S. Air Force; see Blaufarb, op. cit., p. 299.

6. In contrast with guerrilla warfare, in "mobile warfare" the insurgents actively seek battle, putting aside concealment, dispersion, and other methods of avoiding combat. See, for example Vo Nguyen Giap's *Military Art of People's War: Selected Writings,* (New York: Monthly Review Press, 1970).

7. Military Assistance Command, Vietnam Center for Military History, *Lessons Learned* No. 35, "Clear and Hold Operations," 10 January 1964. The necessity to *hold* "cleared" territory was explained in this pamphlet as follows: "The people will not cooperate with friendly forces when they know that several days later they will be abandoned to the mercy of the Viet Cong."

8. Blaufarb, op. cit., pp. 256–258; Lewy, op. cit., pp. 116–117.

9. Commander of the United States Military Assistance Command in Vietnam, COMUSMACV, from June 1964 to June 1968.

10. Lewy, op. cit., pp. 118–119.

11. Blaufarb, op. cit., p. 268; Lewy, op. cit., pp. 134–139.

12. Brian M. Jenkins, "The Unchangeable War," RM-6278-1-ARPA; Santa Monica, California: The Rand Corporation, September 1971, p. 3.

13. Robert W. Komer, "Bureaucracy Does Its Thing: The Institutional Constraints on U.S. GVN Performance in Vietnam," R-967-

ARPA; Santa Monica, California: The Rand Corporation, 1973, p. 145.

14. "The Army's New Fighting Doctrine," *The New York Times Magazine,* 28 November 1982, p. 36ff.

15. *The New York Times,* 30 July 1983.

16. *The New York Times,* 29 June 1983.

17. *U.S. News and World Report,* 11 July 1983.

18. *The New York Times,* 12 June 1983.

19. *The New York Times,* 19 July 1982.

20. *The New York Times,* 4 October 1982.

21. *The New York Times,* 19 July 1982.

22. *The New York Times,* 3 August 1983.

23. *The New York Times,* 19 July 1982.

24. The Jenkins analysis is described in *The New York Times,* 21 August 1982.

25. *The New York Times,* 21 August 1982.

Chapter Five: Guatemala

1. Testimony of Robert Maurer, Acting Executive Director, Amnesty International, U.S.A., *Human Rights in Guatemala,* Hearings Before the Subcommittees on Human Rights and International Organizations and on Inter-American Affairs of the Committee on Foreign Affairs of the House of Representatives, Ninety-Seventh Congress, First Session, Washington, D.C.: Government Printing Office, 30 July 1981.

2. In a May 16 interview with the Associated Press, see *Uno más Uno,* 19 May 1982.

3. *The New York Times,* 20 May 1982.

4. Ibid.

5. Lewy, op. cit., pp. 107–114 and 226–230.

6. International Committee of the Red Cross, *Draft Rules for the Limitation of Danger Incurred by the Civilian Population in Time of War,* Geneva, 1956; Article 11 of this document required belligerents to "protect the civilian population subject to their authority from the dangers to which they would be exposed in an attack—in particular by moving them from the vicinity of military objectives and from the threatened areas."

7. *Report of the Secretary General,* "Respect for Human Rights in Armed Conflicts," U.N. Doc. A/8052 (1970), 18 September 1970, p. 15.

8. *Military Assistance Command, Vietnam* (MACV) Directive 525-13, Change 1, 14 February 1969, p. 1.

9. Ellsworth Bunker, (then U.S. Ambassador to South Vietnam),

"The Vietnam Refugee Problem," November 1969, COWIN Ref. Doc. 36 (COWIN: *Conduct of the War In Vietnam* is a report commissioned in 1971 by the U.S. Army Deputy Chief of Staff for Military Operations.)

10. MACCORDS-RE, "The Refugee Operation: National Overview," Refugees 1967 file, CMH, December 1967. (MACCORDS: Civil Operations and Revolutionary Development Support Division of MACV; CMH: Center for Military History.)

11. Lewy, op. cit., p. 65.

' 12. SACSA Report, 13 December 1967; and draft of Memo for Secretary of Defense, n.d., Refugees 1967 file, CMH.

13. *Massive Extra-Judicial Executions in Rural Areas Under the Government of General Efraín Ríos Montt,* (London: Amnesty International, July 1982).

14. *Time,* 23 May 1983.

15. *The New York Times,* 8 May 1983.

16. *The New York Times,* 9 August 1983.

17. *Uno más Uno,* 19, 20, 22, 24, and 27 October 1982.

18. *Uno más Uno,* 30 October 1982.

19. Norman Chomsky and Edward Herman, *The Washington Connection and Third World Fascism,* (South End Press: Boston, 1979), pp. 192-204.

20. *Latin American Regional Reports, Mexico and Central America,* 24 September, 1982; *Informe de un Genocidio, Los Refugiados Guatemaltecos,* Federación Editorial Mexicana, 1982, p. 33–34.

21. For further details and documentation, see two recent books: Stephen Kinzer and Stephen Schlesinger, *Bitter Fruit,* (Garden City, New York: Doubleday, 1982), and Richard H. Immerman, *The CIA in Guatemala,* (Boston: University of Texas Press, 1982).

22. For further details, see David Wise and Thomas B. Ross, *The Invisible Government,* (New York: Random House, 1964).

23. "U.S. Military Assistance and the Guatemalan Armed Forces," Brian Jenkins and Caesar D. Sereseres, *Armed Forces and Society,* Vol. 3, No. 4, 1977, pp. 575–594.

24. Norman Gall, "Slaughter in Guatemala," *The New York Review of Books,* 20 May 1971, pp. 12–17.

25. Jenkins and Sereseres, op. cit.

26. "Guatemala: The Roots of Revolution," *Washington Office on Latin America Special Update,* February 1983, p. 9.

27. Gall, op. cit., p. 13.

28. Jenkins and Sereseres, op. cit.

29. "Guatemala: The Roots of Revolution," op. cit., p. 10.

30. *Time,* 26 January 1968.

31. Jenkins and Sereseres, op. cit.

32. Tape-recorded interview, U.S. Embassy, San Salvador, 21 January 1983.

33. *Latin American Press,* 19 March 1970.

34. "Guatemala: The Roots of Revolution," op. cit., p. 11, citing statistics provided by the Committee of Relatives of Disappeared Persons.

35. Testimony of Lars Schoultz, Associate Professor, Department of Political Science, University of North Carolina, *Human Rights in Guatemala,* U.S. House of Representatives, Hearings (q.v.), pp. 113–115.

36. Maurer, op. cit., p. 136.

37. Washington Office on Latin America Press Release, 4 September 1981; *Under the Eagle: U.S. Intervention in Central America and the Caribbean,* Latin America Bureau, London, 1981, p. 275.

38. Comité pro Justícia y Paz, "Genocidio y Tierra Arrasada," Jan.– July, 1982; *Notícias de Guatemala,* Jan.–Oct. 1982, nos. 75–85.

39. *The New York Times,* 15 September 1982; however, the Dutch-based Catholic organization *Pax Christi* put the figure at 1,500 per month. See *Uno más Uno,* 26 August 1982.

40. *Massive Extra-Judicial Executions in Rural Areas Under the Government of General Efraín Ríos Montt,* op. cit.: A revision, which appeared on 10 October 1982, updates the figure to more than 2,600 killed; see The Washington *Post,* 12 October 1982.

41. *Comité pro Justícia y Paz; Notícias de Guatemala,* op. cit.

42. *New York Times,* 15 July 1982.

43. "Guatemala Can't Take Two Roads," Allan Nair, *The New York Times,* 20 July 1982; reprinted in *Uno más Uno,* 9 August 1982; in *Excélsior,* 12 August 1982, and in *Noticias de Guatemala* n. 83, 15 August 1982.

44. Ibid.

45. *El Día,* 7 August 1982.

46. Lewy, op. cit., p. 232.

47. *Geneva Convention Relative to the Protection of Civilian Persons in Time of War,* 12 August 1949.

48. Lewy, op. cit., p. 225.

49. See *The Laws of Armed Conflicts, A Collection of Conventions, Resolutions and other Documents,* edited by Dietrich Schindler and Jiri Toman, (Geneva: Leiden/Henry Dunant Institute, 1973), pp. 163–177.

50. Interview with residents of Las Pacayas, 28 January 1983.

51. Tape-recorded interview, San Salvador, 21 January 1983.

52. *Prensa Libre,* Guatemala City, 23 February 1983.

53. Tape-recorded interview with the commander of El Quiché, Colonel Roberto Matta. Santa Cruz del Quiché Army Headquarters, 27 January 1983.

54. As reported in various international newspapers and magazines; e.g., see *Uno más Uno,* 29 March 1983. For another detailed firsthand account of a similar massacre, see the Amnesty International Report, *Massive Extra-Judicial Executions in Rural Areas under the Government of General Efraín Ríos Montt,* op. cit. According to eye-witnesses, "Civil Defense patrol members from Baja Verapaz admitted that they acted under the orders of military commanders who instructed them to consider 'involved' anyone they found over the age of 12 in areas or houses considered suspicious by the commanders. They were told to seize such people and kill them. Even younger children, if they too were felt to be involved, were to be summarily executed."

55. Tape-recorded interview with Secretary of Public Relations Gonzalo Astudios, National Palace, Guatemala City, 15 February 1983.

56. Edgar O'Balance, *Malaya: The Communist Insurgent War, 1948–60,* (London: Faber & Faber, 1966).

57. Robert Thompson, *Defeating Communist Insurgency,* (New York: Praeger Press, 1966); see especially Chapter 11, 'Strategic Hamlets.'

58. Ibid., p. 130. "Without the people's support, the Viet Cong cannot win, but if they attack strategic hamlets they are attacking and antagonizing the people."

59. Ibid., p. 124. "The most vital aspect of protection . . . is the elimination within the hamlet of the insurgent underground organization."

60. *Notes on Strategic Hamlets,* United States Operation Mission, Saigon: Office of Rural Affairs, May 1963.

61. Dennis Duncanson, *Government and Revolution in Vietnam,* (Oxford, England: Oxford University Press, 1968), p. 316.

62. *The Pentagon Papers,* Gravel, op. cit., Vol. II, p. 150.

63. Douglas Pike, *Viet Cong,* (Cambridge: M.I.T. Press, 1966), p. 67.

64. Milton E. Osborne, *Strategic Hamlets in South Vietnam, A Survey and a Comparison,* Data Paper No. 55, Southeast Asia Program, Department of Asian Studies, Cornell University, Ithaca, N.Y., 1965, p. 32.

65. Ibid, p. 32; and Thompson, op. cit., p. 138.

66. According to the United Nations Demographic Yearbook, 1976.

67. Thompson, op. cit., p. 141.

68. Blaufarb, op. cit., p. 123; see especially Ch. 4, "Vietnam and Strategic Hamlets."

69. Unless otherwise cited, the information presented in this section was obtained through on-site investigation in Guatemala.

70. *El Gráfico*, Guatemala City, 8 October 1982.

71. *El Gráfico*, Guatemala City, 25 August 1982.

72. Tape-recorded interview with Colonel Juan Marrorquín, Cobán Army Base, 28 January 1983.

73. *Excélsior*, 7 May 1983.

74. *Inforpress Centroamericana*, No. 605, 19 August 1982.

75. "Guatemala: The Sacred Evangelical War in El Quiché," Shelton H. Davis, *The Global Reporter*, Vol. 1, No. 1, March 1983.

76. *The New York Times*, 18 July 1982.

77. *The New York Times*, 9 August 1983.

78. Stephen C. Schlesinger, "Guatemala's Coup II," *The New York Times*, 11 August 1983.

79. *Central American Report*, Vol. X, No. 3, 21 January 1983, p. 22.

80. *Central American Update*, Vol. IV, No. 5, 5 April 1983.

81. *Uno más Uno*, 4 June 1983.

82. Tape-recorded interview with President Ríos Montt, National Palace, Guatemala City, 28 January 1983.

83. For a discussion of the March 1983 reforms and their implications, see Sergio Aguayo and Alberto Cabral, "Guatemala: El evangelio del genocidio," *Nexos*, No. 66, June 1983, pp. 35–41.

84. *Time*, 23 May 1983.

85. The Washington *Post*, 5 January 1983.

86. *Congressional Presentation: Security Assistance Programs*, FY 1984, p. 353.

87. House of Representatives Resolution 2992, passed 17 May 1983; *The New York Times*, 27 July 1983.

88. *The New York Times*, 10 August 1983.

89. *The New York Times*, 9 and 15 August 1983.

90. *The New York Times*, 30 June 1983.

91. *The New York Times*, 1 July 1983.

92. *The New York Times*, 2 July 1983.

93. The Boston *Globe*, 9 August 1983.

94. The Boston *Globe*, 10 August 1983.

95. *The New York Times*, 13 August 1983.

96. *The New York Times*, 9 August 1983.

97. The Boston *Globe*, 10 August 1983.

98. *The New York Times*, 10 August 1983.

99. The Boston *Globe,* 10 August 1983.
100. *The New York Times,* 11 August 1983.
101. *The New York Times,* 13 August 1983.
102. *The New York Times,* 10 August 1983.
103. *The New York Times,* 13 August 1983.
104. *The New York Times,* 15 August 1983.
105. *The New York Times,* 4 October 1983.

Chapter Six: El Salvador

1. Tape-recorded interview with General José Alberto Medrano, San Salvador, 24 July 1980.
2. *The New York Times,* 19 August 1983.
3. *The New York Times,* 21 February 1981.
4. U.S. Department of Defense, *Congressional Presentation: Security Assistance Fiscal Year 1982,* Washington D.C., 1981, p. 417.
5. U.S. Department of State, *"U.S. Assistance to El Salvador, Fact Sheet,"* 1981.
6. *The New York Times,* 1, 10, 19 and 29 March 1981 and 8 and 13 July 1981; The Washington *Post,* 3, 10 and 18 March 1981 and 7 June 1981.
7. Testimony of Under Secretary of State for Political Affairs, Walter J. Stoessel, Jr., before the Senate Appropriations Committee, 13 March 1981.
8. The Washington *Post,* 15 May 1981.
9. *The New York Times,* 13 July 1981.
10. The Oakland *Tribune,* 23 July 1981.
11. *Inforpress Centroamericana, Centroamérica 1982,* "El Salvador," pp. 30–32.
12. *The New York Times,* 2 August 1982.
13. Testimony of Representative Gerry Studds, Barbara Mikulski, and Robert Edgar, U.S. Congress, House Subcommittee on Foreign Operations, Hearings, *Foreign Assistance and Related Programs Appropriations for 1982;* 97th Congress, 1st. session, 25 February 1981, p. 29.
14. Ibid.
15. *Inforpress Centroamericana, Centroamérica 1982,* op. cit. See also, *NACLA Report on the Americas,* Vol. XVI, No. 2, March–April 1982, pp. 26–27.
16. *Latin America Weekly Report,* 4 June 1982; *The New York Times,* 13 June 1982.
17. The Washington *Post,* 10 June 1982; *Excélsior,* 10 June 1982.

18. *The New York Times,* 18 April 1982; Blaufarb, op. cit., pp. 125–126.

19. *Uno mías Uno,* 3 July 1982.

20. The Washington *Post,* 15 June 1982 and 4 July 1982; *El Día,* 17 June 1982.

21. *The New York Times,* 14 and 15 June 1982.

22. *The New York Times,* 14 June 1982.

23. Testimony of General Wallace H. Nutting given before the Senate Foreign Relations Committee, *The New York Times,* 4 August 1982.

24. *Time,* 25 April 1983.

25. Tape-recorded interview with a ranking military adviser, U.S. Embassy, San Salvador, 21 January 1983.

26. *El Día,* 30 July 1982.

27. *The New York Times,* 26 September 1982.

28. Ibid. See also, *El Día,* 1 December 1982, Gregorio Selser's interview with U.S. Lieutenant Colonel John Buchanan (Ret.).

29. The Washington *Post,* 5 November 1982; *Excélsior,* 5 November 1982.

30. *The New York Times,* 26 September 1982.

31. *El Día,* 1 July 1982; *Uno más Uno,* 2 July 1982.

32. *El Día,* 16 and 17 July 1982; *Uno más Uno,* 16 July 1982.

33. *Uno más Uno,* 22 July 1982.

34. *El Día,* 30 July 1982 and 3 August 1982.

35. *Uno más Uno,* 27 August 1982 and 7 September 1982; *El Día,* 31 August 1982 and 4 September 1982.

36. *Uno más Uno,* 17 September 1982; *El Día,* 21 September 1982 and 5 October 1982; *Inforpress Centroamericana,* No. 515, 21 October 1982.

37. The Associated Press, 20 July 1983.

38. *U.S. News and World Report,* 6 June 1983.

39. *The New York Times,* 23 August 1983.

40. *The New York Times,* 19 August 1983; *Newsweek,* 5 December 1983.

41. Tape-recorded interview with Colonel Jaime Flores Lima, 20 January 1983.

42. *U.S. News and World Report,* 22 August 1983.

43. Associated Press, 20 July 1983.

44. *Central American Report,* Vol. X, No. 21, 3 June 1983, p. 162.

45. *Central American Report,* Vol. X, No. 3, 21 January 1983, p. 22, citing statistics from the United Nations' Economic Commission for Latin America.

46. In addition to on-site observation and interviews with both insurgent and government military commanders, to establish the facts and construct the chronology of the offensives and counteroffensives beginning in October 1982 and lasting until the end of 1983, along with other sources, the following five newspapers were consulted on a daily basis: *Excélsior, Uno más uno, El Día, The New York Times,* and The Washington *Post.*

47. According to the Washington *Post,* 15 October 1982, around 700 guerrilla fighters participated in this attack.

48. *Latin American Weekly Report,* 22 October 1982.

49. The Washington *Post,* 16 and 17 October 1982; *The New York Times,* 17 October 1982.

50. *Uno más Uno,* 23, 28 and 29 November 1982.

51. *Radio Venceremos,* 15 November 1982; The Washington *Post,* 15 June 1983.

52. *Uno más Uno,* 13 and 14 November 1982.

53. *Uno más Uno,* 13 October 1982.

54. The Washington *Post,* 7 November 1982.

55. Ibid.

56. *El Día,* 13 January 1983.

57. *Excélsior,* 14 January 1983.

58. *Excélsior,* 18 January 1983.

59. *Excélsior,* 20 January 1983.

60. *El Día,* 25 January 1983.

61. *Uno más Uno,* 25 January 1983.

62. Ibid.

63. *El Día,* 27 January 1983.

64. *Uno más Uno,* 28 January 1983.

65. *El Día,* 29 January 1983.

66. *Uno más Uno,* 29 January 1983.

67. *Excélsior,* 30 January 1983.

68. *Uno más Uno,* 30 January 1983.

69. *El Día,* 31 January 1983.

70. *Uno más Uno,* 2 February 1983.

71. *The New York Times,* 13 February 1983.

72. *Uno más Uno,* 4 February 1983.

73. *Uno más Uno,* 5 February 1983.

74. *Newsweek,* 7 February 1983.

75. *The Nation,* 12 March 1983.

76. *Uno más Uno,* 1 April 1983; *The Nation,* 16 April 1983.

77. *The New York Times,* 3 February 1983.

78. *The New York Times,* 11 February 1983; see also *Time,* 8 August 1983.

79. *The New York Times,* 12 August 1983.

80. The Washington *Post,* 15 June 1983.

81. *Central American Update,* Vol. IV, No. 5, April 1983, p. 28.

82. *The New York Times,* 12 August 1983.

83. *Newsweek,* 21 March 1983.

84. *Central American Update,* op. cit.

85. Cynthia Arnson, "The Vietnam Syndrome in El Salvador," *The Nation,* 30 April 1983.

86. *Central American Update,* op. cit.

87. Tape-recorded interview, U.S. Embassy, San Salvador, 21 January 1983.

88. Although numerous journalists and other visitors have reported virtually identical statements, this exact quotation comes from an article in *The New York Times,* 12 August 1983.

89. *U.S. News and World Report,* 6 June 1983; *The New York Times,* 12 August 1983.

90. As cited in *U.S. News and World Report,* 22 August 1983.

91. The regular army is made up of 22,400 troops. The remainder of the armed forces, while including a tiny air force and navy, is made up of security forces, primarily the national guard, but also small corps of national police and treasury police.

92. According to the government report during this period, the armed forces suffered 3,557 casualties: 1,073 killed and 2,484 wounded.

93. According to the government report during this period, the armed forces suffered 6,487 casualties: 2,292 killed and 4,195 wounded.

94. *Central American Update,* op. cit.

95. *The New York Times,* 23 August 1983.

96. The Washington *Post,* 11 June 1983.

97. The Washington *Post,* 28 May 1983.

98. The Washington *Post,* 11 March 1983.

99. The Washington *Post,* 3 June 1983.

100. *The New York Times,* 28 May 1983.

101. *Central American Report,* Vol. X, No. 23, 17 June 1983, p. 179; and *The New York Times,* 21 July 1983.

102. *The New York Times,* 5 June 1983.

103. *U.S. News and World Report,* 22 August 1983.

104. The Washington *Post,* 15 June 1983.

105. *The New York Times,* 16 July 1983.

106. *The New York Times,* 12 August 1983.

107. *U.S. News and World Report,* 16 June 1983.

108. *The New York Times,* 12 August 1983.

109. *The New York Times,* 4 August 1983.

110. *The New York Times,* 16 July 1983.

111. *Central American Report,* Vol. X, No. 21, 3 June 1983, p. 182.

112. *The New York Times,* 25 August 1983.

113. Tape-recorded interview with Colonel Jaime Flores Lima, 3rd Battalion Headquarters, San Miguel, El Salvador, 20 January 1983.

114. *The New York Times,* 25 August 1983.

115. *The New York Times,* 27 August 1983.

116. United Press International, 1 September 1983.

117. For examples, see the United Press International reports of 20, 23, 27, and 31 August 1983; *Central American Report,* Vol. X, No. 33, 26 August 1983, p. 258; *The New York Times,* 30 August 1983.

118. *The News,* 27 November 1983.

119. *Newsweek,* 5 December 1983.

120. Horacio Castellanos Moya "Avanza la unidad militar de las fuerzas rebeldes," *El Día,* 3 December 1983.

121. According to Sam Dillon of the *Miami Herald,* one training camp that he visited graduated 150 combatants per month; as cited in Gino Lofredo, "Reconocen en EU los avances de la guerrilla," *El Día,* 3 December 1983.

122. *Central American Report,* Vol. X. No. 34, 2 September 1983, p. 267.

123. *The New York Times,* 5 September 1983.

124. *Central American Report,* Vol. X. No. 35, 9 September 1983, p. 273–27.

125. *The New York Times,* 6 September 1983.

126. Interview with FMLN commanders, Mexico City, 10 November 1983.

127. Ibid.

128. See the almost daily reports of such actions in *Excelsior, El Día,* and *Uno más Uno,* during the months of June–August 1983.

129. *The New York Times,* 11 September 1983.

130. *Central American Report,* Vol. X. No. 33, 26 August 1983, p. 257.

131. *Cable Network News,* 27 September 1983; Associated Press, 29 September 1983.

132. *CBS Nightly News,* 10 October 1983.

133. The Associated Press, 26 September 1983.

134. See the frequent small articles scattered in *Excelsior, El Día, Uno*

más Uno, during the months of September and October. See also, the infrequent U.S. wire service stories during this same period, e.g., Associated Press, 5 October 1983 and United Press International, 8 October 1983.

135. *Newsweek,* 31 October 1983.

136. *Uno más Uno,* 31 October 1983.

137. *Uno más Uno,* 3 November 1983.

138. Ibid; *El Día,* 4 November 1983.

139. *Uno más Uno,* 8 November 1983.

140. *El Día,* 12 November 1983.

141. *Uno más Uno,* 13 November 1983.

142. *Uno más Uno,* 14 November 1983; *El Día,* 11 and 14 November 1983.

143. *El Día,* 11 November 1983.

144. Washington *Post,* 6 November 1983.

145. Washington *Post,* 13 November 1983, as cited in *Uno más Uno,* 14 November 1983.

146. *Uno más Uno,* 13, 16, 18 and 19 November 1983.

147. *El Día,* 18 November 1983.

148. *El Día,* 22 November 1983.

149. *El Día,* 5 November 1983.

150. *Uno más Uno,* 17 and 18 November 1983; *El Día,* 18 through 22 November 1983.

151. *El Día,* 22 and 23 November 1983.

152 *U. S. News and World Report,* 5 December 1983.

153. *Radio Venceremos* Broadcast, 5 December 1983, as reported in *El Día,* 6 December 1983.

154. *U.S. News and World Report,* 5 December 1983.

155. *El Día,* 18 November 1983.

156. In addition to sources already cited in this section, see *El Día,* 21, 22 and 27 November 1983, for specifics on these military aspects of the war.

157. *Uno más Uno,* 23 November 1983.

158. Gino Lofredo, "Reconocen en EU los avances de la guerrilla," *El Día,* 3 December 1983.

159. *Uno más Uno,* 8 December 1983.

160. *Uno más Uno,* 14 December 1983; *El Día,* 16 December 1983.

161. *Uno más Uno,* 15 December 1983.

162. *El Día,* 18 December 1983.

163. *ABC Nightly News,* 2 January 1984.

164. *The New York Times,* 31 December 1983.

165. *CBS Nightly News,* 30 December 1983.

166. United Press International, 30 and 31 December 1983.

167. United Press International, 1 January 1984.

168. Robert E. White, "Salvadoran Impasse," *The New York Times,* 30 November 1983.

169. United Press International, 2 December 1983, as cited in *El Día,* 3 December 1983.

170. *El Día,* 27 November 1983; *The News,* 27 November 1983.

171. *Uno más Uno,* 23 November 1983.

Chapter Seven: Honduras

1. The Honduran labor unions held a different view. They described the same period as one characterized by a brutal "wave of repression." See the *Miami Herald,* 13 April 1979.

2. *Latin American Political Report,* 14 September 1979.

3. Even more generally, it should be noted that between 1975 and 1979 Honduras was the largest importer of arms in Central America. See *World Armaments and Disarmament Yearbook,* (London: Stockholm International Peace Research Institute [SIPRI], 1980), p. 97.

4. *Foreign Military Sales and Military Assistance Pacts,* Department of State, Security Assistance Agency, December 1980, pp. 67–68.

5. Michael T. Klare and Cynthia Arnson, *Supplying Repression* (Washington, D.C.: Institute for Policy Studies, 1982), p. 51.

6. Testimony of Deputy Assistant Secretary of Defense Franklin Kramer before the House Appropriations Subcommittee on Foreign Relations, 25 March 1980, as cited in Cynthia Arnson, "Background Information on Honduras and El Salvador and U.S. Military Assistance to Central America," Update #5, Washington, D.C.: (*Institute for Policy Studies Resource,* August 1981), p. 4.

7. Arnson, op. cit., Update #6, March 1982, p. 9.

8. Arnson, op. cit., Update #5, August 1981, p. 4.

9. The Miami *Herald,* 8 October 1980.

10. Ibid.

11. *The New York Times,* 18 August 1981.

12. The Washington *Post,* 28 March 1980.

13. For information contained in this and the following paragraphs, unless otherwise cited, see Gregorio Sleser, "Si hay intervención, Honduras será las base come in 1954. El coronel Alvarez Martínez la está urgiendo," *El Día,* 14 March 1982; Gregorio Selser, "Honduras: sigue fortaleciendo su poder en la cúpula militar el general Alvarez," *El Día,*

12 December 1982; *Newsweek,* 5 September 1983.

14. *Inforpress Centroamericana,* No. 519. 18 November 1982.

15. *Inforpress Centroamericana,* No. 520, 25 November 1982.

16. *Latin American Weekly Report,* 24 September 1982.

17. *Excélsior,* 31 August 1982.

18. *Latin American Weekly Report,* 24 September 1982.

19. *El Día,* 29 October 1982.

20. *Uno más Uno,* 5 November 1982; *El Día,* 5 November 1982.

21. In addition to the sources cited in Ch. 6, see also, The Washington *Post,* 15 June 1983.

22. *Uno más Uno,* 3 December 1982.

23. *El Día,* 21 November 1982; see also, *Uno más Uno,* 30 November 1982.

24. *El Día,* 21 November 1982.

25. Among which there were national guard and army soldiers, as well as members of the paramilitary organization ORDEN.

26. See Philip E. Wheaton, *The Iron Triangle: The Honduran Connection,* (Washington, D.C.: EPICA, 1981), pp. 2–3; see also, "The Iron Triangle," *The News,* Mexico City, 14 October 1982, pp. 22–23.

27. *Latin American Weekly Report,* 22 August 1982; *The New York Times,* 11 July 1982.

28. *The New York Times,* 6 July 1982.

29. *The New York Times,* 4 July 1982.

30. *El Día,* 11 July 1982.

31. *Central American Update,* Vol. V, No. 1, August 1983.

32. For more details on the plight of the Salvadoran refugees in Honduras, see *Salvadoran Refugees in Honduras,* Hearing Before the Subcommittee on Inter-American Affairs of the Committee on Foreign Affairs, House of Representatives, 97th Congress, 1st Session, 17 December 1981, (Washington, D.C.: U.S. Government Printing Office, 1982).

33. *U.S. News & World Report,* 15 August 1983.

34. *Time,* 13 June 1983. The economically active population does not include peasants, the chronically unemployed, or other marginal citizens; nor, of course, does it take into account the minimally 40 percent of the work force that is underemployed.

35. *Inforpress Centroamericana,* No. 514, 14 October 1982.

36. *Central American Report,* Vol. X, No. 3, 21 January 1983, p. 22, citing statistics from the United Nations' Economic Council on Latin America.

37. *Inforpress Centroamericana,* No. 514, 14 October 1982.

38. *Newsweek,* 5 September 1983.

39. *Inforpress Centroamericana,* No. 518, 11 November 1982.

40. See Table 7, page 237.

41. *Central American Report,* Vol. X, No. 12, 25 March 1983, p. 95, citing the IDB 1982 Annual Report.

42. *The News,* Mexico City, 14 October 1982.

43. *Inforpress Centroamericana,* No. 518, 11 November 1982, citing the Honduran Ministry of the Treasury and Public Credit Statistics.

44. The Washington *Post,* 15 October 1982.

45. *The New York Times,* 15 April 1982.

46. U.S. Department of State, Congressional Presentation, Security Assistance Programs, Fiscal Years 1981–1984, Washington, D.C.

47. *Newsweek,* 5 September 1983.

48. *The New York Times,* 25 June 1983.

49. *Central American Report,* Vol. X, No. 5, 4 February 1983, p. 33.

50. *Latin American Weekly Report,* 30 July 1982.

51. Ibid.

52. *The New York Times,* 5 August 1982.

53. The Washington *Post,* 25 July 1982.

54. *The New York Times,* 5 August 1982.

55. The Washington *Post,* 4 November 1982.

56. *Central American Report,* Vol. X, No. 5, 4 February 1983, p. 33.

57. *The New York Times,* 23 July 1983.

58. *The New York Times,* 19 July 1983.

59. *The New York Times,* 23 July 1983.

60. *Time,* 8 August 1983.

61. *The New York Times,* 23 July 1983.

62. *The New York Times,* 27 July 1983.

63. *The New York Times,* 26 July 1983; *U.S. News & World Report,* 29 August 1983.

64. *The New York Times,* 7 August 1983, claims that 21 ships are involved; the Boston *Globe,* 9 August 1983, places the total number at 19.

65. *The New York Times,* 4 August 1983.

66. *The New York Times,* 20 July 1983.

67. *The New York Times,* 30 July 1983.

68. *The New York Times,* 31 July 1983.

69. *The New York Times,* 26 July 1983.

70. *The New York Times,* 15 August 1983.

71. *U.S. News & World Report,* 29 August 1983.

72. Personal conversation with a ranking Sandinista official.

73. *The New York Times,* 29 July 1983.

74. See, for example, the articles in *The New York Times,* 21, 22, 23, 24, and 27 July 1983 and 2 and 3 August 1983.

75. See, for example, *The New York Times,* 7 August 1983, editorial.

76. *The New York Times,* 3 August 1983.

77. *The New York Times,* 7 September 1983.

78. *Newsweek,* 5 September 1983. Since Big Pine II involves far greater U.S. forces, this should be considered an extremely low estimate. Moreover, the figure of 165 million dollars for operational expenses is an appropriation based on the 5.2 million dollars that the one-week Big Pine maneuver cost. This figure does not include the expenses for the naval battle groups or the ordinary cost of maintaining the other U.S. forces involved in Big Pine II.

79. *The New York Times,* 3 and 21 August 1983.

80. *U.S. News & World Report,* 15 August 1983.

81. Ibid.

82. *Newsweek,* 5 September 1983.

83. *New York Times,* 21 August 1983.

84. *Newsweek,* 5 September 1983.

85. *The New York Times,* 3 August 1983.

86. *The New York Times,* 31 July 1983.

87. *The New York Times,* 5 September 1983.

88. The Washington *Post,* 29 April 1983; *The New York Times,* 31 July 1983; *U.S. News & World Report,* 22 August 1983.

89. *The New York Times,* 3 August 1983.

90. *The New York Times,* 5 October 1983.

91. *The New York Times,* 21 August 1983.

92. *The New York Times,* 26 July 1983.

93. *The New York Times,* 21 August 1983.

94. *The New York Times,* 23 July 1983.

95. *The New York Times,* 21 August 1983.

96. *The New York Times,* 23 July 1983.

97. *Newsweek,* 5 September 1983.

98. *The New York Times,* 21 July 1983.

99. The Washington *Post,* 10 June 1983.

100. *The New York Times,* 19 and 23 July 1983.

101. *Havana Convention on Civil Strife,* Article 1 (1), 1928.

102. *The Charter of the Organization of American States,* Article 15.

103. *The Charter of the United Nations,* Article 2 (4).

104. *The Inter-American Treaty of Reciprocal Assistance,* Article 1, Rio de Janeiro, 1947.

105. *Inforpress Centroamericana,* No. 519, 18 November 1982.

106. *The New York Times,* 15 April 1982.

107. *Inforpress Centroamericana,* No. 520, 25 November 1982.

108. *The News,* Mexico City, 7 June 1983.

109. *Central American Report,* Vol. X, No. 6, 11 February 1983, p. 43.

110. *The New York Times,* 23 July 1983.

111. *Central American Report,* Vol. X, No. 9, 4 March 1983, p. 71.

112. *Newsweek,* 5 September 1983.

113. *The News,* Mexico City, 7 June 1983.

114. *The New York Times,* 25 June 1983.

115. Tom Wicker, "Irony in Honduras," *The New York Times,* 5 August 1983.

116. Honduras is a signatory, since September 1977, of the *American Declaration of the Rights of Man.* Its constitution also guarantees basic human rights.

117. *Inforpress Centroamericana,* No. 507, 26 August 1982.

118. *The New York Times,* 9 November 1982.

119. *Inforpress Centroamericana,* No. 507, 26 August 1982.

120. *The News,* Mexico City, 14 October 1982.

121. *Central American Report,* Vol. X, No. 15, 15 April 1983, p. 109.

122. *The New York Times,* 7 October 1982; *El Día,* 12 October 1982; *Inforpress Centroamericana,* No. 514, 14 October 1982.

123. *Central American Report,* Vol. X, No. 9, 4 March 1983, p. 71.

124. The Washington *Post,* 11 June 1983. See also, *The New York Times,* 21 August 1983, which quotes Alvarez as claiming that another "three hundred leftists recently entered Honduras after being trained in Nicaragua."

125. *Time,* 13 June 1983.

126. *Newsweek,* 5 September 1983.

127. *Central American Report,* Vol. X, No. 14, 15 April 1983, p. 109.

128. *Central American Report,* Vol. X, No. 18, 13 May 1983, p. 142.

129. Barbara Crossette, "Tensions Rise in Honduras As Bastion of Washington," *The New York Times,* 10 July 1983.

Chapter Eight: Costa Rica

1. Carol Thompson, Mary Anderberg, and Joan Antell, eds., *Encyclopedia of Developing Nations,* (New York: McGraw-Hill, 1982).

2. The Washington *Post,* 14 May 1983.

3. Mitchell A. Seligon and William I. Carroll III, "The Costa Rican Role in the Sandinista Victory," in *Nicaragua in Revolution,* Thomas

W. Walker ed., (New York: Praeger Press, 1982), pp. 331–344.

4. *Central American Report,* Vol. X, No. 3, 21 January 1983, p. 22.

5. *The New York Times,* 21 November 1982.

6. *The Encyclopedia of Developing Nations,* op. cit., p. 287.

7. Shirley Christian, "Careworn Costa Rica," *The New Republic,* 6 December 1982.

8. *Central American Report,* Vol. X, No. 19, 20 May 1983, p. 151.

9. *Central American Report,* Vol. X, No. 22, 10 June 1983, p. 172.

10. *Central American Report,* Vol. X, No. 18, 13 May 1983, p. 143.

11. Christian, op. cit.; *Central American Report,* Vol. IX, No. 44.

12. *Central American Report,* Vol. X, No. 1, 7 January 1983, p. 8.

13. *The New York Times,* 21 November 1982; and Tables 6, 7, and 8, pages 234–238.

14. *Central American Report,* Vol X, No. 1, 7 January 1983, p. 8. This figure does not include any repayment of the principal of Costa Rica's foreign debt.

15. Christian, op. cit.

16. See for example, *Uno más Uno,* 12 and 19 December 1982, and *The New York Times,* 30 July 1983.

17. *Excélsior,* 15 September 1982; Christian, op. cit.

18. *Uno más Uno,* 19 December 1982.

19. *The Nation,* 21 May 1983.

20. *Central American Report,* Vol. X, No. 22, 10 June 1983, p. 172.

21. *The Christian Science Monitor,* 4 November 1982.

22. *El Día,* 30 November 1982.

23. *Uno más Uno,* 19 December 1982.

24. According to the Los Angeles *Times,* as quoted in *El Día,* 23 October 1982.

25. The Washington *Post,* 14 May 1983.

26. *Central American Report,* Vol. X, No. 22, 10 June 1983, p. 172. The five countries are Israel, Taiwan, South Korea, Panama, and Venezuela.

27. *The New York Times,* 9 September 1983; Associated Press, 20 September 1983.

28. *The New York Times,* 30 July 1983.

29. *The New York Times,* 20 September 1983.

30. The Washington *Post,* 13 May 1983.

31. *The New York Times,* 20 September 1983 and 13 October 1983.

32. *The New York Times,* 20 September 1983.

33. Unless otherwise cited, information for this section is based upon

the two-part series by Heinz Dieterich, *Uno más Uno,* 5 and 6 November 1983.

34. United Press International, 1 October 1983.

35. *The New York Times,* 13 October 1983.

36. *Uno más Uno,* 6 November 1983.

37. *El Día,* 18 November 1983.

38. *Uno más Uno,* 19 November 1983.

39. *La Nación,* San José, Costa Rica, 19 November 1983.

40. *El Día,* 4 December 1983.

41. *El Día,* 4 December 1983; *Central American Report,* Vol. X, No. 18, 18 May 1983, p. 143.

42. *El Día,* 5 December 1983.

43. *Uno más Uno,* 5 December 1983; *El Día,* 5 December 1983

Chapter Nine: Reform Versus Repression

1. The Washington *Post,* 12 February 1981.

2. This and the following quotations, unless otherwise indicated, are taken from Robert E. White, "Central America: The Problem that Won't Go Away," *The New York Times Magazine,* 18 July 1982.

3. Robert E. White, "Perilous Latin Policy," *The New York Times,* 2 May 1983.

4. During personal conversations with Ambassador White, he has repeatedly referred to Roy Prosterman as a "genius."

5. In "Perilous Latin Policy," op. cit. White again condemns human rights violations not on moral grounds but within the pragmatic context that it promotes insurgency. Referring to the people of Honduras who demand social change and oppose their government's militaristic policies, he states that "these dissidents are now treated as subversives, and, for the first time in its history, the Honduras military has begun to abduct and kill labor union leaders, intellectuals, and others who dissent from official policy. This is the way revolution took hold in El Salvador—with popular outrage against officially sponsored disappearances."

6. James L. Buckley, Under Secretary of State, "Arms Transfers and the National Interest," United States Department of State Bureau of Public Affairs publication, *Current Policy* Number 279, 21 May 1981. Emphasis in the original.

7. Ibid. Emphasis in the original.

8. Thomas O. Enders, Assistant Secretary of State, "Building the Peace in Central America," United States Department of State Bureau of Public Affairs, *Current Policy* Number 414, 20 August 1982.

Chapter Ten: It Depends on the Way You Count

1. The Washington *Post*, 29 April 1983. Again, for example, during his 26 July 1983 speech the President made virtually the same claim when he announced that "for every one dollar we provide for security assistance to that region, we provide three dollars for economic and human development"; *The New York Times*, 28 July 1983.

2. One of the few articles that did not accept the government's distorted calculations of military and economic aid to Central America is Joanne Omang, "Nation-by-Nation Survey of Southern Neighbors," The Washington *Post*, 12 June 1983.

3. The two programs are the Foreign Military and Construction Sales Agreement Program (FMSA) and the Commercial Exports License under Arms Export Control Act (AECA).

4. Under Section 502-B of the 1974 Foreign Assistance Act, the Economic Support Fund is by law one of the five elements of the Security Assistance Program, along with MAP, IMET, FMS, and Peacekeeping Operations.

5. The Washington *Post*, 12 June 1983.

6. AID Memo, 1 October 1983, Washington, D.C.: Center for International Policy.

7. Ibid.

8. *Congressional Presentation: Security Assistance Programs,* Fiscal Year 1983, U.S. Department of State, Washington, D.C., 1982, p. 457.

9. Tape-recorded interview, U.S. Embassy, San Salvador, 21 January 1983.

10. Ibid.

Chapter Eleven: Rationalizing Washington's Policy

1. George P. Shultz, "Reflections Among Neighbors," before the General Assembly of the Organization of American States, Washington, D.C. *United States Department of State,* Bureau of Public Affairs, *Current Policy* No. 432, 17 November 1982.

2. Thomas O. Enders, "Areas of Challenge in the Americas," before the Inter-American Press Association, Chicago, Illinois, *United States Department of State,* Bureau of Public Affairs, Washington, D.C. *Current Policy,* No. 424, 30 September 1982.

3. Thomas O. Enders, Testimony before the House of Representatives by the Assistant Secretary of State for Inter-American Affairs, 1 March 1983, as cited in "Background Information on U.S. Policy and U.S. Military Assistance to Central America," Update #8, Cynthia Arn-

son, *Institute for Policy Studies,* March 1983; see also *Newsweek,* 14 March 1983.

4. Lewis A. Tambs and Frank Aker, "Shattering the Vietnam Syndrome: A Scenario for Success in El Salvador," unpublished position paper, 1982. Tambs' disciple, Frank Aker, accompanied the Ambassador on his mission to Colombia.

5. Ibid.

6. In October 1983, for personal reasons, Clark left NSC to become Secretary of the Interior, being replaced by Robert McFarlane.

7. *Time,* 8 August 1983.

8. The Washington *Post,* 29 April 1983.

9. *The New York Times,* 19 July 1983.

10. *The New York Times,* 20 July 1983.

11. Although this quote has been widely cited, for a specific reference see William Shawcross, *Sideshow: Kissinger, Nixon and the Destruction of Cambodia,* (New York: Simon and Schuster, 1979), pp. 304–305.

12. Tom Wicker, "Hiding Behind Henry," *The New York Times,* 19 July 1983. Emphasis in the original.

13. "The Refugees Are Coming!", *The New York Times,* 24 June 1983.

14. The Washington *Post,* 2 June 1983.

15. *The New York Times,* 11 March 1983.

16. *The New York Times,* 21 June 1983.

17. *The New York Times,* 27 July 1983. On July 28 the House voted 221 to 205 to stop covert funding of the contras, and although this demonstrated growing opposition to Reagan's "secret war," in practical terms of actually stopping the money it had no effect because the Republican-controlled Senate refused to support the decision.

18. *The New York Times,* 16 August 1983.

Conclusion

1. *Inforpress Centroamericana,* No. 478, 28 January 1983. These three nations are also commonly referred to as the Northern Tier states or the Iron Triangle.

2. *Inforpress Centroamericana,* No. 478, 28 January 1983.

3. Because of U.S. domestic and international political considerations, Guatemala did not formally join the CDC. However, in July 1982 the founding members invited the new Guatemalan regimes to join the CDC because this country's new leader, General Efraín Ríos Montt, expressed an interest in cooperating with the other three nations

in fighting "subversion and terrorism." By contrast, at this time, then president of Panama, Aristides Royo, described the CDC as "an arrow aimed at the heart of Nicaragua." He also declared that he was not "enthused with the idea of belonging to the CDC." *Inforpress Centroamericana,* No. 501, 15 July 1982.

4. *Inforpress Centroamericana,* No. 478, 28 January 1983.

5. *The New York Times,* 4 October 1983.

6. *The New York Times,* 6 October 1983.

7. "Remarks Prepared for Delivery by the Honorable Fred C. Iklé, Under Secretary of Defense for Policy," *Office of Assistant Secretary of Defense (Public Affairs) News Release; The New York Times,* 12 and 18 September 1983. See also, Tom Wicker, "A Policy Revealed," *The New York Times,* 19 September 1983.

8. *The New York Times,* 20 September 1983.

9. "Remarks Prepared for Delivery by the Honorable Fred C. Iklé," op. cit.

10. *"A Symposium:* Vietnam-Era Aides Explore Parallels and Differences, Some Applied History for Central America," *The New York Times,* 21 August 1983.

11. *The New York Times,* 11 March 1983.

INDEX

Abrams, Creighton, 80
Acajutla, El Salvador, 152
Afghanistan, 245, 246, 265
Agency for International
    Development, U.S., *see* AID
agrarian reform, *see* land reform
Agrarian Reform Law (1980), 19, 135
agriculture:
    in Costa Rica, 212, 213, 215
    elite's dominance in, 2–3, 99, 124
    in El Salvador, 151–152, 169, 176
    in Guatemala, 123, 125
    international market of, 3, 18, 215
    in South Vietnam, 117
Agroville program, 114
Ahuras Tara, see Big Pine maneuvers
AID (Agency for International
    Development, U.S.), 19, 36, 50,
    114, 233*n*
    El Salvador and, 135–136, 164
    Honduras and, 208–209, 242
    Office of Public Safety of, 36–37,
    101, 185
AIFLD (American Institute for Free
    Labor Development), 19
Air America, 50, 69
Air Force, U.S., 197, 198
    Special Operations Wing (Air
    Commandos), 6, 7, 86, 204
AirLand Battle Doctrine, 82, 83
Alfonsin, Raul, 30
Allende, Salvador, 251
Alvarez Martínez, Gustavo Adolfo,
    73, 184–189, 191–192, 195,
    205
    independence of, 187–188

Alvarez Martínez *(cont'd)*
    military training of, 185
    Monge compared to, 220–221
    Negroponte's relationship with, 59–
    60, 184–185
    political polarization caused by,
    209–211
American Institute for Free Labor
    Development (AIFLD), 19
Amnesty International, 99, 104, 105
Anamoros, El Salvador, mass
    surrender in, 174, 175
Anderson, Jack, 184
Arana Osorio, Carlos, 103–104
Araujo, Arturo, 131
Arauz, Fernando, 223
Arbenz, Jacobo, 101
Arce Brigade, 167, 171, 174
ARDE (Democratic Revolutionary
    Alliance), 53, 56–57, 63, 66, 68–
    70, 221–223
    aircraft supplier of, 68–69
    "Blazing Tooth" Operation of, 73,
    223
    Monge's crackdown on, 221–222
    strike of, 64
ARENA (Nationalist Republican
    Alliance), 25, 31–32
Argentina, 29–30, 49, 90
    Alvarez in, 185, 186
    contras and, 54, 60
    in Malvinas/Falkland Islands war,
    54, 60, 218, 246
armed forces, U.S.:
    competition in, 81
    hierarchy of, 6

armed forces, U.S. *(cont'd)*
  see also Air Force, U.S.; Army,
    U.S.; Navy, U.S.
Army, U.S., 77, 198
  High Command of, 87
  Hondurans trained by, 182–184,
    196
  insurgency theory of, 88–94
  School of the Americas of, 8, 148,
    182, 185
  Southern Command of, 129, 130,
    146–147
  Special Forces of, *see* Green Berets
assassinations, 88, 221
  of Diem, 22
  of Kennedy, 7, 76, 117–118
  of Romero, 135
  selective, 100, 103
Associated Press, 166
Atlacátl Battalion, 139, 140, 144, 145,
    151
  massacres of, 173–174, 178
  Ramón Belloso compared to, 143
  reenlistment in, 161
Atonal Battalion, 144, 145, 155, 156
Austin, Hudson, 10

Bader Meinhof, 89
Baker, Howard, 72
bankers, international, debtor nation's
    cartel feared by, 216–217
Bank of the Army, Guatemalan, 103
Basic Law of Agrarian Reform
    (1980), 19, 135
Batista, Fulgencio, 93
Bay of Pigs invasion, 15, 63, 101, 260
Berlín, Battle of (1983), 157
Bermudez, Enrique, 57, 60
Bianchi, Francisco, 105
Big Pine maneuvers *(Ahuras Tara)*,
    65, 73, 198–206, 253
  cost of, 204
  duration of, 200, 203–204
  effects of, 201–203
  military operations of, 204–206
  postponement of, 198
  Reagan's views on, 200–201
Bishop, Maurice, 10

Black, Eli M., 181n
Blandón, Adolfo, 178
"Blazing Tooth" Operation (ARDE),
    73, 223
Bodden Cacacers, Hubert, 186
Boland Amendment, 54–55, 203
Bolivia, reform in, 16n
Bolsones Territorial, 191
"bomb and talk" strategy, 249–250
bombing policy, 7, 221
  Big Pine II and, 205
  in El Salvador, 149, 150, 151, 155
  saturation, 76–77, 78, 149, 265–266
  in Vietnam war, 76–77, 78, 148–
    149, 251, 265–266
Bonner, Raymond, 58
Brezhnev, Leonid, 267–268
bridges, FMLN's destruction of, 152,
    153, 156, 169, 177
Briggs, Sir Harold, 113, 114
Buckley, James L., 230

Cabel Bridge, murders at, 113
Cacaopera, El Salvador, FMLN's
    capture of, 156
Cackchiquel Indians, 99
Calero Portocarrero, Adolfo, 67
Calley, William, Jr., 137
Cambodia, bombing of, 251, 265–266
capitalism, peasant, 17–19
CAPs (Combined Action Platoons),
    79–80, 86
Carazo, Roberto, 214–215
Caribbean Basin Initiative, 216, 256n
Caritas, 123
Carranza, Nicolas, 31
Carter, Jimmy, 23, 126, 136–137, 193
  CIA's covert operations limited by,
    50–51, 52
Carter Administration, 35, 239, 254–
    255
  Costa Rica and, 214
  El Salvador and, 18–20, 23–24,
    133–135, 136–137, 226–227, 229,
    255
  Guatemala and, 23–24, 103, 104,
    126, 255
  Honduras and, 180–184, 190–191,

Carter Administration *(cont'd)*
     193, 255
  human rights policy of, 23–24, 103,
     104, 126, 229, 255
  land reform encouraged by, 18–20,
     181, 229
  Nicaragua and, 55–56, 133–134,
     180
Casey, William J., 50, 51–52, 53–54,
     63
Castro, Fidel, 201, 213, 262, 264
Catholics, Catholic Church, 26, 123,
     190, 211
  in El Salvador, 43, 133
  in Guatemala, 121, 122, 124
  liberation theology of, 3–4, 90, 264,
     267
  in Vietnam war, 35, 49
CBS Nightly News, 63
CDC (Central American Democratic
     Community), 127, 217–218, 254,
     256, 257
Cedar Falls operation, 97
Central America:
  Cuban role in, 65, 183, 199, 200,
     201, 214, 248, 256, 266
  East-West conflict and, 1–2, 12,
     38–39, 65, 85, 189, 199, 203, 213,
     217, 220, 225, 229, 230, 245, 252,
     254, 260–262, 264–265
  economic vs. military aid to, 183
  legitimizing of governments in, 4,
     20, 35–39, 95, 181
  problems of U.S. direct
     intervention in, 11
  U.S. investment in, 260
  Vietnamization of, 224
  see also specific countries
Central American Defense Council,
     130, 254
Central American Democratic
     Community (CDC), 127, 217–
     218, 254, 256, 257
Central American Economic
     Community, 254, 256*n*
Central Intelligence Agency, *see*
     CIA
Cerezo Arévalo, Venicio, 128

Chalatenango, El Salvador:
  FMLN's successes in, 140, 154–
     155, 156–157, 177
  government offensives in, 143–144,
     145, 150–151
  massacres in, 173–174
  in National Plan, 159
"Chalatenango and Morazán, Unidos
     Vencerán" (FMLN offensive),
     150
Chammorro Coronel, Edgar, 84
Chapin, Frederic L., 129
Chile, 49, 251
China, People's Republic of, 246, 266
  Soviet relations with, 15, 265
"Chiul massacre," 112
Christian Base Communities, 90
Christian Democratic party,
     Salvadoran, 27, 38, 135
Church, Frank, 50
CIA (Central Intelligence Agency), 5–
     6, 40–74, 240
  budget of, 51
  contras sponsored by, 5, 52–74; *see
     also* ARDE; contras; FDN
  Operation Phoenix of, 5, 40–43, 45,
     160
  Operations Directorate of, 5, 51–
     52, 87
  Salvadoran elections and, 243
  in Vietnam war, 5, 40–43, 45, 49–
     50, 160
CIC (Communal Institutional
     Coordinators), 121, 122
CIM (Municipal Institutional
     Coordinators), 121, 122
Cinchoneros guerrillas, 89
CIR (Regional Institutional
     Coordinators), 121, 122
Citizens Irregular Defense Groups, 50
Ciudad Barrios, El Salvador, 171
civic action, 34–35, 91, 96, 102, 160,
     163, 164
Civil Defense Corps, Guatemalan,
     102, 108–113
  conditioning of, 110–113
Civil Defense Corps, Salvadoran, 108,
     133, 164–165, 169–170

Civil Guards, Costa Rican, 219, 222
Civil Operations and Rural
    Development Support program
    (CORDS), 8, 9, 35, 159, 160,
    162, 168
Civil War, U.S., 81, 82
Clark, William P., 63, 249
Clarridge, Dewey, 54
clear-and-hold operations, 79, 159
COHA (Council on Hemispheric
    Affairs), 73
Cojutepeque, El Salvador, 171
Colby, William E., 42
collectives, agricultural, 18
colón, devaluation of, 215
Combined Action Platoons (CAPs),
    79–80, 86
Combined Movement maneuvers,
    196–197, 198, 199
Commander of U.S. Military
    Assistance Command Vietnam
    (COMUSMACV), 80
commando-style raids, 8, 79, 89
Committees of Civil Defense,
    Honduran, 210
Communal Institutional Coordinators
    (CIC), 121, 122
Communism:
    conspiracy theory of, 15, 189, 267
    expansion of, 1–2, 12, 14, 38–39,
        85, 189, 199
    peasants vs., 17, 133
    see also Soviet Union
"Communist Intervention in El
    Salvador," 38–39
Communist Party, Malay, 113–114
Communist Party, Salvadoran, 131–
    132
communitarianism, 96
COMUSMACV (Commander of U.S.
    Military Assistance Command
    Vietnam), 80
concentration camps, 100
CONDECA (Council of Central
    American Defense), 71, 73, 74,
    179, 196, 218, 257
Conference of the American Armies
    (1981), 256

Congress, U.S., 4, 34, 126, 136, 161,
    183
    contras and, 53–55, 58, 62, 63, 67–
        68, 70, 72, 73–74, 203, 253
    human rights and, 24, 26–28, 102–
        103, 164, 180, 196
    Office of Public Safety dismantled
        by, 36–37, 185
    Reagan's Central American policy
        opposed by, 1–2, 26, 31, 39, 68,
        84, 126, 162, 197, 203, 220, 253
    Suazo Córdova's address to, 208–
        209
    see also House of Representatives,
        U.S.: Senate, U.S.
Conservatives, U.S., foreign policy
    views of, 225–226, 229–231
Constituent Assembly, Guatemalan,
    127
Constituent Assembly, Salvadoran,
    25, 30, 32, 38
Contadora Group, 39, 127
contras, 5, 52–74, 179
    in Costa Rica, 5, 56, 57, 63, 66,
        68–70, 73, 199, 214, 219, 221–
        223, 258
    economic-sabotage campaign of,
        67, 68, 70–71
    in Honduras, 5, 54–55, 56–63, 66,
        67, 69–70, 72, 73, 179, 190, 192,
        196, 197, 198, 199, 207, 209, 221,
        257, 258
    ideological differences overcome
        by, 66
    optimism of, 66–67
    popular uprising expected by, 63,
        64
    Sandinista counterattack of, 70
    statistics on, 61, 62, 63, 64
    war of attrition fought by, 64–65
    see also ARDE; FDN
Convention On the Prevention and
    Punishment of the Crime of
    Genocide (1948), 107
cooperatives, agricultural, 25
COPREFA (Salvadoran Armed
    Forces Press Committee), 145,
    146

CORDS (Civil Operations and Rural Development Support program), 8, 9, 35, 159, 160, 162, 168
Corinto, Nicaragua, 221
corporations, transnational, agriculture and, 2–3
Costa Rica, 127, 212–224
  army abolished in, 212, 213
  CIA-sponsored contras in, 5, 56, 57, 63, 66, 68–70, 73, 199, 214, 219, 221–223, 258
  civil war in, 212, 213
  class structure in, 213
  East-West conflict and, 213, 217–220
  economic crisis in, 214–217, 220, 221, 224
  economic development in, 213
  interventionists in, 222–223
  neutrality of, 212, 214, 219, 222–223, 224
  Nicaragua's relations with, 214, 217–219, 221–223
  political polarization in, 217, 221, 222–223, 263
  as pro-Yankee country, 213–214
  Reagan in, 198, 218
  rightist trend in, 214, 217
  Sandinista operations in, 180, 219
  security requirements of, 219
  as Switzerland of Central America, 212–213
  U.S. economic aid to, 216, 217, 233
  U.S. military aid to, 219–220
Council of Central American Defense (CONDECA), 71, 73, 74, 179, 196, 218, 257
Council of the Americas, Enders's speech to, 17
Council on Hemispheric Affairs (COHA), 73
counterinsurgency:
  elite's resentment of, 6
  financial web of, 232–244
  first use of term, 13
  infrastructure building and, 240–242

counterinsurgency (cont'd)
  Kennedy's interest in, 13–15, 20–22, 23, 28, 85
  liberals vs. conservatives on, 225–231
  military strategy of, 2, 7–8, 75–94
  origins of, 13–15
  political effects of, 262–263
  public's misunderstanding of, 2
  reform side of, 16–39; see also land reform; political reform; reform
  repressive side of, 2, 4, 5, 7, 40–74, 89–90, 91, 96–124, 225–226
  see also specific topics
"Counterinsurgency, Yes—But with Controls" (Maechling), 226
Crossette, Barbara, 211
Cuba, 93, 110, 183, 248, 256, 266
  Bay of Pigs invasion and, 15, 63, 101, 260
  isolation of, 213, 217
  Nicaragua's relations with 65, 199, 200, 201, 214
Cuban missile crisis, 39, 203, 261
Cunén, Guatemala, 123
curfews, 89, 115, 117
currency controls, 125
currency devaluation, 215
Cusculatán, El Salvador, 170, 171, 173–174
Cusculatán suspension bridge, FMLN's destruction of, 177
Custodio, Ramón, 210

Dada, Hector, 135
d'Aubuisson, Roberto, 25, 28–29, 30–32
death squads, 2, 5, 89–90
  army massacres vs., 47
  in El Salvador, 19, 24, 28, 38, 43–47, 137, 159
  in Guatemala, 95, 101–102
  in Honduras, 210
  in Vietnam war, 42–43
Declaration of San José (1961), 213
Defense Department, U.S., 11, 15, 51, 73, 126, 129
  Big Pine maneuvers and, 198, 201

Defense Department, U.S. *(cont'd)*
  Central American intervention
    opposed by, 84
  generational change in, 83
  Honduran policy of, 183, 186, 197,
    198, 201, 204
  inertia of, 81–82
  Salvadoran army and, 138, 139,
    161, 178
  traditionalists in, 7, 75, 76, 77, 79,
    81, 117–118, 141
Defense Guidance paper, 83, 85–86
Defense Intelligence Agency, 240
de la Madrid, Miguel, 202
democracy, Costa Rica as, 212, 213
Democratic National Organization
    (ORDEN), 132–133, 135, 164,
    192, 210
Democratic Revolutionary Alliance,
    see ARDE
Democratic Revolutionary Front, *see*
    FDR
Depression, Great, 131
D'Escoto, Miguel, 74
Diem, Ngo Dinh, 20–22, 31, 35
  fall of, 22, 116–117, 128
Dien Bien Phu, French defeat at, 92
"disappearance" of people, 5, 29, 30,
    47–49, 90, 186
Doctrine of Attrition, 82
Dodd, Christopher, 158
domino theory:
  Central America and, 12, 247–249,
    265–267
  Vietnam war and, 265–266
Duarte, José Napoleón, 27, 30, 135,
    136
Durzuna, Honduras, U.S. base in, 7,
    196–197

East Timor, massacre in, 113
Echéverria, Juan, 219
economic aid, U.S.:
  to Costa Rica, 216, 217, 233
  as counterinsurgency aid, 242–244,
    247
  to El Salvador, 93–94, 242–243

economic aid, U.S. *(cont'd)*
  to Honduras, 193–194, 208–209
  military aid vs. 232–240, 242–244
economics, economy, 3, 18
  agricultural base of, 2–3
  of Costa Rica, 213, 214–217, 220,
    221, 224
  of El Salvador, 94, 135, 140, 151–
    154, 155–156, 169, 170–171, 177,
    243
  of Guatemala, 122–123, 124–125
  of Honduras, 193–194, 195
  of Nicaragua, 65, 66, 67, 68, 70–71
Economic Support Fund (ESF), 233
El Carrizal, El Salvador, 150
elections:
  as counterinsurgency measures, 4,
    25, 27, 37–38, 91, 95, 125–126,
    181
  in El Salvador, 25, 27, 38, 91, 242–
    243
  in Honduras, 181, 184
  Sandinistas and, 65–66
elections, U.S.:
  of 1980, 1, 136, 231
  of 1982, 27, 28
  of 1984, 2
electrical system, 164
  FMLN's disruption of, 152–153
elite class:
  agriculture and, 2–3, 99, 124
  in Costa Rica, 213
  in El Salvador, 132, 134, 136, 138
  military's relationship to, 103, 132
  reform resisted by, 4, 22–25, 28–
    29, 103, 138
  Ríos Montt opposed by, 124–125
El Jícaro, El Salvador, 154
El Paraíso military base, 177
El Salvador, 12, 22, 131–179
  air force of, 153, 170, 171, 258
  army of, *see* Salvadoran army
  contras vs., 53–54
  contras resupplied from, 67, 73
  coups in, 131, 133, 135, 255
  death squads in, 19, 24, 28, 38, 43–
    47, 137, 159

El Salvador *(cont'd)*
  economy of, 94, 135, 140, 151–154,
    155–156, 169, 170–171, 177, 243
  "fourteen families" in, 132, 134,
    136
  frustration of U.S. advisers to,
    147–149
  Guatemala's relations with, 127,
    129–130, 179, 258
  Honduras's collaboration with,
    146, 150, 155, 157, 179, 188–192,
    204–205, 207, 208, 258
  Honduras's 1969 war with, 191,
    255
  human rights in, 26–29, 32, 45, 46,
    144, 180
  insurgents in, *see* FMLN
  juntas in, 19, 38, 45, 135, 136
  land reform in, 17, 18–20, 24–26,
    28, 32, 135, 136, 229
  massacres in, 43–47, 132, 135, 137,
    144, 159, 173–174, 190, 191
  military's role in, 131
  National Guard in, 9, 29, 33, 48,
    136, 168
  National Plan in, 9, 159–179
  news blackouts in, 173–174, 177
  Nicaragua's influence on, 131–132,
    133–135
  nuns killed in, 9, 29, 136
  Operation Well-Being in, 35, 160,
    162–163, 165, 172
  political parties in, 27, 31–32, 38,
    45, 131–132, 135
  propaganda in, 36–37, 38, 173
  self-reform in, 23–24
  social structure in, 132, 134, 164
  stalemate in, 142–143, 150
  U.S. advisers killed in, 6, 136
  U.S. congressional delegation to,
    141
  U.S.-sponsored elections in, 25, 27,
    38, 91, 242–243
  White as ambassador to, 226–227
Encyclopedia of Developing Nations,
  212*n*
Enders, Thomas O., 17, 56, 231, 247–

Enders, Thomas O. *(cont'd)*
  248, 249–250
Ernesto Cruz, Ramon, 181*n*
ESF (Economic Support Fund), 233
Excélsior (Mexico City), 188

Fagoth, Steadman, 56–57
Falkland Islands War, 54, 60, 218,
  246
Farabundo Martí National Liberation
  Front, *see* FMLN
FDN (Nicaraguan Democratic Force),
  53, 56–63, 64, 66–67, 69–71, 72,
  72
  arms suppliers of, 58–59, 197
  command structure of, 59–60
  full-scale invasion by, 62
  in Nueva Segovia, 61–62
  officer corps of, 57–58
FDR (Frente Democrático
  Revolucionario—Revolutionary
  Democratic Front), 136–137,
  150, 165–166, 192
  kidnapping of, 27, 48, 136
FEDEFAM (Latin American
  Federation of Family
  Associations of the Detained-
  Disappeared), 48–49
FFZs (free-fire zones), 97
Fiallos Navarro, Francisco, 68
15th of September Legion, 57
1st Infantry Battalion, Honduran, 186
Flores Lima, Jaime Erneto, 32, 165,
  178
FMLN (Frente Farabundo Martí de
  Liberación Nacional—Farabundo
  Martí Liberation Front), 132,
  138, 139–159, 163, 165–179, 191,
  192, 199
  Civil Defense units vs., 165, 169–
    170
  composition of, 27*n*
  coordination of, 154
  economic sabotage campaign of,
    140, 151–154, 169, 170–171, 177,
    243
  first offensive of, 136–137

FMLN *(cont'd)*
  Force Concentrations of, 167
  Green Beret's views on, 161
  Heroes and Martyrs of October
    1979–1982 offensive (October
    offensive), 149–150, 151–155,
    188
  intelligence operations of, 161, 168
  military gains of, 1, 9–10, 139, 140,
    142, 176, 177
  military strategy of, 139–140, 144–
    145, 147–159, 165–166, 167,
    168–169, 172
  peace offer of, 27
  political maturity of, 176
  popular support for, 64, 164, 166–
    167, 175
  prisoners of war and, 174–175, 177
  structure of, 40–42, 47, 137, 166,
    167
  supply lines of, 183, 190, 204–205
  in urban vs. rural areas, 142–143
  zones controlled by, 139, 140,
    143*n*, 176
FMS (Foreign Military Sales
    program), 232*n*
food, as weapon, 123
Ford Administration, Vietnam policy
    of, 93
Foreign aid, U.S., *see* economic aid,
    U.S.; military aid, U.S.
Foreign Assistance Act, 233
Foreign Military Sales program
    (FMS), 232*n*
foreign policy, basis of, 227
foreign policy, U.S.:
  liberals vs. conservatives on, 225–
    231
  rationalizing of, 245–253
  self-fulfilling prophecy and, 12,
    262–268
  *see also specific countries and
    presidential administrations*
Fort Benning, Ga., 162, 185
Fort Bragg, N.C., 7, 13*n*, 143
  Special Warfare Center at, 87, 88

Forum for Peace and Democracy
    (San José forum), 217–218
FUSEP (Public Safety Force), 186,
    188

Gairy, Sir Eric, 10
Galbraith, John Kenneth, 23
García, José Guillermo, 9, 27, 30–33,
    136, 148, 155–156, 157, 188–189
  replacement of, 158, 249
GDP (gross domestic product), 193,
    215
General Uprising and General
    Offensive ("Tet" offensive), 92–
    93, 97–98
genocide, 98, 106–108, 118, 164
  defined, 108
Giap, Vo Nguyen, 92
Golcher, Rinaldo, 162
Golden Bridge, demolition of, 153
Gomez, Lionel, 136
Gorman, Paul F., 129, 203, 205, 257
Gospel Outreach, 123
Great Britain:
  in Malvinas/Falkland Islands War,
    54, 60, 218, 246
  strategic hamlet strategy of, 113–
    114
Great Depression, 131
Green Berets (Special Forces), 6, 7
  Border Patrol Unit of, 183
  in Costa Rica, 220
  El Salvador and, 139, 144, 147–
    148, 159, 160–161, 162, 172
  establishment of, 87
  expansion of, 87–88
  in Guatemala, 102
  in Honduras, 182–184, 204, 205,
    · 257
  military strategy of, 81, 88–92
  teaching role of, 87, 91, 139, 144,
    162, 182–183, 257
Grenada, U.S. invasion of, 10–11, 71,
    73, 85, 247
gross domestic product (GDP), 193,
    215

Guanacaste, Costa Rica, Sandinistas in, 214
Guatemala, 12, 54, 64, 73, 91, 95–130
army of, 120, 122, 123, 124, 125, 179, 189
CIA role in, 101, 129
civic action in, 35, 96, 103
coups in, 22, 95, 96, 101, 123–130, 257
death squads in, 95, 101–102
disappearances in, 49, 103
economy of, 122–123, 124–125
Electoral Tribunal in, 127
El Salvador's relations with, 127, 129–130, 179, 258
genocide in, 98, 106–108, 118, 164
history of state terrorism in, 101–105
human rights in, 23–24, 95, 102, 103, 104, 120*n*, 180, 255
Indians in, 98, 99–100, 104–106, 121, 123
massacres in, 35, 96–108, 111–113, 126
patterns of land ownership in, 103, 105
propaganda in, 37
reform in, 35, 95–96, 102, 118, 125–128
reform resisted by elite in, 23–24, 103
scorched earth in, 95, 106–108
social class in, 99, 103
strategic hamlets in, 95, 100, 108, 113–123
system of state terrorism in, 100
U.S. Embassy in, 128
U.S. support of, 11, 96, 102, 120, 126, 258
Guatemala City, Guatemala, 122, 129, 130, 257
occupation of OAS office in, 88
Guerrilla Army of the Poor, 106
guerrilla warfare, *see* insurgency, insurgent organizations
Guevara, Ché, 88

Haig, Alexander, 59, 84, 227, 249
Hammer, Michael, 16
hammer-and-anvil tactic, 142, 146, 150, 155, 191
Havana Convention on Civil Strife, 207
"Hawks View" exercises, 196
health-care system, in Costa Rica, 212
Hernández Martínez, Maximiliano, 131–132, 136
Heroes and Martyrs of October 1979–1982 offensive (October offensive), 149–150, 151–155, 188
Hickory operation, 97
Hilsman, Roger, 75–76, 261–262
Hinton, Deane R., 27–28, 33, 45, 163, 250
Hitler, Adolf, 47
Ho Chi Minh, 88, 262
Honduran Anti-Communist Movement (MACHO), 210
Honduran army, 179
1st Infantry Battalion of, 186
Green Berets and, 182–184
reorganization of, 187
rules of promotion in, 186
in Salvadoran territory, 146, 150, 155, 157, 188–189, 191–192
6th Battalion of, 155
U.S. war games with, 195–206, 257–258
Honduras, 89, 180–211
air force of, 182
border patrols in, 183–184
CIA-sponsored contras in, 5, 54–55, 56–63, 66, 67, 69–70, 72, 73, 179, 190, 192, 196, 197, 198, 199, 207, 209, 221, 257, 258
congress of, 209, 210
coups in, 181*n*, 182, 187
disappearances in, 186, 211
economic problems of, 193, 194
elections in, 181, 184
El Salvador's border with, 150, 181, 183–184, 190, 191

Honduras *(cont'd)*
  El Salvador's collaboration with,
    146, 150, 155, 157, 179, 188–192,
    204–205, 207, 208, 258
  El Salvador's 1969 war with, 191,
    255
  human rights in, 209–210
  international treaties signed by, 207
  Mejía Víctores in, 128–129
  in military alliances, 127, 130, 255,
    256, 257
  military domination in, 185, 187
  political polarization in, 206–211,
    263
  Reagan in, 198
  reform in, 181, 187, 208–209
  refugees in, 99, 190, 192
  Sandinista operations in, 180
  secret police in, 186, 188
  stability of, 181, 192–193
  "tank road" in, 242
  U.S. aid to, 182–184, 192–197, 204,
    208–209, 257
  as U.S. forward base, 85, 161, 180–
    184, 207, 257
  U.S. relations with, 5, 11, 59, 60,
    180–211, 257–258
hostages, taking of, 88–89
House of Representatives, U.S., 67–
  68, 72, 203, 253
Hudson Institute, 88
human rights:
  Carter Administration and, 23–24,
    102–103, 104, 126, 229, 255
  in El Salvador, 26–29, 32, 45, 46,
    144, 180
  in Guatemala, 23–24, 95, 103,
    120*n*, 180, 255
  in Honduras, 209–210
hunter-killer units, 160, 162, 163,
  169, 170–171, 174

IDB (Inter-American Development
  Bank), 194, 240
Iklé, Fred C., 27, 173, 188, 259, 260
IMET (International Military and
  Training program), 232*n*

IMF (International Monetary Fund),
  215–217, 224, 240
"Independence, Liberty and
  Democracy for El Salvador"
  (FMLN offensive), 167
infant mortality, in Costa Rica, 212
Institute for Military Assistance, 88
insurgency, insurgent organizations:
  Communist exploitation of, 14–15,
    38–39
  conventional warfare used by, 91–
    92
  financing of, 89, 90
  Kennedy's views on, 13–14
  military methods of, 7–8, 139–140,
    144–145, 147–159, 165–166, 167,
    168–169, 172
  popular base of, 8, 11, 16, 42, 63,
    64, 90, 97, 115, 164, 166–167, 175
  proof of membership in, 42–43
  structure of, 40–43, 47, 64, 89, 90,
    98, 105, 137, 166, 167
  summary of causes of, 2–4
  U.S. Army's theory of, 88–94
  variety of names for, 13
  see also specific topics
Inter-American Development Bank
  (IDB), 194, 240
Inter-American Foundation, 34
Inter-American Press Association,
  Enders's speech to, 247–248
Inter-American Treaty of Reciprocal
  Assistance (Río Treaty), 207,
  256*n*
Intermountain Aviation Company, 69
"Internal War" (Hilsman), 75–76
International Military and Training
  program (IMET), 232*n*
International Monetary Fund (IMF),
  215–217, 224, 240
International Red Cross, 97, 175, 177
Investair Leasing Corporation, 69
Israel, 209, 215, 233
  military aid of, 24, 59

"January Heroes and Revolutionaries
  Offensive" (FMLN), 149*n*

Jenkins, Brian, 81, 88–92, 101, 102
Jocoatique, El Salvador, 156
Johnson, Lyndon B., 93
Johnson, U. Alexis, 23
Johnson Administration, Guatemala and, 102
Joint Chiefs of Staff, U.S., 197, 204, 240
Joyabaj, Guatemala, repopulation of, 118–119

Kaibiles, 98, 108
Kampuchea, 266
Kassebaum, Nancy L., 162
Keitel, Wilhelm, 47–48
Kekchi Indians, massacre of, 104
Kennedy, John F., 75, 245
    assassination of, 7, 76, 117–118
    counterinsurgency doctrine of, 13–15, 20–22, 23, 28, 85
Kennedy, John F., School of Special Warfare, 7, 13n
Kennedy Administration, 14–15, 39
    civic action programs in, 34
    counterinsurgency strategy in, 75–76, 77
    South Vietnam and, 20–22, 23, 31
Khmer Rouge, 266
Khrushchev, Nikita, 14–15
kidnappings, 49, 67, 89, 221
    in El Salvador, 27, 29, 48, 136
Kirkpatrick, Jeane, 158
Kissinger, Henry A., 249, 251
Kissinger commission, 39
Korean conflict, conventional warfare in, 6, 76, 82
Kristol, Irving, 230
Kruster, Thomas J., Jr., 90
Ky, Nguyen Cao, 38

labor, labor unions, 122, 133
    in Costa Rica, 217, 224
    in Honduras, 181, 186, 211
Labor Party, Salvadoran, 131
landholding patterns:
    in Costa Rica, 213
    in Guatemala, 103, 105

land reform, 16n
    as counterinsurgency measure, 4, 17–20, 24–26, 125, 181, 208, 229
    in El Salvador, 17, 18–20, 24–26, 28, 32, 135, 136, 229
    in Honduras, 181, 208
land-to-the-tiller program, 19, 25–26
Lao Communist National Liberation Front (Pathet Lao), 49–50
Laos, bombing of, 251, 265–266
La Sociedad, El Salvador, FMLN in, 156, 174
Las Pacayas, Guatemala, 108–109, 110
Las Vueltas, El Salvador, FMLN's capture of, 150, 154
latifundia, expropriation of, 19, 25
Latin American Federation of Family Associations of the Detained-Disappearred (FEDEFAM), 48–49
Laugerud, Kjell, 103
Lewy, Gunter, 98
Liberal Party, Honduran, 184, 208
liberals, U.S., foreign policy views of, 225–229
liberation theology, 90, 264, 267
    appeal of, 3–4
life expectancy, in Costa Rica, 212
literacy campaigns, 110
literacy rate, in Costa Rica, 212n
Littoral Highway, 152, 155
loans, foreign:
    to Costa Rica, 215–217, 224
    interest on, 3, 193, 194, 215–217
    moratorium on repayment of, 216–217
    as security assistance, 240
Lodge, Henry Cabot, 21–22
López Arellano, Oswaldo, 181n
López Fuentes, Héctor Mario, 120
Lucas García, Romeo, 95, 104, 250, 255
Lutz, Joseph C., 86

McDonald's, 152
McEnry, John, 189

MACHO (Honduran Anti-Communist Movement), 210
McLaughlin, Bill, 63
Maechling, Charles, Jr., 226
Magaña, Alvaro, 25, 30–33
Majano, Adolfo, 136
Malay peninsula, strategic hamlets on, 113–114
Malaysia, 266
Malvinas/Falkland Islands War, 54, 60, 218, 246
Managua, Nicaragua, bombing of, 221
Mao Tse-tung, 16
MAP (Military Assistance Program), 102, 232n
Marighella, Carlos, 88
Marines, U.S., 132, 205, 227
  in CAPs, 79–80, 86
  special operations unit of, 86–87
Mariola Battalion, 157
Marrorquín, Juan, 120
massacres:
  of Atlacátl Battalion, 173–174, 178
  "Chiul," 111–112
  conditioning function of, 110–112
  death squads vs., 47
  of Kekchi Indians, 104
  My Lai, 137
  Parraxut, 111
  Río Sumpúl, 190, 191
  see also specific countries
Matanza, La (The Killing), 132
Matta, Roberto, 110–111
Meanguera, El Salvador, FMLN's capture of, 156–157
Medrano, José Alberto, 132–133
Mejía Víctores, Oscar Humberto, 123–124, 127–129, 257
Mekong Delta, configuration of villages in, 117
Melgar Castro, Juan, 181n
Méndez Montenegro, Julio César, 101
Meo tribesmen, 5, 49–50, 57
Mercado, William, 129
Mexico, 202, 218
  refugees in, 106, 252
Meyer, Edward C., 84

Miami, Fla.:
  as refuge for dictators, 93
  Somocistas in, 60–61, 93
Middle East, Central America compared to, 2, 63
Military Advisory Group, U.S., 6, 35, 36, 160
military aid U.S., 232–244
  to Costa Rica, 219–220
  economic aid vs., 232–240, 242–244
  to El Salvador, 9, 26–29, 30–31, 84, 102, 136–139, 142, 143, 144, 145, 158, 160–162, 164, 172–173, 177–179, 229, 246, 247–248, 249
  to Guatemala, 102, 120, 126, 258
  to Honduras, 182–184, 192–193, 195, 196–197, 204, 257
  human rights and, 23–24, 26–29
  Reagan's calls for increases in, 2, 158, 249
Military Assistance Command, U.S., 78
Military Assistance Program, U.S. (MAP), 102, 232n
military strategy, counterinsurgency, 2, 7–8
  development of, 75–94
  of Green Berets, 81, 88–92
  Hilsman's views on, 75–76
  Jenkins's views on, 88–92
Minh, Duong Van, 22
Miskito Indians, 5, 49, 54, 56, 57, 197, 198
Misurasata (Indian coalition), 56, 66
Mitchel, Edgar L., 69
MLN (National Liberation Movement), 101
Mocorón, Honduras, 197, 198
Mondale, Walter, 84
Monge, Luís Alberto, 215–216, 217, 218, 220–224
  white paper of, 218–219
Montagnards, 5, 50, 57
Monterroso, Domingo, 173, 178
Montoneros, 90
Morazán, El Salvador, 191–192
  Cacahuatique volcano in, 171, 176

Morazán, El Salvador *(cont'd)*
    FMLN offensives in, 145–146, 150,
        151, 154–155, 156, 157–158, 172,
        174
    freedom of guerrillas in, 166–167
    in National Plan, 159
Motley, Langehorne A., 17n, 250
Municipal Institutional Coordinators
    (CIM), 121, 122
My Lai massacre, 137

Nacht und Nebel, 47–48
National Bipartisan Commission on
    Central America, 250–251
National Campaign Plan, Salvadoran,
    9, 159–179
    civic action in, 160, 163, 164
    military zones established by, 159
    phases of, 159–160
    weaknesses of, 163–165
National Committee for
    Reconstruction, Guatemalan,
    121–122
National Conciliation Party,
    Salvadoran, 132
Nationalist Republican Alliance
    (ARENA), 25, 31–32
National Liberation Movement,
    Guatemalan (MLN), 101
National Liberation Party, Costa
    Rican, 217
National Military Academy,
    Argentinian, 185
National Plan for Security and
    Development, Guatemalan, 96,
    101, 104–105, 108–113, 118–124,
    159
    "rifles" clause of, 118
national security, U.S., Reagan's
    views on, 2, 83, 193, 248
National Security Agency, U.S., 240
National Security Council, U.S.
    (NSC), 9, 15, 21
    contra plan of, 53–54
National Unity Directorate of the
    Revolutionary Movement of
    Honduras, 210

NATO (North Atlantic Treaty
    Organization), 83
Navy, U.S., 129
    in Big Pine maneuvers, 198, 201,
        204
    off Nicaragua, 71, 73
    unconventional warfare sections
        (SEALs), 6, 7, 86, 204
Nazism, 93, 185
    crimes of, 47–48
Negroponte, John D., 59–60, 184–
    185, 195
Nentón, Guatemala, "repopulation"
    of, 119
*New Interamerican Policy for the 80's,
    A* (Santa Fe document), 198–199
Newsweek magazine, 55–56, 58, 59,
    158, 166, 171
    Somocistas' plan "number one" in,
        61
New York Times, 19, 53, 58, 68–69,
    211, 252
New York Times Magazine, 52, 227–
    228
Nicaragua, 110, 244, 248
    Alvarez's war preparations against,
        187–188
    CIA's "secret war" against, 1, 5, 39,
        52–74, 259–260, 264; *see also*
        ARDE; contras; FDN
    civil war in, 11, 36, 62, 89, 131–
        132, 133–134, 180
    Costa Rica's relations with, 214,
        217–219, 221–223
    counterrevolution in, 5, 52–74
    Cuban assistance to, 65, 199, 200,
        201, 214
    destruction of ports in, 70–71
    economy of, 65, 66, 67, 68, 70–
        71
    fall of Somoza in, 93
    Honduran insurgents trained in,
        210
    Honduras's relations with, 187–
        188
    massacres in, 61
    National Guard of, 5, 53, 56, 57–

Nicaragua: National Guard of *(cont'd)*
    58, 60, 61, 62, 66, 134, 136
  Salvadoran history influenced by,
    131–132, 133–135
  Somoza dictatorship in, 5, 53, 134,
    180, 194, 214, 254–255
  State Department's media attack
    on, 39
  U.S. invasion plans for, 71–74
  see also Sandinista government
Nicaraguan Democratic Force, *see*
    FDN
night fighting, 7, 79, 81, 85
"9 March 1981 Presidential Finding
    on Central America," 53
Nixon Administration, Vietnam
    policy of, 93
Non-Aligned Movement, 264
nuclear power, 14, 83, 261
Nueva Concepción, Guatemala, 110
Nuremberg trials, 47–48
Nutting, Wallace H., 146–147, 188

OAS (Organization of American
    States), 65–66, 88, 191, 213, 255
  Charter of, 207
  Honduran peace doctrine to, 208
  Schultz's speech to, 246
Ochoa Pérez, Sigfrido, 32–33
Oduber, Daniel, 213
Office of Public Safety (AID), 36–37,
    101, 185
Office of Strategic Services (OSS), 75,
    87
Office on Latin America, 48
oil imports, 3, 193, 215
Ojos de Agua, El Salvador, 150
OPEN (Organization for National
    Emergencies), 219, 220
"Operation Blazing Tooth" (ARDE),
    73, 223
"Operation Pegasus" (invasion plan
    for Nicaragua), 73
Operation Phoenix (CIA), 5, 40–43,
    45, 160
Operation Sunrise, 116
Operation Well-Being, 35, 160, 162–
    163, 165, 172

ORDEN (Democratic National
    Organization), 132–133, 135,
    164, 192, 210
Organization for National
    Emergencies (OPEN), 219, 220
Organization of American States, *see*
    OAS
Ortega, Daniel, 66
Ortega, Humberto, 70, 71
OSS (Office of Strategic Services), 75,
    87

Panama, 8, 148*n*
  U.S. aid to, 182
Panama Canal Zone, 159, 182, 185
Pan American Highway, 113, 152,
    153, 177
Parraxut massacre, 112
Pastora, Edén, 56, 57, 63, 64, 89, 214,
    219, 221
Pathet Lao (Lao Communist National
    Liberation Front), 49–50
Páz García, Policarpio, 181*n,* 182,
    184
Peace and Justice Committee,
    Guatemalan, 111
peace concept, in superpower
    propaganda, 246–247
Pearlman, Mark, 16
peasants, 3, 9, 35, 43, 114–115
  conservatism of, 17
  in El Salvador, 133, 152, 153, 190,
    191
  in Guatemala, 96, 102, 103, 109
  in Honduras, 181, 186, 208, 211
  land reform and, 17–19, 208
"Pegasus Operation" (invasion plan
    for Nicaragua), 73
Peñas Blancas, Nicaragua, 222–223
Pentagon Papers, 5, 50, 130
People's Revolutionary Army, 90
Perquín, El Salvador, 145–146, 154,
    158
Peruvian Superior War College, 185
Peterson, Mark J., 69
Phoenix Operation (CIA), 5, 40–43,
    45, 160
Pickering, Thomas R., 27*n,* 250

Pinochet, Augusto, 251
piston-and-cylinder tactic, 142
Political Action and Census
    Grievance teams, 35
political prisoners, 46, 89
political reform, 16n, 20–22
    elections as, 4, 25, 27, 37–38, 91,
        95, 125–126, 181
Popular Liberal Alliance, Honduran,
    208
population:
    of Central America, 11
    of El Salvador, 18, 45
    of Nicaragua, 62
"preventive terror" actions, 100
prisoners of war, in El Salvador, 174–
    175, 177
propaganda, 35–39, 89, 173
Prosterman, Roy L., 18–20, 25, 229
Protestants, 121
    evangelical, 122, 123, 124
public opinion, U.S., 36
    Central American policy and, 1, 2,
        29, 39, 73
    Vietnam war and, 2, 4, 21, 92–93
Public Safety Force (FUSEP), 186,
    188
Puerto Castilla, Honduras,
    counterinsurgency facility in, 7,
    87, 162, 171, 204, 209, 249

quadrillage technique, 76

racism, massacres and, 106
Radio Venceremos, 146
Rama Indians, 56
Ramón Belloso battalion, 87, 143–
    144, 145, 151, 156, 158
Rand Corporation, 88
Ranger, U.S.S. (aircraft carrier), 201
"Rapid Reaction Battalions," 36
Raúl (FMLN political officer), 147,
    148
RDF (Rapid Deployment Force), 7,
    83
Readiness Command, 83n
Reagan, Ronald, 1–2, 126, 164n, 193,
    232, 233, 245

Reagan, Ronald (cont'd)
    alarmism of, 2, 248, 252
    contras and, 5, 53, 63, 65
    election of, 136, 182, 203
    Latin American trip of, 198, 218
    political appointments and
        replacements of, 17n, 27n, 39,
        250
    press conferences of, 200–201
    speeches of, 252–253, 261
Reagan Administration, 83
    CIA's clandestine operations
        refurbished by, 5–6, 39, 51–52,
        87
    Costa Rica and, 5, 214–224, 256
    distribution of foreign aid in, 232–
        244
    El Salvador and, 1, 24–34, 38–39,
        137–147, 152, 159–164, 172–
        173, 177–179, 246–249, 256, 257,
        266
    Grenada and, 10–11, 71, 73, 85,
        247
    Guatemala and, 12, 124, 126, 127,
        128–130, 256–257
    Honduras and, 5, 182, 184–190,
        193–206, 256, 257–258
    human rights and, 24, 26–29, 32
    Khmer Rouge supported by, 266
    liberal critics of, 225, 227–228, 239
    military escalation in, 1–2, 11–12,
        39, 87–88
    military pacts encouraged by, 255–
        256
    Nicaragua and, 1, 5, 39, 52–74, 245
    unconditional military victory as
        goal of, 258–260
    unconventional warfare sections
        rejuvenated by, 6–7
    White fired by, 227
recession, 3, 83, 124, 215, 221
Red Cross, 97, 175, 177
reform, 2, 4–5, 7, 16–39, 40, 91, 95–
    96, 102, 118, 136, 225–229
    civic action as, 34–35, 91, 96, 102,
        160, 163, 164
    contradiction inherent to, 4, 23
    elite's resistance to, 4, 22–25, 28–

Reform: elite's resistance *(cont'd)*
29, 103, 138
idealistic base of, 16
propaganda and, 35-39
repression vs., 225-231
revolution vs., 11-12
self-, during crisis, 22-34
see also land reform; political
reform
refugees:
Costa Rica as haven of, 212
Guatemalan, 97-100, 106, 108-
109, 112, 118, 123
in Mexico, 106, 252
Salvadoran, 190, 192
in United States, 248-249, 251-252
Vietnamese, 97-98
Regional Institutional Coordinators
(CIR), 121, 122
Regional Military Training Center,
U.S. (Puerto Castilla), 7, 87, 162,
171, 204, 209, 249, 257
retirement, in Costa Rica, 212, 213
revolution:
Central American tradition of, 180
Kennedy's views on, 13-14, 15
reform vs., 11-12
Soviet support of, 14-15
terrorism vs., 89
White's views on, 228, 229
Revolutionary Organization of the
People in Arms, Guatemalan,
106
Revolutionary Popular Bloc,
Salvadoran, 133
Riding, Alan, 19, 53
Ríos Montt, Efraín, 95-101, 105, 108,
122, 256-257
as born-again Christian, 95, 96,
122, 123, 124
elections promised by, 95, 125-127
fall of, 22, 123-130
Río Sumpúl massacre, 190, 191
Río Treaty (Inter-American Treaty of
Reciprocal Assistance), 207, 256*n*
Rivard, Robert, 166-167
Rivera, Brooklyn, 56-57

Rivera y Damas, Arturo, 157, 170,
173-174
Rodas, Modesto, Jr., 208
Romero, Carlos Humberto, 22, 45,
135
Romero, Oscar, 20, 135
Romero, Peter, 176
Rommel, Erwin, 185
Rules of Engagement, in Vietnam
war, 97
Rural Patrols, Salvadoran, 164
Rusk, Dean, 21

Salvadoran Armed Forces Press
Committee (COPREFA), 145,
146
Salvadoran army:
in Bolsones Territorial, 191
casualty rates of, 161, 166, 174
FMLN's superiority to, 161, 168
four-phase plan of, 140-142
García's purge of, 31, 136
incompetence of, 8-9, 138, 139,
142, 146-147, 160-161
influence of U.S. military doctrine
on, 132, 137-147
massacres by, 45, 46-47, 132, 135,
137, 144, 159, 173-174
National Plan and, 159-179
U.S. training of, 138-139, 143, 144,
160-162
warfare methods of, 77, 80, 147-
159, 168-169, 170-171
Sandinista commando raid (1977),
89
Sandinista government, 5, 11, 52-74,
197, 245
Alvarez vs., 187-188
Big Pine and, 198-203
Costa Rica's criticism of, 214, 218-
219, 223
elections promised by, 65-66
Mejía Víctores's attack on, 129
nation mobilized by, 73-74
regionalization of civil strife
threatened by, 202-203
Sandino, Augusto, 131-132

San Esteban Catarina, El Salvador,
    170
San Fernando, El Salvador, 145–146,
    154
San Francisco Gotera, El Salvador,
    146, 156, 158, 168
San José forum (Forum for Peace and
    Democracy), 217–218
San Miguel, El Salvador, 151, 155,
    166
    FMLN attacks in, 167–168, 171
    3rd Infantry Battalion in, 165, 167,
    178
San Miguel Acatán, Guatemala,
    repopulation of, 118–119
San Nicolás, El Salvador, 173
San Pedro Sula, Honduras, 89, 185,
    211
San Salvador, El Salvador, 9, 16, 19,
    30, 172
    FMLN assaults on, 155, 157
    occupation of Spanish Embassy in,
    88
    U.S. Embassy in, 6, 30–31, 33, 35,
    36, 227
Santa Fe Committee, 199
Santa Fe document, 198–199
San Vicente, El Salvador, 151, 159
    Chinchontepec volcano in, 169
    Civil Defense in, 164–165, 170
    Operation Well-Being in, 162–163,
    165, 172
saturation patrolling, small-unit, 7–8,
    80, 115, 160
Schaufelberger, Albert A., III, 6
Schlossberg, Arnold, 206
School of the Americas (Panama), 8,
    148, 182, 185
scorched earth tactic, 95, 106–108
sea lines of communication (SLOCs),
    260
SEALs (Sea, Air, and Land teams), 6,
    7, 86, 204
search-and-destroy operations, 7, 76,
    77–78, 80, 81, 98, 113, 115
    in El Salvador, 141–142, 173, 176–
    177

"search-and-evade" missions, 140
security aid, U.S., see military aid,
    U.S.
Senate, U.S., 69, 70, 72, 203, 250
    Foreign Relations Committee of,
    162
    Intelligence Committee of, 58, 67–
    68, 240
Sharon, Ariel, 185, 209
Shultz, George P., 161, 246
SLOCs (sea lines of communication),
    260
SOC (Special Operations Command),
    86
social class:
    agriculture and, 2–3, 213
    death squads and, 43, 45
    of Indians, 99
    see also elite class; peasants
Social Democrats:
    in Costa Rica, 212, 217
    in El Salvador, 45, 135
social injustice, as basis for
    insurgency, 2–4, 13–14
socialism, appeal of, 3–4
social security, in Costa Rica, 212
Solano Calderón, Angel, 222, 223
Somoza Debayle, Anastasio, 5, 53,
    66, 93, 134, 180, 214, 254–255
Somoza García, Anastasio, 214
South Vietnam:
    army of, 78, 79, 81, 93, 107, 140
    civic action programs in, 35
    fall of, 93
    internal refugees in, 97–98
    Kennedy's visit to, 13
    Minh's coup in, 22
    reform in, 16n, 18, 20–22, 23, 35,
    37–38
    strategic hamlets in, 95, 114–118,
    169–170
    see also Vietnam war
Soviet Union, 213
    Afghanistan and, 245, 246, 265
    in Central America, 2, 38–39, 65,
    85, 199, 203, 225, 260–261, 264–
    265

318

INDEX

Soviet Union *(cont'd)*
China's relations with, 15, 265
nuclear weapons of, 83, 261
wars of liberation supported by,
14–15
Special Operations Command (SOC),
86
Starry, Don A., 83
State Department, U.S., 19, 21, 27,
38–39
fall of Ríos Montt and, 128–129
pragmatists vs. ideologues in, 249–
250
Refugee Affairs Office of, 251–252
White Papers of, 38–39
Stone, Richard B., 39, 250
strategic hamlets, 100, 114–123
in El Salvador, 160, 169–170
theory of, 114–115
strikes, 185, 217, 224
of ARDE, 64
general, 19, 20, 91, 136
Suazo Córdova, Roberto, 59–60, 186,
195, 208–209
election of, 59, 184
Suma Indians, 56
Swartztrauber, Saypre, 189
sweeping operations, 78–79, 98, 151,
159
in Guatemala, 109, 111–112, 119

Tambs, Lewis A., 248–249, 251
taxes:
in Costa Rica, 213
in Guatemala, 122, 125
Tegucigalpa, Honduras, 211
Tejeira, José María, 210
Tenancingo, El Salvador, 170
"Tet" offensive (General Uprising
and General Offensive), 92–93,
97–98
Thailand, 266
Thayer, Paul, 259
Thieu, Nguyen Van, 38
Third World nations, economic
dependency of, 216
*This Government Has the
Commitment to Change,* 37

Thompson, Sir Robert, 114, 117
Torres Arias, Leonidas, 186, 188
Tracy, Larry, 178–179

unemployment, 91, 152, 193, 212
Union of Rural Workers, 133
unions, labor, 122, 133, 211
United Nations, 49, 97, 210
Charter of, 207
General Assembly of, 107
World Food Program of, 123
United Press International, 177
United Provinces of Central America,
180
upper class, *see* elite class
USIA (United States Information
Agency), 36–37
USIS (United States Information
Service), 36, 160
Usulután, El Salvador, 151, 155, 157,
165, 172

Vaky, Viron, 181–182
Venezuela, 214, 218
Veterans of Foreign Wars, Reagan's
address to, 253
Vides Casanova, Carlos Eugenio, 9,
33–34, 162–163, 178, 249
Viera, José, 16
Viet Cong, 18, 21, 50, 97, 98, 107
infrastructure of, 42–43
strategic hamlets and, 114, 116–117
Viet Minh, 92
Vietnam, Democratic Republic of, 18
Vietnam press, 116
Vietnam war:
bombing policy in, 76–77, 78,
148–149, 251, 265–266
counterinsurgency in El Salvador
and, 79, 80, 140–141, 148–149,
159, 162
counterinsurgency in Guatemala
and, 95, 97–98, 107–108,
114–118, 128, 130
death squads in, 42–43
dispute over military strategy in,
7–8, 77–82
domino theory and, 265–266

Vietnam War *(cont'd)*
   infrastructure building and, 240
   massacres in, 137
   Operation Phoenix in, 5, 40–43, 45,
     160
   public opinion and, 2, 4, 21, 92–93
   scorched earth tactic in, 106–108
   U.S. defeat in, 8, 93
Vitelio Alas, Santiago, 174
Volio, Fernando, 223

Waghelstein, John D., 84
Wall Street Journal, 39
warfare, conventional vs.
     unconventional, 6–8, 75–82, 91–
     92, 117–118, 147–159
war lords, in El Salvador, 9, 32–33,
   149
Warsaw Pact, superiority of, 82–83
Washington *Post,* 39
Watergate, reform of CIA and, 5, 50,
   52
Weathermen, 89

Weber, John, 102
Weinberger, Caspar W., 72, 85, 176,
   246
welfare system, in Costa Rica, 212,
   217, 221
Westmoreland, William, 80
White, Robert E., 178, 226–229
White Hand, 101–102
"Why Another Somoza?" (Anderson),
   184
Wicker, Tom, 251
Wickham, John, 83
Winsor, Curtis, 222, 223
World Bank, 240
World Court, 207
World War I, 82
World War II, 87
   conventional warfare in, 6, 76, 81,
     82
   war crimes in, 47–48

Zacapa-Izabal campaign, 102
Zamora, Rubén, 165–166, 167